THE ILLUSTRATED
ENCYCLOPEDIA OF THE
DOG

THE ILLUSTRATED
ENCYCLOPEDIA OF THE
DOG

Oceana

AN OCEANA BOOK

This book is produced by
Quantum Publishing Ltd.
6 Blundell Street
London N7 9BH

Copyright © 2005 Quantum Publishing Ltd.

This edition printed 2005

BAM 1-84573-077-1

QUMTIEP

Manufactured in Singapore by
Pica Digital Pte. Ltd.
Printed in China by
CT Printing Ltd.

CONTENTS

INTRODUCTION

Before buying a dog, it is essential to get as much information as possible about all the different breeds, as this will help you select a dog that meets your requirements. This is important in terms of not only looks and size, but also character and temperament, so that the dog can fulfil the role you have in mind.

Ownership of a dog is a serious undertaking. It requires a long-term commitment, bearing in mind that some breeds, the Miniature Poodle for instance, may live for 17 years or more. Twelve years is the average canine lifespan, during which time the dog must be fed, exercised, and groomed, receive veterinary attention for accidents and illnesses, and be taken into consideration whenever its owner is planning to be away from home for more than a matter of hours.

Owners should also consider their dog's welfare when making out their will. If a dog should survive its owner, clear instructions should be available stating whether the dog is bequeathed to an animal charity, with a suitable donation if possible, or to a named friend or relative.

A long-term commitment

Many dog owners do not take such a responsible attitude. This does not mean that they are bad or uncaring. More likely, they made the decision to buy a dog in the belief that the requirements and temperament of one canine were much the same as another, and that the only consideration was whether the dog looked big and tough or small, cute and cuddly. Yet some big, macho-looking dogs are great big softies, and some small breeds are famed for ill-humor. Only by studying the characteristics of different breeds can you find out which ones are really suitable for you.

In addition, before buying a dog you must make sure, unless you own your home, that the landlord does not object to its presence. Most standard leases preclude the keeping of pets without the written consent of the landlord.

The therapeutic value of dogs is being increasingly recognized—indeed there is an International Association of Human-Animal Interaction Organizations—with dogs playing their part in comforting residents in hospices and nursing homes, as hospital visitors (Pro-Active Therapy Dogs), and as Hearing Dogs for the Deaf. At the same time, however, the laws concerning dogs are becoming ever more stringent, with some breeds being outlawed in certain states and countries. Laws relating to dog ownership vary from state to state in the United States, for example, a very strict "poop and scoop" law is in operation in the UK, and in others a limitation on the number of dogs that any individual may keep.

If you think much of this legislation is unnecessary, bear in mind that up to 10,000 cats and dogs are born every hour in the USA and that 200,000 animals pass through the hands of the American Society for the Prevention of Cruelty to Animals each year. For this reason alone it is vital to make the right initial choice, so that the partnership between dog and owner is a happy and long-lasting one.

The first dogs

Canidae, the family of beasts of prey from which dogs and wolves are descended, first began evolving from prehistoric mammals some 60 million years ago. The *Cynodictis*, a strange-looking creature with a long body, sabre tail and short legs, is generally credited with being the original predecessor of the dog as well as other canines such as the wolf and fox. The dog family, *Canis familiaris*, can be traced back to the Miacis, a tree-climbing, weasel-like carnivore that lived around 50 million years ago. However, the Tomarctus, a fox-like animal that appeared 35 million years later, is believed to be the true ancestor.

The Tomarctus had disappeared by the middle of the Pleistocene age, one million years ago, and today it is agreed that the more recent ancestor of the dog is the social wolf, with which it shares both a great many characteristics and the same dental patterns.

Precisely how dogs became the companions of

humans can only be surmised. Remains found in Denmark show that dogs were domesticated by the time of the Neolithic. Some say this came about when people threw scraps of meat to the wild dogs that crept up to their camp fires, and that later they recognized the value of dogs as hunters and protectors. Others believe that humans began the domestication and breeding of dogs by removing litters of pups from their lairs, irrespective of whether the young were wolves, jackals or wild dogs, all of which would interbreed in domestic conditions.

Breeding for diversity

Certainly, humans would have discovered that, by selective mating, certain traits could be bred in or perpetuated. In this way they were able to produce dogs that were not only a desired color and size, but which had inbred characteristics: for example, strong guarding instincts or keen eyesight.

The first dogs were bred selectively for a specific purpose. The earliest recorded history of dogs, by the Greek Xenophon (c. 430–350 BC, was devoted to hunting and hunting dogs. Not until the Swedish naturalist Carolus Linnaeus (1707–73) produced his *Systema Natura* (*The Order of Nature*) in 1735 were dogs classified other than as workers.

By the middle of the 19th century, with interest in dogs steadily increasing, the need for a Group system became apparent. There were attempts at classification by appearance and according to archaeological evidence for evolution of the species. The current, universally acknowledged, system has generally been developed to take into account the type of work, if any, and the size of breeds.

Miacis   *Tomarctus*

ORIGINS OF THE FAMILY OF DOG

Although a mystery still surrounds its origin, the dog was probably the first animal to be domesticated. Over the years, since the first taming of the wolf and the use of dogs for hunting, a close relationship has evolved between dogs and man. Today, the dog is not only a workmate, but friend, companion, and part of the family.

The family of dog

The pet dog is known by scientists as *Canis familiaris* and as such it is classified together with 35 other species in the family *Canidae*. Well-known members of this family include the wolf, coyote, jackal, fox, and cape hunting dog. As a family, the *Canidae* are found in the wild on all continents with the exception of Antarctica. In Australia, the sole representative is the dingo, which was introduced by man relatively recently, but now lives wild.

Canid species live in a wide range of habitats, from the Sahara desert which is the home of the fennec fox, a small creature with large bat-like ears, to the cold northern wastes where the arctic fox is found. Because of its attachment to man, the domestic dog is distributed more widely than any of its wild relations. However, after thousands of years of domestication, it is now highly dependent on man for food and shelter.

The closest relatives of the domestic dog are the coyote, four species of jackal and the two species of wolf, the common or grey wolf and the red wolf, which is found only in Texas and Louisiana in the USA.

Wolves were once found across all the temperate and sub-arctic areas of the northern hemisphere. Their distribution is now considerably reduced; they disappeared from the UK in the Middle Ages, and from much of Europe and North America during the present century. Nevertheless, the wolf figures in the folklore and legend of the many countries which it once inhabited, and it is generally reputed to be an animal to be feared. However recent studies of wolf behavior suggest that for centuries the animal has been a victim of irrational prejudice. It is, in fact, a highly social, co-operative hunter, which usually feeds on large game animals.

The cape hunting dog and the dhole, or Asiatic wild dog, hunt in packs and are therefore able to kill prey considerably larger than themselves. The other members of the *Canidae* sometimes may hunt in pairs or, like the coyote and some species of jackal, in families.

THE MOST LIKELY ANCESTOR

The mystery of the dog's origin remains, but at present, by majority consent, the wolf is considered the most likely ancestor. However, it is likely that the domestic dog has interbred with different races of wolf and perhaps with the jackal at various times, and that this has produced some of the variations seen in the domestic dog.

Although the dog is man's best friend, and as such the subject of much observation and scientific study, a great mystery still surrounds his origin. This is largely because the dog was domesticated at least 12,000 years ago, and some authorities put it at even longer ago than that, at 15,000 years or more. In fact the dog was probably the first species to be domesticated, although the pig, duck, reindeer, sheep, and goat are other contenders for this distinction.

Charles Darwin, the founder of modern evolutionary theory, suggested that the dog was descended from more than one species of wild canid, putting forward the wolf, coyote, and various species of jackal among others. A modification of this theory was put forward by the eminent living zoologist Konrad Lorenz, who suggested that some breeds, such as Chow and Husky, derive from the wolf, while the majority of breeds evolved from the golden jackal. Lorenz has now altered this view; he still considers that the dog has a multiple origin, but that its ancestors are simply the different races of wolf, which are indeed quite different from one another in size and color.

Another major problem in determining with any certainty the ancestor, or ancestors, of the dog is that there are few significant differences in terms of anatomy, behavior, or genetics between many of the canid species. Indeed it has been found that in certain circumstances the wolf, coyote, and jackal will breed with each other and with the domestic dog. Moreover, the resultant offspring are generally fertile, unlike the mule which is the result of a liaison between a horse and a donkey. This is not surprising in the light of the fact that the chromosomes in the cells of all these species appear to be almost identical when examined under a microscope.

A strong argument in favor of the wolf as the dog's ancestor is that, like the domestic dog but unlike the jackal or coyote, it is a highly social animal. However, the debate goes on and will doubtless continue for many years. In 1977 the zoologist Bouquegneau argued that the jackal will display dog-like social behavior in certain circumstances and should therefore be considered a possible ancestor of the domestic dog.

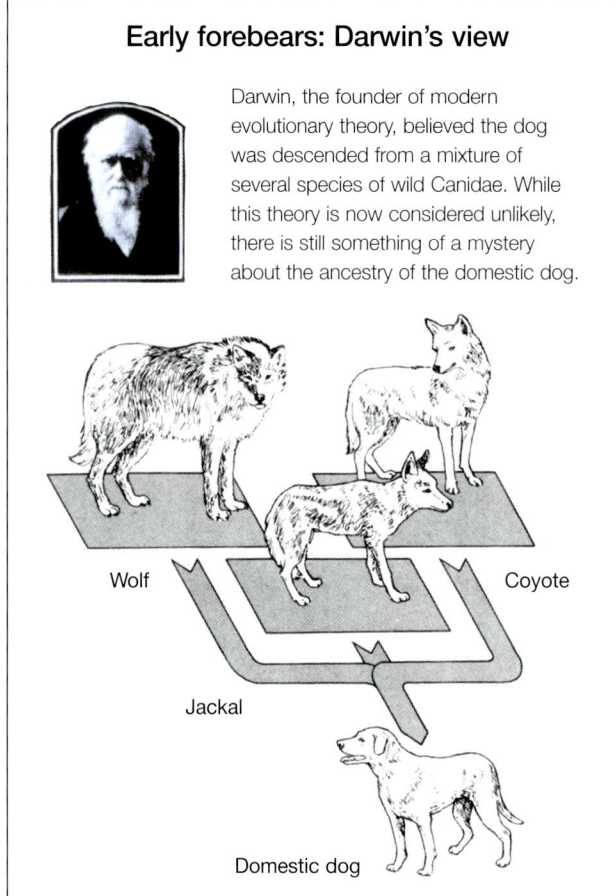

Early forebears: Darwin's view

Darwin, the founder of modern evolutionary theory, believed the dog was descended from a mixture of several species of wild Canidae. While this theory is now considered unlikely, there is still something of a mystery about the ancestry of the domestic dog.

Wolf

Coyote

Jackal

Domestic dog

A quite different suggestion, for which there is little evidence at present, is that there was a dingo-like dog living in Europe and Asia in prehistoric times and that the domestic dog is derived from this.

The huge variations between breeds can also be explained by the theory that the dog was domesticated in several parts of the world at around the same time; different peoples practised selective breeding with these early domestic dogs, but with very different ends in mind.

The likely lineage

The wolf has nearly 40 recognized races. The four shown on this map represent those which have been most often reported as likely later ancestors of the domestic dog, with some mixing of the races.

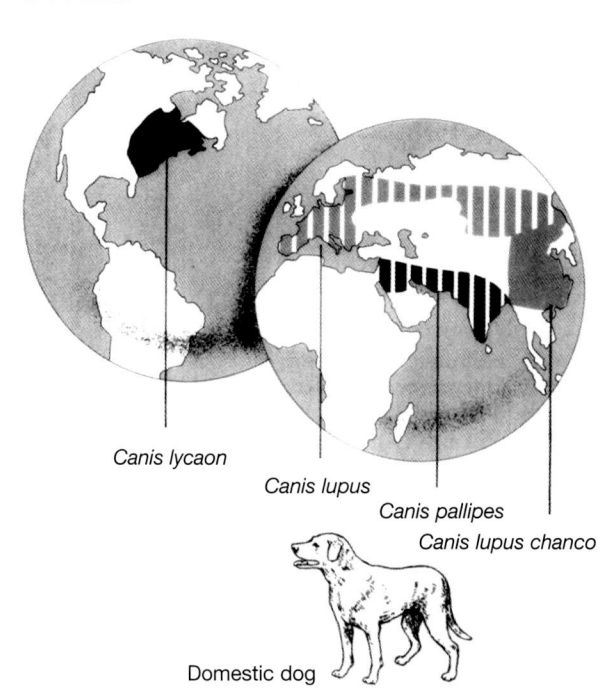

Canis lycaon

Canis lupus

Canis pallipes

Canis lupus chanco

Domestic dog

The dog in ancient times

Once the wolf had been tamed, specialist breeds of what was by then a dog seem to have developed quite quickly. Egyptian pottery, 7,500 years old, shows a dog of the Greyhound/Saluki type, which had almost certainly been bred to chase game in the desert. Greyhounds and Salukis therefore have the longest known pedigrees of all modern breeds, although they have undoubtedly changed since their early days in the desert.

All the evidence suggests that the ancient Egyptians cared as much for their dogs as most modern civilizations, if not more so. Many of their towns had special dog graveyards, and Anubis, the jackal-headed god of death, was the object of devout worship and reverence.

Frescoes, bronzes, carvings, and written references reveal that by 2000 BC the Egyptians had mastered the principles of breeding and developed it to a high level of sophistication; several breeds are depicted, and these include a toy dog, similar to a Maltese, bred almost certainly as a pet and not for any practical purpose.

Sculptures from Babylon, which date from around 2000 BC, show dogs very similar to modern Mastiffs. It seems these were trained to fight in battle, as well as being used for hunting. It is likely that, at a given command from their handlers, they would run ahead and attack the enemy. The use of dogs in this way spread later on to Europe, and even to England, where it is reported that dogs were used against the invading Romans in 55 BC.

The use of dogs for domestic purposes, such as herding and guarding, is not so well documented. Peaceful activities of this kind are not represented as frequently in ancient art as religious ritual, war, and hunting. However, it is certain that dogs for these purposes have been bred in Europe and elsewhere for thousands of years. The Romans had separate descriptive names for house dogs, shepherd dogs, sporting dogs, war dogs, dogs which would fight in arenas as a spectacle, dogs which hunted by scent, and those which hunted by sight. Some of these dogs had specific names which related to regions of the Roman Empire.

The Malamute, the sled and guard dog of the North American Eskimos, was present when Europeans first reached America. It is thought that they have remained close to their present form for several thousand years.

Some of the dogs depicted by Egyptian artists appear to be pet dogs. However, definite evidence of selective breeding for pets dates from a few hundred years BC in Greece. Again, these appear to be of the Maltese type and they were obviously widespread, since similar dogs are reported in Rome a few hundred years later.

Quite separately, the Chinese developed their own famous breed of pet dog, the Pekingese. These miniature dogs were bred during the T'ang dynasty, beginning in the seventh century AD, and were closely associated with the ruling emperors. Pekingeses were also called lion dogs, because the objective was to breed them to look as much like miniature lions as possible.

The taming of the wolf

As discussed in the section on the dog's most likely ancestor, its origins date from its domestication at least 12,000 years ago, some authorities even say 15,000. This suggests that the dog was the first species to be domesticated, before the pig, duck, reindeer, sheep, or goat. The recent discovery in Israel of a man's skeleton buried with his hand resting on a four to five-month old puppy indicates that there was already an affectionate relationship between the two and the dog's teeth indicate that it had already undergone some domestication.

The geographical spread of fossil sites, and the distribution of certain breeds across the world today, suggest that domestication almost certainly took place at a number of different times and places. If dogs are descended from wolves, as seems likely, it is easy to see how this happened.

Man would have lived close to wolves in most parts of the world, and if early man was anything like modern man, it is probable that stray wolf cubs were brought home and looked after by children and their mothers. After all, stray badgers, foxes, deer and other wild species are frequently reared and kept as household pets today.

Attempts have been made to tame wolves in recent years, and these have shown that they are much less docile than dogs and more fearful of anything unfamiliar. However, not all wolves are the same, some being more amenable and well disposed towards humans than others. If wolves of favorable temperament had been selectively bred, a strain of tame wolves could have been established very quickly.

A group of Russians have done just this very recently with silver foxes. The tamest individuals from a group were bred with each other over about 12 generations; the resulting foxes were just as tame as domestic dogs, and quite unlike their wild counterparts.

Clearly, then, the offspring of abandoned wolf cubs could have become pet wolves over a small number of generations; but there is an argument against this theory

Left *Of the nearly 40 races of wolf recognized around the world, four—Canis lycaon, Canis lupus, Canis pallipes and Canis lupus chanco—are thought to be the most likely ancestors of the domestic dog.*

It has to be assumed that the pet wolf began to earn his keep very quickly. He may well have been useful as a guard, alerting his masters to the approach of dangerous animals, or indeed humans. He may have been used as a work animal, pulling sleds for example, and his skin would almost certainly have provided clothing. Other functions could have quickly evolved: guarding flocks; catching game; tracking and flushing out prey using his superior sense of smell.

The long association between man and his best friend must have started in some such way as this. But why, of all the carnivorous species that he might have tamed, did man choose only the wolf and much later the Kaffir cat of the Middle East? In the case of the wolf the answer must lie in the social nature of this animal in the wild.

By selecting the tamest wolves and rearing them with humans from puppyhood, the social dependence of the wolf on other members of the pack, especially the head wolf, could easily have been transferred to man. Treating man as the pack leader, the domestic wolf would have given him total obedience and support, the very qualities which have long endeared the dog to man.

of the dog's origin. Not only would a pet wolf have offered no economic benefit to his masters, but, as a carnivore, he would have eaten a significant quantity of scarce food.

WHO DOMESTICATED THE DOG?

In 1979, Israeli archaeologists digging in the Middle East found the remains of a man and a puppy in close proximity. The hand of the man was resting on the puppy. This was among the remains of a 10,000-year-old Natufian settlement!

It is likely that prehistoric people, realizing they had nothing to fear from the dogs that crept toward their cave or camp fire seeking food and warmth, threw them some scraps of meat. The dogs, realizing, in turn, that humans were not predators, crept closer until a bond of companionship and mutual affection developed.

As time went on, humans would have recognized the value of the dog as a guard, beast of burden, sled dog and hunter, and later would have made the first crude attempts at selective breeding in a desire to perpetuate those traits of conformation, temperament, and ability which they most admired.

Dogs, as we have seen, are descendants of the wolf and it is still possible today to see the result of some of the early attempts at selective breeding. Eskimo dogs are by no means dissimilar to the northern races of the wolf. They were frequently crossed with wolves to maintain their size and stamina. The Samoyed is a descendant of the Siberian Wild Dog. Dogs owned by the North American Indians tend to be smaller animals—likely descendants of the coyote or prairie wolf. Of all European dogs, the German Shepherd is certainly the most wolf-like. It was once known as the Alsatian Wolf Dog.

Early man's best friend

It is apparent that in the early days of domestication, and despite the friendship that had developed between humans and dogs, little or no effort was made to produce anything other than "useful" breeds. The written history of domesticated dogs is, for a thousand years, starting with a work by Xenophon (c. 430–350 BC), essentially about hunting and hunting dogs. Indeed, it was not until 1685, in Nuremberg, that the first encyclopedia of dogs was published: the *Cynographia Curiosa oder*

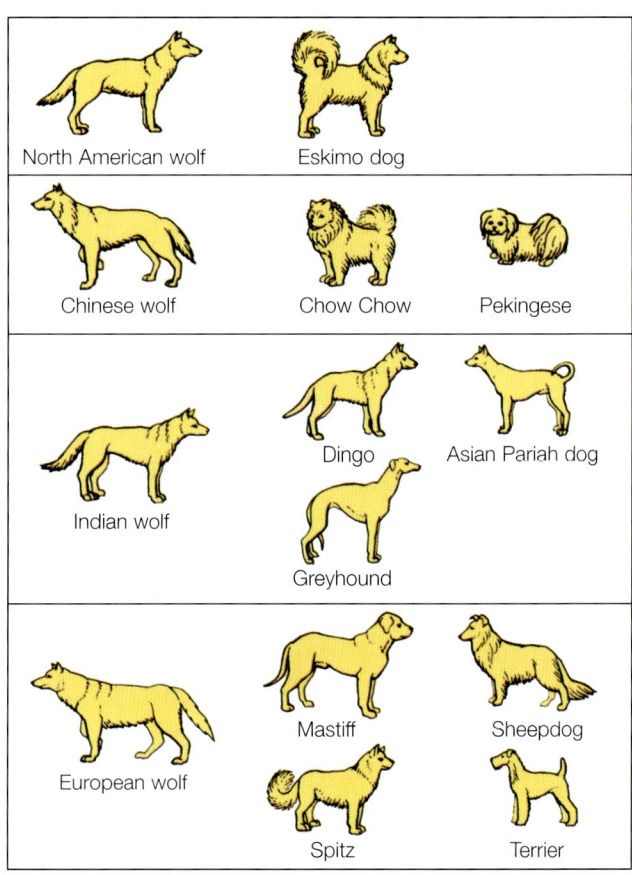

Hundebeschreibung, by Christian Franz Paullini.

A glimpse, however, of the changing role of the dog to meet social requirements, fashion and fancy, can be detected in a letter penned in 1560 by the Cambridge scholar John Caius to the Swiss naturalist Gesner, in which he outlined the breeds of dog in England at that time: *"we also have a small race of dogs that are specially bred to be the playthings of rich and noble ladies. The smaller they are, the more perfectly suited to their purpose, which is to be carried at the breast, in the bedchamber or in the lap, when their mistresses sally forth."*

Hunting and watch dogs still predominated, but the lap dog had begun to make its mark.

THE EVOLUTION OF DOG BREEDS

Today, the pet-seeker has a wider range of breeds, both ancient and modern, to choose from than at any stage in the past. But it is important to study carefully the history of any breed which you are thinking of choosing as a pet, to ensure that it fits into your lifestyle.

Many of today's 300 or so breeds were originally developed in particular countries of the world, for specific purposes in that area. Since then, many have become known to a wider dog-owning public. Keen breeders first usually arrange for the import of these new breeds, establishing a foundation stock in the new country. Although these dogs cannot be shown in their own classes at this stage, there are usually opportunities for them to be exhibited in mixed classes of rare breeds. Then if they prove popular, they are recognized by the governing canine authority and are allotted their own classes at shows, once sufficient numbers have been built up. It can therefore be a lengthy process to establish a new breed and then see it in the show ring.

As might be expected, a number of breeds have remained scarce, and achieved relatively little recognition among the dog-owning public at large. The popularity of a breed tends to rise and fall in accordance with fashion, but there will always be a dedicated core of breeders looking after its interests.

During recent years, the Hungarian breeds have become much better known outside the native land. Despite their long history—the origins of the Komondor date back over 1,000 years—they have been seen in the USA only since the 1930s, and are even less common in Europe.

The appearance of the Komondor may not appeal to everyone, as they have a dense, corded coat. But this served to protect them from the climate, and enabled them to blend in among the sheep flocks which they guarded against wolves and other predators. It also helped to protect them from attacks by wolves.

The smaller version of the Komondor is called the Puli. This breed was used essentially for herding sheep, rather than defending them from attack. The traditional form of the Puli's coat is again corded, but in the combined interests of fashion and expediency some breeders have encouraged owners to simply brush the coat Afro-style, rather than retaining the cords. Coat care in this case, as with the Komondor, is a lengthy process.

These utilitarian breeds lack the sleek appearance of the hunting dog of the Hungarian nobles, known simply as the Vizsla, which translates as "alert and responsive." The native form of the Vizsla is smooth-coated and varies in color from shades of sandy yellow through to gold. It was only during the 1930s, by which time the breed had become scarce, that the wire-haired form was produced. It involved the crossings of Vizslas with German Wire-haired Pointers.

These Hungarian examples give an insight into the development of breeds in other countries. There were those produced for looking after flocks, which called for bravery at a time when wolves and bears were far more numerous, especially in Europe, than they are today. Smaller breeds actually managed the livestock, while for recreation, the nobility bred hounds. As hunting patterns changed, and firearms became more reliable for hunting game, so gundogs, working either individually or in small groups, came into existence.

Today, the pet-seeker has a wider range of breeds, both ancient and modern, to choose from than at any stage in the past. But it is important to study carefully the history of any breed which you are thinking of choosing as a pet, to make sure that it fits into your lifestyle. Only in the last 100 years or so have dogs evolved away from their working ancestries to become primarily companion animals—and for some breeds, this transition has been more difficult than others.

THE DEVELOPMENT OF THE PURE-BREED DOG

Below The Bulldog's shoulders are broad, sloping, and deep. They are also very powerful and muscular, giving the appearance of having been tacked on to its body.

Localized forms obviously tended to evolve into dogs of recognizable type, although they were not breeds in the sense that we understand it today. These dogs were bred for particular purposes rather than to conform as closely as possible to a prescribed ideal form in terms of their appearance, as pure-bred dogs are today. Interest in this field arose largely during Victorian times, when "fancying," or the selective breeding of livestock for particular features, became highly fashionable. This was coupled to the rise of dog shows, where the various breeds were paraded and judged, with prizes being given to the winners in each category.

The most famous dog show in the world, organized by Charles Cruft, began in 1890. Originally, this had started as a show for the terrier breeds, which were extremely popular in Victorian England, but soon it began to cater for all other breeds as well. Indeed, Queen Victoria herself entered some of her Pomeranians in 1891, and this royal link with dogs has continued right through to the present day.

The foundation of the Kennel Club in the UK, which became the governing body in the canine world, took place in 1873. This was to prove the major influence in the development of pure breed dogs: from its inception, it began to establish stud books for the various breeds. The Kennel Club was also instrumental in establishing the standards against which the various breeds are judged. Once the Kennel Club had defined the required characteristics of the different breeds, it became possible for breeders to assess their dogs against the "ideal" for their breed, as laid down in the standards.

Since those early years, various modifications to the individual standards have been made, and dog breeding has become much more international. As a result, many breeds have become available, and the Kennel Club has helped to nurture their development in the UK, in conjunction with the breeders themselves and the breed societies. The influence of the Kennel Club has also spread far afield. In the USA, the American Kennel Club was established during 1883, on similar lines to its British equivalent, and a Canadian counterpart was set up four years later. Today, similar organizations are to be found throughout the world where dog showing is popular.

WERE DOGS ALWAYS POPULAR?

Even in astrology, dogs are a force to be reckoned with and there is more than a little truth in the saying that "every dog has its day." There are 40 "dog days" between July 3rd and August 11th, when Sirius, the Dog Star, rises and sets with the sun. The superstition that Sirius greatly influences the canine race is found in Greek literature, as far back as Hesiod in the eighth century BC.

There have always been dog lovers and dog haters. Indeed, the recent rebellion in the UK against the proposed registration of dogs is nothing new. In 1796 there was a motion to introduce the first duties on dogs in England, five shillings on "outdoor" dogs, three shillings on "indoor" dogs. It was proposed by one George T. Clark, who was rewarded for his trouble with the receipt of dozens of dead dogs in hampers, packed as game. There was a massacre of dogs by owners who objected to paying the dues.

On balance the dog has been more revered than reviled through the ages. The ancient Egyptians are known to have had faithful dogs buried alongside them, a practice also followed in ancient America by the Toltec people, and later by the Aztecs, whose dogs were sacrificed at funerals in the belief that they would guide their masters to a better world.

Holy dogs

We know that the dog has played a large part in Eastern religions and that although it is considered by Moslems to be an outcast of Allah, and unclean, the fleet-footed Saluki is still prized with pure-bred Arab horses.

Hindus believe that a person who ill-treats a dog will be punished by returning to earth in canine form. It is often the fear of the unknown that has made humans behave unreasonably towards animals. Here lies the source of totemism—the identification of themselves by human families with an animal family—and of metempsychosis—the belief in the transmigration of human souls, and the return in an animal's body. The importance of shepherd dogs and guard dogs was stressed in the teachings of the Persian prophet Zoroaster (Zarathustra), almost 3,000 years ago. Zoroaster's doctrine, which spread widely in the East, bore many references to dogs and their importance. He decreed: "If these two dogs of mine, the shepherd dog and the guard dog, pass the house of any of my faithful people, let them never be kept away from it, for no house could exist, but for these two dogs of mine, the shepherd dog and the guard dog."

Dogs were even worshipped by the followers of Mithras, who was aided and accompanied by his dog, and whose cult flourished for almost five centuries in Roman times, spreading from India to Spain and from Egypt to the south of Scotland.

There is a dog-worshipping sect to this day. It is called the Brotherhood of the Essenes. The Essenes maintain that there are animal planes in the celestial Kingdom which they relinquish voluntarily as they journey through the gates of the zodiac into the Earth's sphere. According to their beliefs, dogs are beings without sin, sent to Earth to test humans.

Above *The Saluki is a fleet-footed dog able to keep pace with fast Arab horses. In the Middle East it is still used for hunting gazelle. Elsewhere it is mainly kept as a lean and elegant pet.*

CHOOSING A BREED

During recent years, there has been growing concern about the temperament of some breeds, with Rottweilers in particular gaining a bad reputation in the media for their ferocity. When selecting a pure-bred, you must always consider its ancestry. Inherited traits established over many generations will still influence the behavior of the breed today. The Rottweiler has a long history as a brave and powerful guard dog, and has obviously retained some potentially aggressive traits within its personality.

Aside from providing us with companionship, dogs are still used for various working purposes. The Rottweiler is sometimes employed as a police dog, emphasizing the responsive and intelligent side of its nature. Other dogs, bred primarily for hunting purposes, are much harder to train successfully. Hounds such as the Afghan will prove far less amenable in this regard when compared to other sporting dogs,

Left *Aggression can be a serious problem with powerful guard dogs like the Rottweiler, so it is essential that such a breed be trained responsibly from the start.*

such as members of the retriever group. Throughout their existence, the retriever breeds have worked closely alongside their owners. It is no coincidence that while still fulfilling their traditional role as gun dogs, retrievers are also now used as guide dogs for the blind and for people who are hard of hearing. Their excellent scenting abilities mean that they can also be trained successfully to detect drugs and explosives. Working sheepdogs can still be found throughout the world and they make popular companions, although these dogs may sometimes become rather bored and frustrated in urban surroundings. It is important to consider the individual needs of the breed, together with your own personal surroundings, before making any decision about obtaining a dog. Sadly, too many

Left *Afghans require considerable exercise, but few breeds can rival them for elegance and individuality.*

people base their choice simply on a breed's appearance, without considering its evolution.

While it is obvious that a large dog requires more space, and will prove more costly to feed than a smaller breed, other factors, such as the dog's temperament and ease of training, are likely to be more relevant to the relationship between dog and owner, and, ultimately, to the enjoyment of ownership. Other factors to consider when choosing a breed are the coat care required—the smooth-coated breeds such as the Greyhound being the least demanding in this regard—and, possibly, its lifespan. As a rough guide, the large breeds, such as the Irish Wolfhound, may live for less than a decade, whereas many of the smaller dogs will remain active well into their teens.

The cost of a pedigree dog is influenced by several factors. The relative scarcity of a breed will have a direct impact on its price, as under these circumstances demand will probably outstrip supply and there may well be a waiting list for puppies. The quality of both the bloodline, measured in terms of show performance, and the potential of the individual puppies themselves will also influence the price asked by the breeder. If you are looking simply for a pet dog, rather than a good show specimen, the cost should be correspondingly lower.

Breeders invariably have some surplus puppies that, possibly because of faults in their markings for example, will not do well in the show ring. Such dogs will invariably settle down and give great pleasure as pets, but beware of any individuals with a known physical deformity. These could prove a source of worry and trouble, not to mention veterinary expense, in later life.

Although it is sometimes claimed that cross-bred (mongrel) puppies are healthier than their pure-bred counterparts, there is no real truth in this assertion. They are equally susceptible to diseases such as distemper and the various parasites that may afflict dogs. There is possibly a greater risk, however, that pure-bred dogs may suffer from certain congenital weaknesses such as Hip Dysplasia (HD) or Progressive Retinal Atrophy (PRA). Responsible breeders will have their breeding stock screened for these particular conditions, thus minimizing the risk of the problem occurring later in their offspring.

Below *Poodle puppies at two days old.*

Left *Guide dogs for the blind, or "seeing eyes" as they are called in the USA, must rank as the most valuable group of trained dogs.*

The Airedale Terrier is the largest of the terrier breeds. It is named after the River Aire in Yorkshire, UK, where it was first bred.

CHOOSING AN INDIVIDUAL DOG

Right *A careful veterinary examination is essential before vaccinating a young puppy.*

Below left *Many infectious diseases may cause severe dehydration owing to persistent vomiting and diarrhoea. To replace the fluid an intravenous drip is required.*

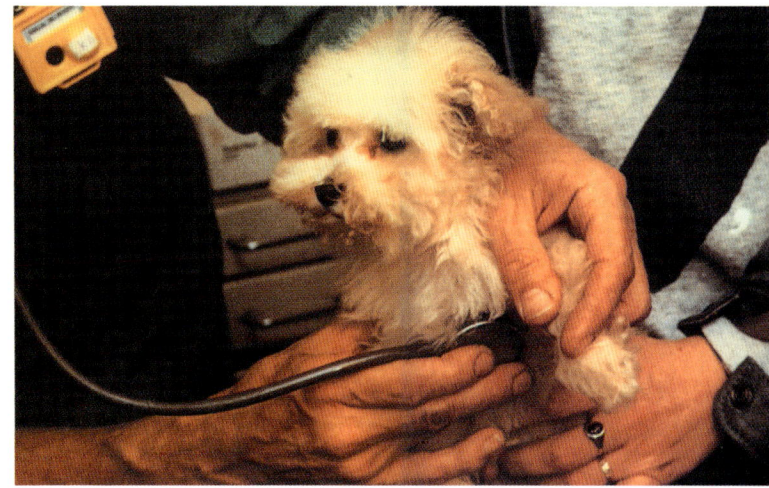

Having decided on a particular breed, you can then track down puppies without too much difficulty in most cases. Your veterinarian may be able to suggest a breeder within your locality, and there are also directories which list breeders of pedigree dogs, often on a regional basis. The various dog magazines and newspapers may also be a useful source of reference. It will obviously make life easier if you obtain your puppy as close to home as possible, although, particularly if you are looking for a potential show dog, you may want to see several litters before taking any decision, and this may entail traveling further afield. In the USA especially, a good range of pedigree puppies are available from pet stores, although you will obviously not have the advantage of seeing their parents or home surroundings if you buy from such a source.

It is obviously vital to select a healthy puppy, and if you are at all concerned, especially when considering a puppy in a pet store, it would be best to delay your

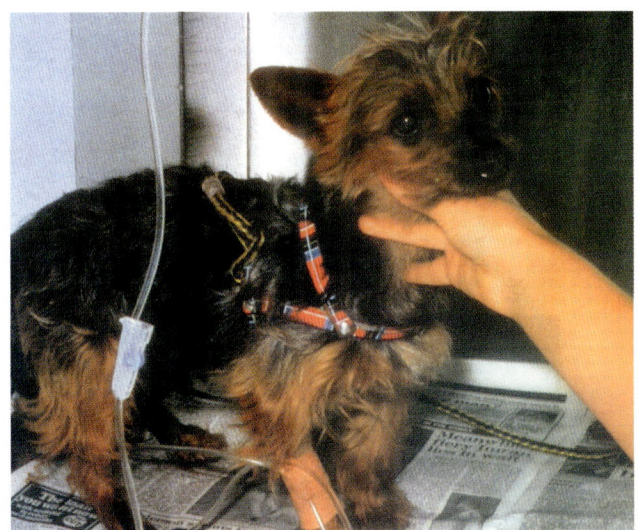

purchase. Puppies are normally lively, but remember that they will sleep for longer than adult dogs. Always watch them running about, as this will reveal any trace of lameness. The puppy's skin should feel quite loose when you handle it, and, over all, it ought to be relatively plump.

There should be no trace of either fleas or lice on the coat. If the pup is distinctly pot-bellied, this tends to be indicative of a heavy burden of intestinal parasites. When you are feeling around in this area, locate the remains of the umbilicus, in the mid-line of the body. In a few cases, a hernia may have occurred during the birth process, creating a swelling that might need to be corrected by surgery later.

The puppy's motions should appear firm, although, occasionally, following deworming, an outbreak of diarrhoea may result. Even so, view any puppies with diarrhoea cautiously, as this could be evidence of a more serious affliction. In any event, always make an appointment to take a newly acquired puppy to a veterinarian at an early opportunity, both for a health check and to discuss the necessary schedule of vaccinations. You must also sort out the paperwork regarding the transfer of ownership of the puppy to you, which will mean notifying the registration authority in the country concerned. The breeder should be able to advise you if you have any doubts about this procedure.

ARE DOGS INTELLIGENT?

One of the reasons why dogs bring great comfort to humans is their uncanny facility of picking up our moods. The dog, in common with its ancestor, the wolf, is sensitive to atmosphere. That is why it will come and sit quietly beside us when we are despondent or jump around enthusiastically when we are in high spirits.

This is a question which scientists have argued over for centuries. We know that dogs are incapable of logical thought as we know it. They cannot reason as we can, but in terms of a "domestic wolf" they are indeed intelligent, relying on association, scent, instinct, and memory. They also display characteristics of guarding, loyalty, and playfulness which are typical of the wolf pack and a keen sense of humor.

It is known that pups untouched by human hands during the first weeks of life never become wholly domesticated. Similarly, the dog that is kennelled, fed, groomed, and exercised, but otherwise given little attention, is unlikely to reach the same potential as its contemporary which is kept as a household pet, spoken to regularly, played with, and introduced to any number of outside influences and experiences.

Teaching your dog

Dog training must be interpreted by the dog as an extension of play learning; however it is largely a matter of association. Some dogs, like some humans, are more intelligent than others, but there are few, given time, which, having recognized the key words, will not react to sentences such as: "Shall we (Let's) go for a WALK, Ben?," "Do you want your DINNER?," "Here's MUM (or Dad)!" and "Let's go and meet JANE." The list is endless and the dog's reaction could reasonably be thought to mean that it understands the meaning of the word spoken. It cannot do so, but associates the key word, whether or not used in conjunction with its name, with the action that takes place thereafter.

Actions rather than words

It is not just the spoken word that brings about this association in the canine mind. Actions can speak as loudly as words. The mere fact of a dog's owner walking into the hall, or kitchen, with a coat on may be enough for the dog to jump up from its basket in anticipation of a walk, while the sound of a car engine in the drive may be sufficient to send it running hurriedly to the door in anticipation of its master's arrival. Undoubtedly the more time one spends with one's dog the more it learns, and the more it learns, the more it endears itself to us. Most pet owners have only one dog. They do not have the same opportunity, as those who keep several, of studying the behavior of the social pack.

Substitute pack leaders

It has been explained how humans became substitute pack leaders, whom our domesticated wolf knows he must respect. Where, however, there are a number of dogs, the biggest, strongest male will generally emerge as the canine pack leader. He will marshal his troops, standing aside, for instance, until all have been accounted for when going out of doors. He will guard the food bowls, sometimes literally forbidding another dog to eat until he allows it to do so—even, on some occasions, giving a disliked subordinate what amounts to the evil eye until the unfortunate animal creeps away into a corner. Much however depends on the breed and temperament of the dog.

RARE AND UNUSUAL DOGS

The world's rarest dog is reckoned to be the Tahltan Bear Dog which, as its name implies, was once used by the Tahltan Indians of western Canada for bear hunting, also against lynx and porcupine. It is understood that the Indians carried these dogs—the weight of which is around 30 lb (13 kg)—in hide sacks on their backs, so as to preserve their strength for when the quarry was sighted, at which time they would promptly be released. The job of the bear dog was to hold the proposed victim at bay, circling it until its masters moved in for the kill. There must be less than a handful of the breed now alive and it is sadly in danger of extinction. This was a fate which threatened the Chinese Shar Pei and the Chinese Crested dog not so long ago, and both are now fairly commonplace, particularly in the British show ring.

The Podengo

It would indeed be true to say that what is rare today may not be rare tomorrow, so one must hope that the future will be brighter for another breed threatened with extinction, the Portuguese Warren Hound or Podengo, which is little known outside its country of origin where it is a hunter of rabbit, hare, and deer. There are three sizes of the variety, the grande (large), which stands 22–27 in (56–58 cm) high, a small variety (pequeno), which resembles a large, smooth coated Chihuahua, and a medium sized dog. The grande is not unlike the Ibizan Hound.

The Portuguese Water Dog

There is another Portuguese dog which is unusual albeit not so rare, and that is the Portuguese Water Dog, a

---

On ice

The Broholmer is a breed recognized only in its native Denmark. It was believed to have become extinct in the 1960s but then, in December 1974, a dog of the breed appeared at the home of a pharmacist in Helsinki, Finland. The Royal Veterinary College in Copenhagen set up a frozen sperm bank for the dog, which was named Bjoern, in the hope that a bitch might eventually be found. But alas, this did not prove to be the case, and Bjoern died in January 1975.

A rock day

The Lundehund is a breed which for centuries has lived solely on two islands in the north of Norway. Unlike other dogs which have four toes, possibly an atrophied fifth, the Lundehund has five toes and an atrophied sixth. Also, unlike other small dogs with five toe cushions, the Lundehund has seven or eight. Because of its small size and this strange foot equipment the dog is enabled to scale rocks and cliffs so as to gently lift a Puffin from its nest and restore it unharmed to his master.

---

fascinating animal, which was once readily to be seen at Portuguese and Spanish seaports working as a fisherman's dog, guarding his nets. It is remarkable in that it will catch an escaping fish in its jaws and swim back with it to its master. There are short, curly-coated and long-coated varieties, but it is the latter that calls for attention when it is presented in a smart lion clip similar to that of the elegant Poodle.

The Lowchen

The Lowchen, a native French breed, registered in its country of origin under the title "petit chien lion," little lion dog, had all but died out little more than 20 years ago, but is now a popular contender in the show ring—though little seen, it must be admitted, being taken for a walk in a park.

WHAT IS A PURE BREED?

A pure breed dog is one whose sire (father) and dam (mother) are of the same breed, the parents having themselves descended from dogs of the same breed. It has been explained how early people would have attempted planned matings of their canine companions so as to perpetuate those traits they admired and desired. They would have experimented with such things as height, weight, and coat-type, with color patterns, with the shape of the dog's head and skull, and the setting of its tail until, in the course of a few generations the desired canine type would breed true.

Doubtless subsequent dog fanciers would have discussed the attributes of their animals much as people do today. However, while we have the legacy of many paintings which depict breeds of dogs that appear to have changed little from those we know now, it is almost impossible to chart their progress. This is because it was not until 1873 that the Kennel Club in London—the first of its kind in the world—was formed. The Kennel Club introduced a registration system, so that one might determine the breeding of every pure-bred canine—in what amounted to its own birth certificate—and also refer to an approved "standard" for each variety of dog that was recognized.

Of course the desire to continue to introduce and improve breeds has continued and there are remarkably few varieties which do not owe their present existence to another breed. The Doberman, for example, owes much to the Rottweiler and Manchester Terrier, and the little Long Coat Chihuahua to the Papillon, or Butterfly dog, so named because of the shape of its ears.

Tallest and shortest

- *The tallest of breeds are the Great Dane, the Irish Wolfhound, the Saint Bernard, the English Mastiff, the Borzoiain, and the Anatolian Karabash (Turkish Shepherd dog). All of these breeds can attain 36 in (90 cm) at the shoulder.*

- *The smallest dog breed is the Chihuahua, the recognized weight of which is between 2 and 6 lb (0.9 and 2.75 kg). Mexico City's natural history museum, however, has the skeleton of a fully grown Chihuahua measuring only 7 in (18 cm) in total length. There is no weight quoted for this dog, which was presented in 1910, but it is estimated that, if its bones are anything to go by, it could not have weighed more than 1 lb (0.45 kg).*

- *The second smallest dog is reckoned to be the Yorkshire Terrier which "officially" should not weigh more than 7 lb (3.2 kg), but many "Yorkies" nowadays tend to be much heavier.*

Right *The Greyhound is a pure breed that has not altered materially from its likeness carved in an Egyptian tomb in the Nile Valley c.4000 BC. It has been used for coursing since Roman times. Nowadays it is bred along distinct lines for showing, coursing and track racing.*

WHAT ARE CROSSBREEDS?

A crossbreed is the progeny of a pure-bred bitch which has mated with a pure-bred dog of another pure breed—for example, the result of a Poodle–Spaniel mating.

There are those who favor a crossbreed believing that they will have the benefit of the attributes of both breeds. In fact, a problem often arises where an owner, having lost a crossbreed of a certain type, wishes to replace it with another, for crossbreeds are rarely intentionally bred.

A mongrel is a dog or bitch whose sire and dam are likely to owe their make-up to any number of different breeds.

Feet first

The best way to determine how large a mongrel puppy is likely to grow is to look at the size of its feet. A pup with really large feet is destined to be a mammoth-sized dog.

Old wives' tale

There is an old wives' tale that mongrels are more robust then pure-bred dogs. In fact, the mongrel is unlikely to be any tougher, or weaker, than its pure-bred contemporaries.

There is no doubt that mongrels make excellent pets but there is always an element of uncertainty as to how they will turn out in regard to either appearance or temperament.

pure breed of same type = pure breed

pure breeds of different type = "X" breed

"X" breed + "X" breed = mongrel

WHAT IS A CERTIFICATE OF PEDIGREE?

It is a common mistake to refer to a "pedigree" dog. The correct term is a pure-bred dog. A Certificate of Pedigree is the document which should be handed to the buyer of a pure-bred pup at the time of purchase. The buyer should also be given a Transfer form enabling him or her, for a modest fee, to register the pup in the buyer's name, in place of the vendor's, with the respective national kennel club.

The Certificate of Pedigree which, like the Transfer form, should be signed by the breeder, must show the registered name and number of the puppy—obviously you can call your pup whatever pet name you wish—its date of birth, and the registered names and registration numbers of its parents and ancestors for three, or preferably five, generations.

This Certificate of Pedigree is a valuable document which calls for careful scrutiny. Unless the pup's parents are registered, and the signature of the breeder appears, the new owner will be unable to register a transfer of ownership and, perhaps more importantly, will be unable to enter the dog in pure breed show classes, or to register and sell its subsequent progeny as pure-bred.

You will probably notice on a Certificate of Pedigree that most of the dogs' names bear a Prefix, for instance, Merry Max of Penfold, or Penfold Merry Max. This is because breeders, again for a modest fee, are enabled to register a Prefix with their respective kennel club, which enables stock from their kennels to be easily recognized. Where a dog has been bred by the Prefix holder, the word will appear in front of the dog's name (called an Affix). If the dog has been acquired, the Prefix will follow the dog's name, for example "of" or "at," and this is called a Suffix.

How to detect prize winning stock

If you attend dog shows and look at the catalog entries for a specific breed, you may find it interesting to detect, from their affixes, those kennels that predominate and produce considerable prizewinning stock.

Pedigree certificates are usually completed by hand. Those which have entries written in red ink are highly prized, for only the names of champions are thus honored.

The American and British championship systems are different. In the UK, champions are dogs which have been awarded three Challenge Certificates at three different Championship Dog Shows and by three different judges. In the USA, a championship is attained via an accumulation of points. A dog that has accumulated 15 points is designated a Champion. The dog may earn from one to five points at a show, and only one male and one female can win points a show.

It is worth repeating that, when buying a pup, the Certificate of Pedigree warrants careful scrutiny and that even if the pup you intend to buy is an attractive and healthy example of its breed, and you have no intention of exhibiting or breeding from it, if the Certificate is incomplete, the pup should not command as high a price as its fellows which are correctly documented.

MAN'S BEST FRIEND

Right That dogs can be trained to walk on the leash with safety uppermost is shown by this guide dog helping its owner through slippery and snowy territory.

Unlike the cat, which is a natural loner, the dog is by nature a gregarious, friendly animal. As has been seen, the first dogs were very probably descended from tamed wolf cubs, the offspring of social animals who lived in packs. In the absence of the pack these early predecessors of the modern dog gave the allegiance and affection which is a part of their nature, to the humans who reared them. A dog's friend became his human companions, who were themselves social animals, happy to reciprocate the gestures of a friendship made toward them.

And so it has been ever since. The first dogs helped man in many ways—guarding, herding, fighting, and hunting—but man saw the dog as something more than just economically useful and this was revealed early on when he chose to breed dogs specifically as pets. What is a pet, but a friend?

Of course, many dogs still perform a working role as well as providing friendship, but it is significant that in a recent survey 88 per cent of dog owners gave companionship as a reason for keeping their dogs. A much smaller number, 40 per cent, mentioned the protection that the dog afforded them.

In most countries, the number of dogs kept as pets has grown dramatically over the last 50 years. The most dogs per numbers of households are found in the USA and France, where almost one family in three has a dog. The lowest levels of dog ownership are found in Germany and Switzerland, 11 percent of households, and in Japan, 13 percent. In the UK about 25 percent of households have a dog.

Few attempts have been made to explain the growth of dog ownership which has occurred during this century. The scientific studies and surveys that have been made suggest that changes in the organization of society have made more people seek the companionship that a dog offers. Urban man has become separated from his relatives, and neighbourliness too has suffered as people move readily from place to place seeking better jobs, houses, and so on. A man's dog, on the other hand, is always pleased to see him and ready to give and receive affection.

To most ways of thinking, a dog fulfils the role of companion or friend better than a cat, which is by nature a more independent, solitary animal. It is significant then that, in almost every country where statistics exist, dogs are now more popular than cats.

The protection offered by a dog is obviously an important factor, and here again he scores over the cat. His ability to guard his owner and his home was one of the qualities which first endeared him to man thousands of years ago. In those days he afforded protection from wild animals; now he serves to ward off human assailants and intruders.

THE INSIDE STORY

If you take a random selection of pure-bred dogs, you will notice that their faces, ears, eyes, heads, color, even the way in which they move—their gait—differ. As many new breeds have developed over the years, and continue to develop and become recognized as official breeds by the kennel clubs, it has become necessary to standardize the way in which all these differences are described

All dogs, even the Saint Bernard and the Chihuahua, have broadly similar skeletal structure. They all have the same number of bones, and these are of reasonably uniform shape throughout the species. However, centuries of selective breeding have caused the relative lengths of bones to vary immensely from one breed to another. For example, the Scottish Terrier has very short limb bones and a relatively large head, while the Greyhound has very long limb bones and a relatively small skull and body skeleton.

A dog's nails, or claws, are the equivalent of human finger and toe nails, but they are much stronger. Dogs are not good at climbing in part because their claws are not retractile like a cat's. Also, a dog's skeleton has essentially evolved for running long distances over fairly flat terrain. A cat's skeleton, on the other hand, is highly flexible enabling it to turn its whole body and limbs for gripping while climbing, but it is not suited for running in more than short bursts.

A dog's tail performs a different function from that of a cat, which is used largely to help the cat balance as well as for communication. The different breeds of dogs have tails of all shapes and sizes, but they make a limited contribution to the dog's sense of balance. The tail is used primarily for communication; wagging it, letting it droop, and moving it in a variety of ways enables the dog to express his feeling to both humans and other dogs.

Every breed of dog has the same number of the four different types of teeth: incisors, canines, premolars, and molars. The dog's own scientific name is used to describe the pair of large tearing teeth, seen at top and bottom toward the front of a dog's mouth; these are, of course, found in other species including man.

The bite of the incisors at the front of the mouth varies

between the breeds. A level bite is when the six top and bottom incisors meet evenly; if they overlap slightly, this is known as a scissor bite. An undershot bite is where the lower jaw protrudes beyond the upper one, while an overshot bite is the opposite condition.

These jaw differences are caused by the structure of the skull, a part of the dog which has been subject to strong selective breeding. Like the skeleton, there are fundamental similarities between the skulls of all dogs, but selection has produced great variation, from, for

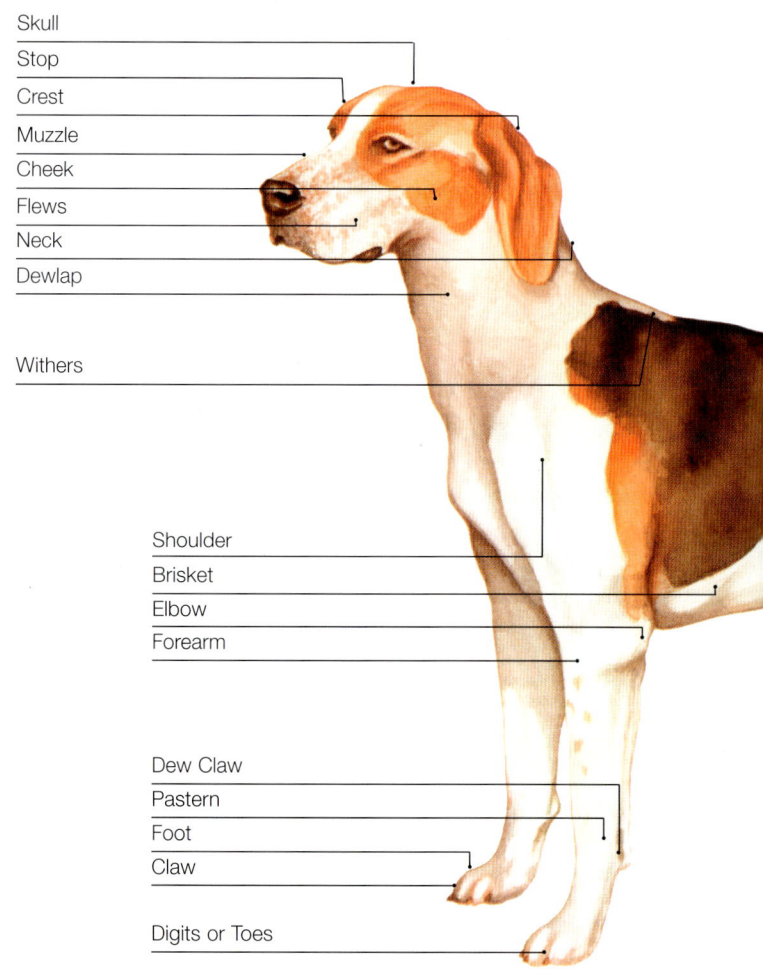

Skull
Stop
Crest
Muzzle
Cheek
Flews
Neck
Dewlap
Withers
Shoulder
Brisket
Elbow
Forearm
Dew Claw
Pastern
Foot
Claw
Digits or Toes

example, the very flat face of the Pekingese to the long face of the Borzoi.

Skulls vary considerably in width, and this is largely determined by what anatomists call the zygomatic arches, the bones below the eyes on the upper jaw. In the Labrador and Saint Bernard these are strong and arched outward, while in the German Shepherd Dog and the Fox Terrier they are much less pronounced.

Although the Labrador's head seems bigger and broader than a Fox Terrier's, this does not mean that his brain is any larger.

Some breeds, including Red Setters and Bloodhounds, have a prominent sagittal crest, the ridge on the top of the skull. Again, this does not mean that they have bigger brains, but it does allow for the attachment of extra muscles which are used for biting.

The scottie's unique bone structure shows how selected breeding results in varied physical types.

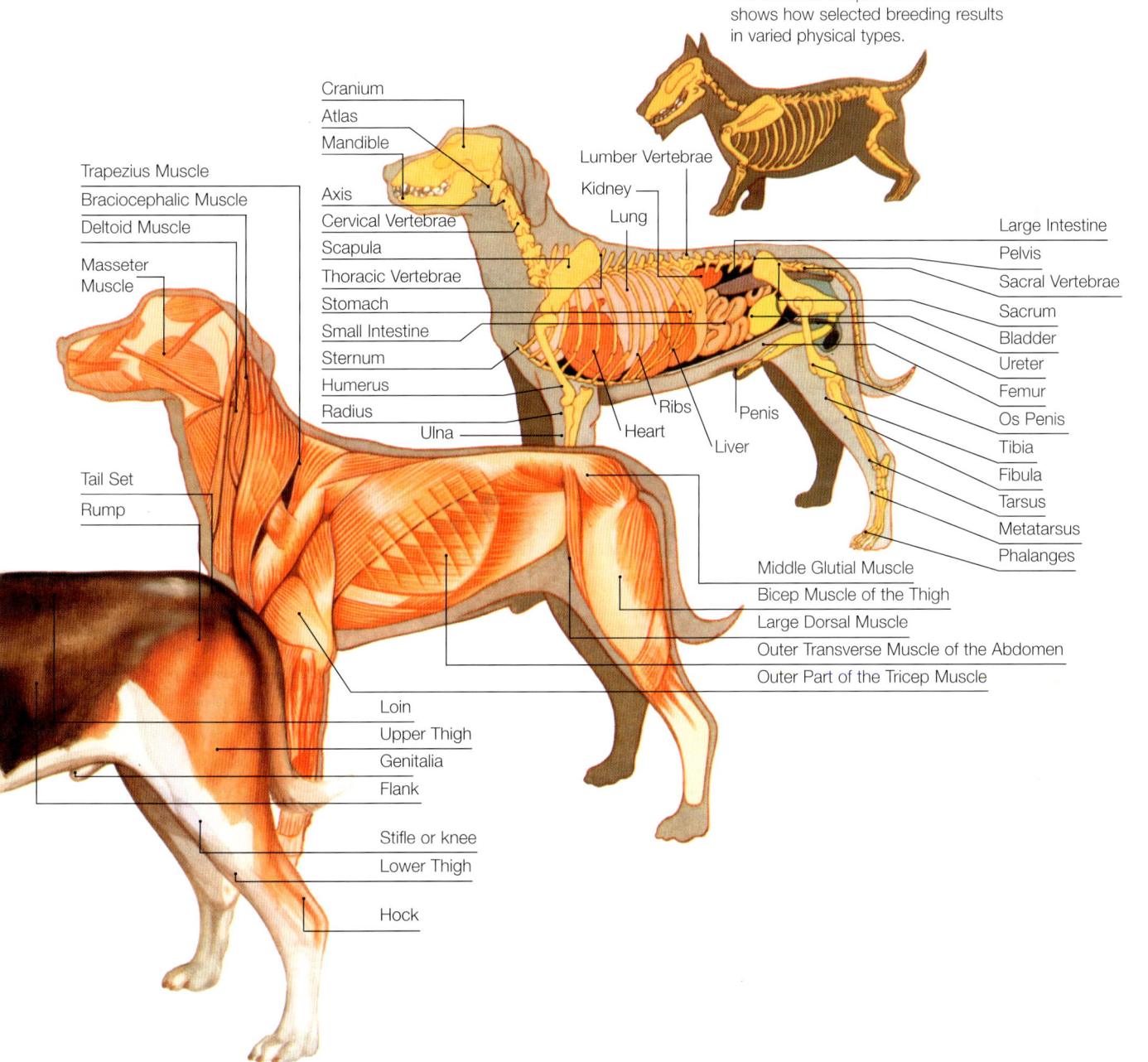

Cranium
Atlas
Mandible
Lumber Vertebrae
Kidney
Trapezius Muscle
Axis
Lung
Braciocephalic Muscle
Cervical Vertebrae
Large Intestine
Deltoid Muscle
Scapula
Pelvis
Masseter Muscle
Thoracic Vertebrae
Sacral Vertebrae
Stomach
Sacrum
Small Intestine
Bladder
Sternum
Ureter
Humerus
Femur
Radius
Os Penis
Ulna
Ribs
Penis
Tibia
Heart
Liver
Fibula
Tail Set
Tarsus
Rump
Metatarsus
Phalanges
Middle Glutial Muscle
Bicep Muscle of the Thigh
Large Dorsal Muscle
Outer Transverse Muscle of the Abdomen
Outer Part of the Tricep Muscle
Loin
Upper Thigh
Genitalia
Flank
Stifle or knee
Lower Thigh
Hock

DOGS' BITE AND HEADS

Bite

A dog's bite is defined by the position of the lower jaw relative to the upper jaw. Not all dogs are required to have an even bite, but in some breeds, for example the Chihuahua, it is a show fault to be either over or undershot.

Heads

There are three skull types. These describe the basic shape of the head which comprises 50 bones. There are many subtypes that come within these basic groups. Heads lacking in refinement are said to be coarse.

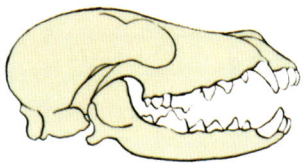

NORMAL

A level bite, where the upper and lower rows of teeth meet up.

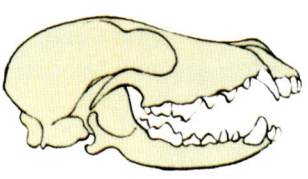

OVERSHOT

A short lower jaw, where the lower incisors (front teeth) protrude beyond the inner surface of the upper incisors.

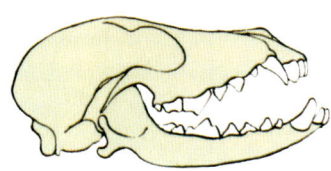

UNDERSHOT

A long lower jaw, with the incisors projecting beyond those of the upper jaw.

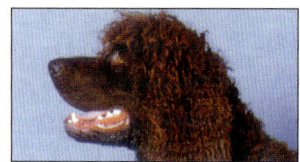

MESOTICEPHALIC

Medium proportions of bone width to overall length of the skull (Irish Water Spaniel).

BRACHYCEPHALIC

Short, compressed head, with a rounded cranium (Pekingese).

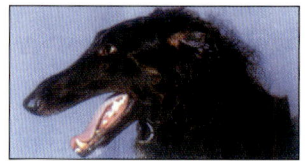

DOLICHOCEPHALIC

Long narrow head, with shallow cranium (Borzoi).

APPLE

Domed and rounded (Chihuahua).

BALANCED

Skull and foreface equal in length to form a consistent whole (Springer Spaniel).

BLOCKY

Square or cube-like formation (Staffordshire Bull Terrier).

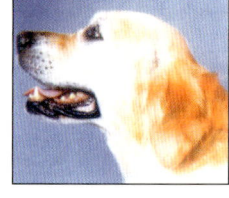

CLEAN

Free from wrinkles or bony or muscular lumps (Golden Retriever).

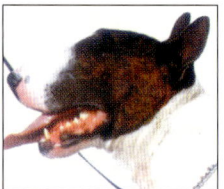

EGG-SHAPED

Strong and deep and free from hollowing, right to the end of the muzzle (Bull Terrier).

FOX-LIKE

Sharp expression, pointed nose, short foreface, and pointed ears (Lapland Spitz).

OTTER

Head shaped like an otter's with broad, flat skull and short, strong muzzle (Border Terrier).

PEAR-SHAPED

Rounded, narrow skull with a tapering muzzle and no stop (Bedlington Terrier).

RECTANGULAR

Head slightly domed, a little narrower at the ears than the eyes (West Highland White Terrier).

FACES, EARS, AND EYES

Faces

The shapes of dogs' faces are influenced to a great extent by the basic skull type, but have changed and been refined over the years as the different breeds have developed.

The descriptive names used to classify the types of faces are derived from the skeletal structure of the head, and from the coloration of the face.

BROKEN-UP
Has a receding pushed-in nose, a deep stop, an undershot jaw, and wrinkles (Pekingese).

CLOWN
Black and white or tan and white markings are more or less symmetrically divided by a line down the face and skull (Smooth-haired Fox Terrier).

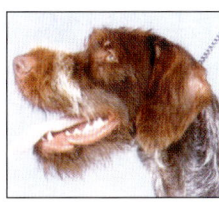

DISH
The nose is higher at the tip than at the stop due to the nasal-bone formation, or the line of the stop to the tip of the nose is slightly concave (German Pointer).

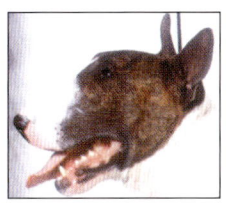

DOWN
Where the muzzle inclines downward from the skull to the tip of the nose (Bull Terrier).

FROG
An extending nose combined with a receding jaw, usually overshot. It is a fault in some breeds, such as French and British Bulldogs (Rottweiler).

Ears

Ears are described in terms of their shape and how they hang from the head. The phrase "set on" refers to the position of the ears in relation to eye level and/or the width of the skull. The ears may be set on high, like those of the Great Dane; set on low, like those of the King Charles Spaniel; or set on wide, as in the case of the German Shepherd Dog. There are three normal ear types and many variations.

BAT
Erect, somewhat broad at the base, rounded in outline at the tip, and with the orifice opening directly to the front (French Bulldog).

BUTTON
The ear flap folding forward and the tip lying close to the skull, covering the orifice and pointing toward the eye (Irish Terrier).

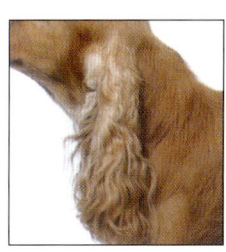

DROP
Where the ends of the ears are folded or droop forward. They may be pendent or pendulous (English Cocker Spaniel).

Ears

Cropped ears involve cutting or trimming the ear to leather so that the ears stand erect. It should only be carried out by a veterinary surgeon. In the USA ear cropping is carried out on several breeds, including Boxer, Doberman, Great Dane, Giant, Standard and Miniature Schnauzers, Griffon Bruxellois, and Manchester Terrier. However, it is not allowed in the UK and a number of other countries.

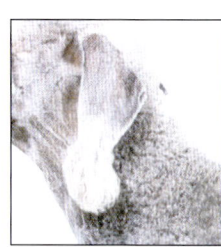

FILBERT-SHAPED
Ears which are hazelnut-shaped (Bedlington Terrier).

HEART-SHAPED
Shaped like a heart (Pekingese).

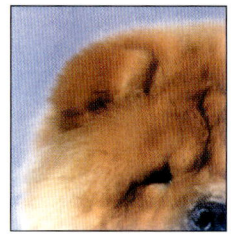

HOODED
Small, triangular and erect, but tilted forward slightly (Chow Chow).

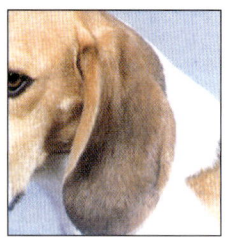

HOUND
Triangular and rounded, the ear flap folding forward and lying close to the head (Beagle).

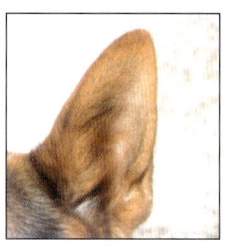

PRICKED
Standing erect and generally pointed at the tips (German Shepherd Dog).

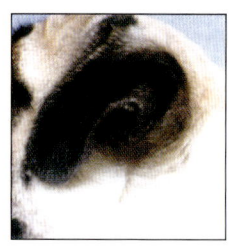

ROSE
A small drop ear that folds over and back so as to reveal the burr (Pug).

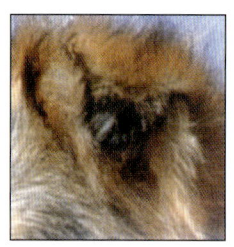

SEMI-DROP
Also called a semi-prick ear, where just the tip of the ears breaks and falls forward (Shetland Sheepdog).

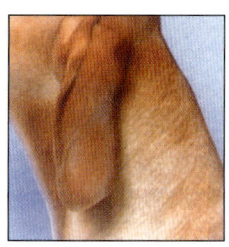

V-SHAPED
Usually, but not always, carried in the dropped position. Also known as Triangular Ears (Hungarian Vizsla).

Eyes

The terminology for eyes is based on the shape of the eyes and how they are set in the skull. Because of the size of the muzzle, dogs have little overlapping sight; that is, they have only a small field of vision covered by both eyes. In breeds like the Bulldog, the eyes are positioned relatively far forward, limiting their total field of vision to 200°. In other breeds, for example the Coonhounds, the field of vision is much greater—270°—because the eyes are set further back on the head. Both glassy and beady eyes are regarded as a fault.

ALMOND
Almond-shaped (German Shepherd Dog).

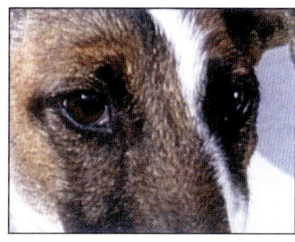

CIRCULAR
As round as possible (Smooth-haired Fox Terrier).

DEEP SET
Sunk well down the eye sockets (Chow Chow).

GLOBULAR
Appearing to protrude, but in fact not bulging when viewed in profile (Chihuahua).

GOGGLY
Round and protruding (Griffon Bruxellois).

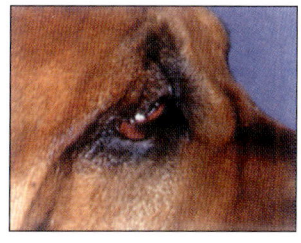

HAW
The term used for the third membrane in the inside corner of the eye. Its appearance is a fault in some breeds (Bloodhound).

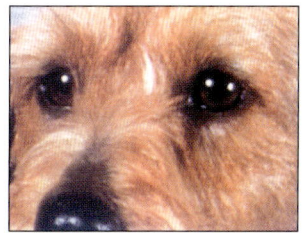

OBLIQUE
Set in the head at an angle from the ear toward the muzzle (Miniature Wire-haired Dachshund).

PIG
Very small and hard. Also describes eyes that are small and close together, a fault in the Miniature Pinscher (Pug).

TRIANGULAR
Set in triangular-shaped tissue (Afghan Hound).

TAILS

Tails

The name given to tails refers to their length, shape, position, and the hair covering them. Retrievers use their tails as rudders when they are in the water, and Deerhounds use theirs to maintain their balance, but, for most breeds, the tail is most important as a means of communication.

The "tail set" refers to the way in which its base is set on the rump; whereas how the tail is "set on" refers to its placement: it may be high, low, and so on.

Tails are docked in some breeds, such as the Doberman, to make them appear more aggressive. They also used to be docked in hunting breeds to prevent damage. About 45 breeds have docked tails. The operation is performed by a veterinary surgeon.

BOBTAIL
A dog that is naturally tail-less or a tail that is customarily docked very short (Old English Sheepdog).

BRUSH
Tail like the brush of a fox (Alaskan Malamute).

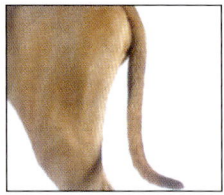

CRANK
Carried down and resembling a crank (Italian Short-haired Segugio).

CURLED
Tail set on high and curled over, either onto the spine or onto one side. There may be single and double curls (Finnish Spitz).

FLAG
Long and carried high (Beagle).

KINK
Sharply bent (Lhasa Apso).

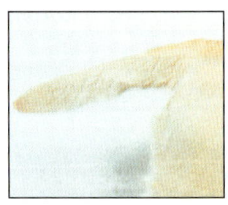

OTTER
Thick at the root, round, and tapering toward tip, with short, thick hair, and used as a rudder when swimming (Labrador).

RING
Carried up and around, almost in a circle (Basenji).

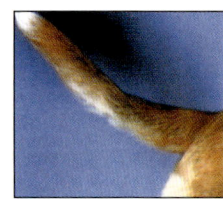

SABRE
Carried like a sabre (Basset Hound).

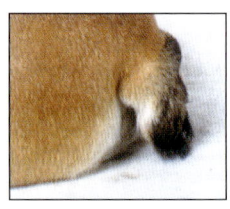

SCREW
Naturally short, twisted in a spiral fashion (French Bulldog).

SICKLE
Carried out and up in a semi-circle (Affenpinscher).

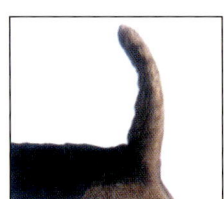

SPIKE
Short and thick, tapering quickly along its entire length (English Lakeland Terrier).

STERN
The technical term for the tail of a sporting dog or a hound (English Pointer).

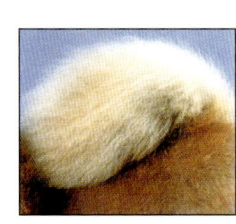

SQUIRREL
Carried up and curving forward (Chow Chow).

WHIP
Carried stiffly straight and pointed (Bull Terrier).

GAIT AND COAT COLORS

BELTON
(English Setter).

BLACK AND TAN
(Hamiltonstövare).

BLUE
(Blue Gascony Basset).

BRINDLE
(Greyhound).

GRIZZLE
(Old English Sheepdog).

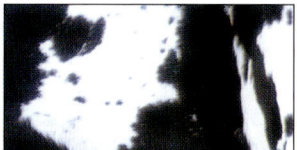

HARLEQUIN
(Great Dane).

PARTI-COLOR
(Swedish Vallhund).

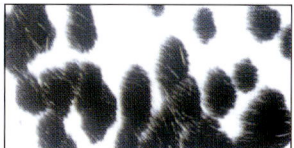

PIEBALD
(Dalmatian).

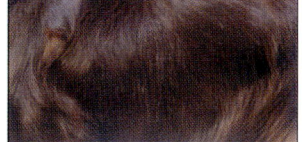

RED
(Irish Setter).

ROAN
(Welsh Corgi).

TRICOLOR
(Beagle).

WHEATEN
(Soft-coat Wheaten Terrier).

Gait

The term gait refers to the pattern of a dog's footsteps at various speeds, and is distinguishable by a particular rhythm and footfall.

Gaiting a dog is a show term meaning to show off its paces. There are a number of faults in movement. Crabbing is where the dog moves with its body at an angle to the line of travel. Other names for this type of action are sidewinding, sidewalking, and yawing. Cow-hocking is where the hocks turn inward, facing one another. Dishing is similar to weaving in the horse, and is an unnatural movement of the forequarters.

The manner—and place—at which dogs are gaited in the show ring differs from breed to breed. Some of the larger varieties are moved around the show ring at a fast pace; others are gaited fairly sedately. For this reason, it is important that the elderly exhibitor who may be new to the game does not select a breed that would prove too tiring to exhibit.

Amble: A relaxed, easy movement, often seen as a transition between the walk and the faster movements. The front and hind legs on either side move in unison.

Trot: A rhythmic, two-beat, diagonal gait during which the feet at diagonally opposite corners of the body strike the ground together—the right hind with the left front, and the left hind with the right front.

Canter: A gait which has three beats to each stride. Two legs move separately and two as a diagonal pair. The movement is reminiscent of a rocking-horse, slower than a gallop and not nearly as fatiguing.

Gallop: The fastest gait, during which all four feet are off the ground at the same time.

Pace: Movement or gait during which the left foreleg and left hind leg go forward in unison, followed by the right foreleg and right hind leg.

Hackney: Almost identical to the action of the Hackney horse or pony, with the same high lifting of the front feet. The Miniature Pinscher has a hackney gait.

HEREBY HANGS A TAIL

The selective breeding of dogs has not just created a variety of skull and skeletal structures. Ears, coat types, and overall colorings also vary immensely.

Above right The bat ears of the neat French Bulldog act as sound reflectors and contrast with the long, hanging ears of the Bloodhound (*below right*). Note the latter's pendulous dewlaps.

Presumably the original dogs had ears much like those of the wolf. These are still seen in some breeds today, especially certain types of Terrier, and are usually called fox ears. In most breeds the ears are now slightly larger, and are termed prick ears. The largest erect ears, such as those of the French Bulldog, are known as bat or tulip ears.

All the breeds with erect ears, and some with button or semi-prick ears, which curl slightly at the top, have retained the wolf's ability to move his ears backward and forward. This enhances the hearing, because the ears act as sound reflectors to concentrate the sound into the inner ear where it is detected.

This is not to say that dogs with hanging ears, such as the Spaniel, Pointer, and Labrador, cannot hear well, but their sensitivity to sound is generally less acute than several of the other breeds. Many dogs with hanging ears have a highly developed sense of smell; the Bloodhound is an obvious example.

The early wolf-like dogs had what is known as a double smooth coat, with a thick, short underlayer and a longer outer coat which was straight and lay close and flat. Selective breeding has created all sorts of variations on this. At one extreme is the Mexican Hairless dog, which may have a few hairs on its head, though many of them have no hair at all. There are more examples at the other end of the scale: the Rough Collie has an extremely long outer coat; two Hungarian breeds, the Komondor and the Puli, have very long and dense outer coats that hang in coarse tassels; the Afghan hound has a fine but very long outer coat, which lends itself to combing.

Short coats, like those of the Weimaraner and Boxer are very common, as are wire-haired coats, where the hairs feel stiff and wavy and point in all directions. There are numerous variations on these basic types: both short and long coats can be wire-haired; long outer coats can be thin or very heavy; hair can be fluffy like a Poodle, woolly like a Husky or frizzy like an Irish Water Spaniel.

The dog's coat, even in the short-haired breeds, acts as an extremely efficient insulator. The hair traps a layer of air between the dog's skin and the outside, protecting it against the cold. This efficient heat control means that heat loss is difficult in hot weather.

The skin of the first dogs was tight and well muscled immediately below the surface. In some breeds it has become much looser, and this is especially evident in some short-haired dogs about the face and neck. The extreme example is the Bloodhound which has what is known as a dewlap neck, layers of loose skin under its throat.

The color and markings of the coat have also become increasingly varied through breeding. The first wolf itself showed some dark markings particularly on the face, and its color is also highly variable across its range. This has formed the basis for all the varied markings seen in breeds of dog today, sometimes with several in one breed.

EMERGENCE OF THE BREEDS

From the long-bodied, short-legged Dachshund, bred for digging, to the huge shaggy rescue dog, the Saint Bernard, each species of dog has its own characteristics, making Canis familiaris *more varied than any other. A dog show such as Cruft's, with dogs of all types and sizes on parade, reveals the great diversity, both genetic and behavioral, of the different breed.*

The broad groupings of sheep-herding dogs, hounds, terriers, and pet dogs arose at an early stage in the development of the domestic dog, simply because dogs were used, and therefore bred, for different purposes. Within these major groupings it is possible to trace smaller groups of breeds which are closely related in origin, and to single out particular breeds which have interesting histories.

The majority of modern breeds are comparatively recent in origin, principally because the desire of owners and breeders to show dogs in which the particular characteristics of a breed have been closely defined is a relatively new phenomenon. Prior to this, the appearances of different dogs belonging to the same breeds were much more varied than today. For example, a hundred years ago the German Shepherd Dog was not a distinct breed, but instead there were German "sheepdogs" of varying sizes and colors.

The German Shepherd Dog was introduced into the UK early this century, but after World War I it became known as the Alsatian; it has recently been officially renamed the German Shepherd Dog to bring the UK into line with the rest of the world.

Of existing breeds, the Greyhound and the Saluki can be traced back farthest; very similar dogs were depicted in middle eastern art several thousand years ago. At the other extreme, one of the most modern breeds is the Australian Terrier. This was developed by breeding between various English terriers including the Yorkshire, Cairn and Dandie Dinmont, and the Australian Silky Terrier—another recent breed. This process began about 100 years ago, but the characteristics of the breed have been firmly fixed only for about 25 years.

In the USA in 1945 the American Cocker Spaniel was given separate breed status from the English Cocker Spaniel. This new breed with its longer, thicker coat had been selectively bred from English stock. The Spaniel itself is an old breed; the name was used by Chaucer in 1340, and some authorities believe the breed originated in Spain even earlier than that. At that time the term Spaniel would have included a fairly mixed-looking group of dogs. It is only in comparatively recent times that

The beautiful Chow Chow, an ancient Chinese breed.

The Golden Retriever combines the qualities of gundog and family pet.

today's dozen or so Spaniel breeds have emerged, each with a well defined appearance.

Many attempts have been made to create ancestral trees showing the supposed relationships of all the breeds to each other. This is a near impossible job because frequently in the past, crossings were made to produce new breeds from quite unrelated dogs. Apart from detailed paintings of a few dogs, it is impossible to say exactly how the ancestors of modern dogs looked, even a few hundred years ago.

Another problem is that there is no international agreement as to how dogs should be grouped for show purposes. The Spitz group of dogs is split up between at least three other groupings for show purposes in the USA and the UK. In Sweden, however, where this group is especially strong, they are shown together as a single group in their own right.

In the USA there are six groupings for show purposes: sporting, non-sporting, working, terriers, hounds, and toys. In the UK and Australia there are also six, but they are not the same: working, utility, gundogs, hounds, terriers and toy. On the continent of Europe, there is some variation between countries, but most frequently seven groupings are used: hounds and greyhounds, gundogs, guard and utility dogs, sheepherding dogs, terriers, large companion dogs, and small companion dogs. This lack of uniformity reflects the difficulties created by the diverse origins and interrelationships of all the breeds.

HOW STANDARDS ARE SET

Dog breeds are divided into groups, and these are of considerable help and importance not only in categorizing the breeds for exhibition purposes, but also in aiding the purchaser to select the breed best suited to the purpose that he has in mind, be it a children's pet, hunting dog, or guard.

All breeds placed by their national kennel club within a specific group are given a breed standard. This sets out a standard of excellence for representatives of that breed, and includes such modifications as ideal height and/or weight, desirable color, conformation points, and so on. Again, there are slight differences in what is deemed ideal from country to country. For instance, while in America the height limit for a Beagle is 15 in (38 cm) at the shoulder, the English call for a height from ground to withers that should neither exceed 16 in (40.5 cm) nor fall below 13 in (33 cm) and they do not allow as great a tolerance in the

case of the Kerry Blue Terrier.

However, differences would not adversely influence an experienced judge adjudicating away from home.

For the older established breeds, standards were set by the appropriate fancier's club when they were founded, some as long ago as the 1870s. Today, when a new breed is accepted for registration, standards from the kennel club of the country of origin are examined by the standards committee, which may also consult with outside experts. An interim standard is used for an imported breed which is not on the full register.

The German Pointer is a long-established, recognized breed.

The American Cocker Spaniel has been bred with specific traits.

The Leonberger is in contention for Kennel Club registration.

BREEDING CHARACTERISTICS

Breeding for appearance was introduced in the 19th century. Up to that time, dog breeding concentrated on producing traits that were useful for work: vermin hunting (terriers), flushing and driving game (pointers, hounds), running down large and small quarry (mastiffs, greyhounds), and guarding (mastiffs). From these basic types were derived more specialist breeds, each ideally suited to work a specific terrain (Saint Hubert Hound) or perform a particular job (Dogue de Bordeaux).

The interest in selective breeding was fostered by the Kennel Club, founded in London in 1873. It established a registration system which enabled breeders to record the lineage of each pure-bred animal, that is, one whose dam and sire were both offspring of pure-bred animals as far back as could be traced.

Characteristics such as size, color, or set of tail can be introduced or altered by breeding from animals with those traits. It is also possible to introduce a feature from another breed—for example, Dingo blood added to the Smooth-coated Collie to produce the Australian Kelpie—and then to breed across enough generations for the trait to run "true." There is always a risk, however, that overbreeding can throw up inheritable weaknesses such as Hip Dysplasia (malformation) and Progressive Retinal Atrophy (blindness). Congenital disorders can only be prevented by stopping all affected animals from breeding.

NON-SPORTING BREEDS

This is the category from which many pet dogs are selected. The breeds within this group may well have performed some task in the past, but in the main they are now the dogs whose sole purpose in life is to be a companion to their owners. There is a large choice, ranging from the lively Dalmatian, a former carriage dog, to the more sedate French Bulldog and the Chow Chow (shown above).

WORKING BREEDS

This group covers the traditional guards and workers—rescue, sled and draft dogs, and those favored by the armed services, such as the Rottweiler (shown above). Bred to work, and in many cases fearsome, natural guards, most are happiest when they are doing the job for which they are bred or at least when in an environment where their abilities will not go to waste.

HERDING BREEDS

The breeds in this group were originally developed to herd and protect sheep, such as the Maremma, Collie, and German Shepherd Dog (the latter is shown above), cattle (the Lancashire Heeler and Corgi) and other stock. Many are still used by shepherds and farmers, but they are also extremely adaptable as pets, often taking it upon themselves to herd the family together.

GUNDOGS

In this group are the pointers, retrievers (shown above is the Golden Retriever), and spaniels—all gundogs are used variously to detect, flush out, and retrieve game. Usually gentle natured, many dogs in this category have the dual role of huntsman's dog and family pet.

TERRIERS

These dogs were bred to go to ground, to hunt vermin. and bolt the fox from its lair. Energetic, sporting, and sometimes noisy, most terriers are affectionate by nature, but they can be nippy. The Yorkshire Terrier (shown above) is a friendly and very popular dog.

HOUNDS

Hounds are often divided into those that hunt by scent (scent hounds), for instance the Bloodhound, Basset and Beagle (the Beagle is shown above), and those that rely on their keen eyesight (sight hounds), such as the Greyhound and the Saluki. Hounds are good natured but have a propensity to roam; many hounds are kept in packs, in outside kennels, rather than living indoors.

TOY BREEDS

Do not be fooled by the fact that the traditional ladies' lap dogs, such as the Pomeranian (shown above) come within this category. Many toy breeds would walk their owners off their feet, if given the chance to do so. Most are splendid guards, keenly intelligent, affectionate, if somewhat possessive, and courageous to the point of stupidity.

Chart showing the rates at which different breeds reach their mature sizes. The fastest growth occurs in the first six months of life, and continues more slowly for the next six months. The smaller breeds reach their full size by this time, although larger dogs continue to grow a little after this point.

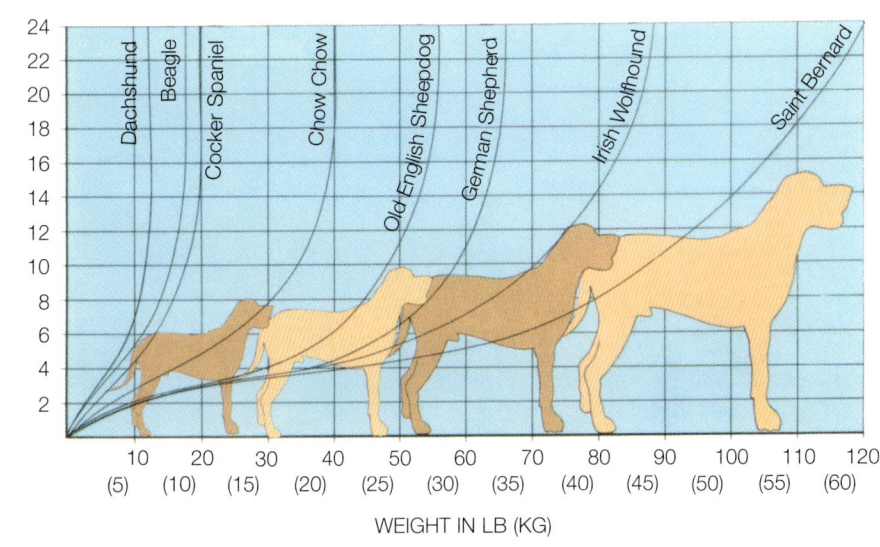

The English Springer Spaniel is one of the largest of the spaniels. It got its name from the fact that it used to be used to flush out or "spring" game.

ENCYCLOPEDIA OF DOG BREEDS

NON-SPORTING BREEDS

TIBETAN SPANIEL

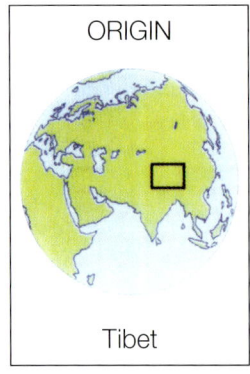

ORIGIN

Tibet

Character charming, independent, self confident, energetic, intelligent, and good with children.

Exercise needs a lot of physical activity.

Grooming coat needs regular grooming.

Feeding moderate appetite.

Longevity average to long lived.

Characteristics mouth is tipped by black nose.

Despite its name, this breed is not related to the spaniels and is not known to have been used as a hunting companion or gundog. The Tibetan Spaniel is thought to have been in existence long before the history of Tibet started to be chronicled in the seventh century, and its origins are therefore obscure. The exchange of dogs between Tibet and China in ancient times means that Chinese dogs, such as early Shih Tzu or Pekingese-like dogs, could have contributed to it. It has also been said that the Tibetan Spaniel was a favorite with monks and was often kept in monasteries. It is said that it turned, and perhaps still turns, the prayer wheel of Tibetans. It is also said that, in common with the Hairless Dog in Mexico, it was used by humans for warmth.

The first Tibetan Spaniel recorded in the UK was brought by a Mr. F. Wormald in 1905, but it seems to have been the late l940s before the breed made any impact there.

This charming, good natured dog is rarely seen outside the show ring. It is intelligent, good with children, and makes a splendid house pet. It is energetic and enjoys a good romp, and its coat needs regular grooming.

TIBETAN TERRIER

In spite of its name, this breed is not derived from terrier stock, but was originally bred in Tibet as a herding dog. There was some confusion among the various Tibetan breeds when they first became more widely known in the West during the early years of the last century, but the Tibetan Terrier was subsequently acknowledged by the Kennel Club in the UK during 1937. In the USA, it was only recognized for showing purposes as recently as 1973.

Aside from their herding activities, these shaggy dogs were highly valued as companions in their homeland, and the reasons for this are not hard to recognize today. They are happy, friendly dogs with a tolerant disposition toward children. Their coat, which is now more profuse than in the past, creating a very elegant appearance, will need daily brushing to prevent it from becoming tangled.

These terriers can be bred in a wide range of colors, with only liver or chocolate being frowned upon in show circles. While in its early days the Tibetan Terrier was shown in a tousled state, many hours of preparatory work are now essential when benching these dogs.

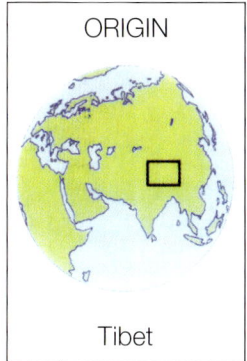

ORIGIN

Tibet

Character loving, loyal, tolerant, devoted to owners and children, a good walker, and an excellent watchdog.

Exercise requires little exercise.

Grooming Tibetan Terriers used to be shown in a tousled state; many hours of preparatory work are now required to give its long coat the regular attention it requires

Feeding average appetite.

Longevity average to good.

Characteristics profuse hair on fairly narrow head.

SHAR-PEI

ORIGIN

China

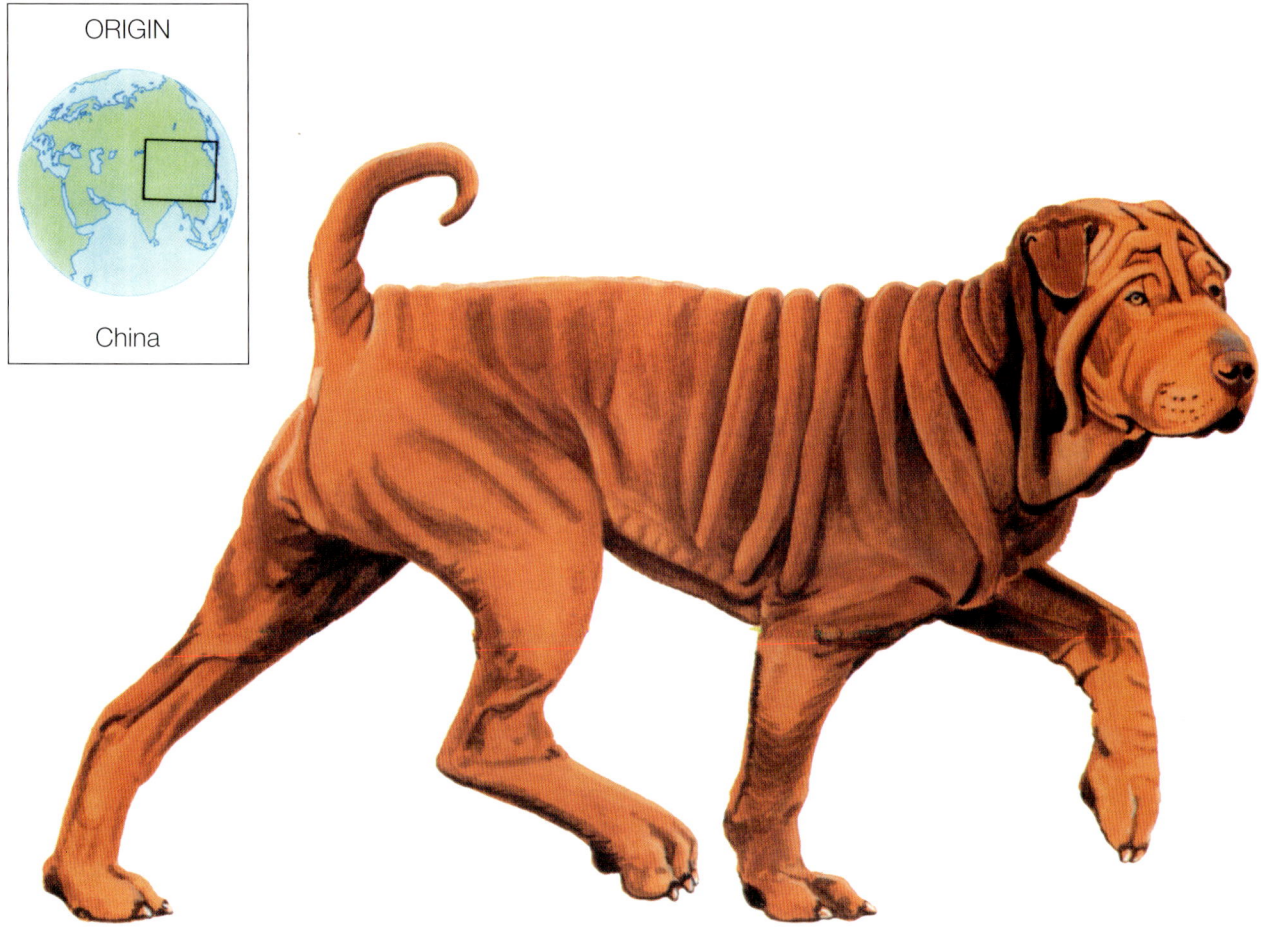

It is not long since the Shar-Pei graced the *Guinness Book of Records* in the World's Rarest Dog slot, but today it has a growing band of devotees in the USA and Canada, and in the UK where it is attracting good show entries.

Despite being bred as a fighting dog, the Shar-Pei is an amiable dog unless provoked. Indeed it is believed that drugs were used to promote aggression, while the breed's success as a fighter was largely due to its folds of loose skin, which made it difficult for an adversary to catch hold.

Likenesses of the Shar-Pei survive from the Han Dynasty (206 BC–AD 220), and it is possible that it originated in Tibet or the northern provinces of China some 2,000 years ago.

The future of the Shar-Pei was in peril in 1947, when the People's Republic of China put such a heavy tax on dogs that very few people could keep them. It is fortunate that a number of fine specimens were smuggled out of China.

The dog, which has wrinkles not unlike those of the

Bloodhound, stands only 18–20 in (46–51 cm) at the withers and weighs up to 50 lb (22.5 kg). It comes in solid colors: black, red, light or dark shades of fawn, and cream.

Character alert, active, calm, and independent. Affectionate and devoted.

Exercise was a wild boar hunter, so needs plenty of it.

Grooming use fairly stiff brush. Rub down with towel or hound glove.

Feeding approximately 1½ cans (14½ oz size) of a branded meaty product, with biscuit added in equal parts by volume. (note in all instances: if your dog is over or under the standard weight for its breed, consult your veterinary surgeon.)

Longevity average.

Characteristics include any sign of irritation of eyeball, conjunctiva, or eyelids.

SHIBA INU

ORIGIN

Japan

The Shiba Inu is an ancient breed associated with the prefectures of Gifu, Toyama, and Nagano in central Japan and the name, in fact, means "little dog" in the Nagano dialect. Remains of a dog of this type were found in ruins dating back to the Joman era (500 BC). The Shiba Inu has, in recent years, become a firm favorite of exhibitors, following closely on the heels of the Japanese Akita onto the international scene. It is an excellent bird dog, guard, and hunter of small game, with a considerable amount of native cunning.

The Shiba is an affectionate, friendly, and sensitive dog that makes a fine pet as well as a show dog and/or hunter. It needs a fair amount of exercise and a good daily brushing to keep it looking trim.

Character affectionate, friendly, sensitive, agile, fastidious, and aloof.

Exercise it needs a fair amount of exercise.

Grooming a good daily brushing.

Feeding moderate exercise.

Longevity 12 to 13 years.

Characteristics thick, strong tail is carried in curl when dog is standing.

BICHON FRISÉ

ORIGIN

Tenerife

Character happy, adaptable, bold, and intelligent, the ultimate companion dog.

Exercise likes plenty, can be trained to herd sheep.

Grooming daily grooming is essential. Teeth and gums need particular attention.

Feeding about ½ can (14½ oz) of a branded meaty product, with biscuit added in equal parts by volume.

Longevity about 14 years.

Characteristics this breed is game and hardy, and has been known to round up sheep in Norway.

The cuddly Bichon Frisé is believed to have originated in Tenerife, one of the Canary Islands off the west coast of Africa. Its ancestors were brought to Europe over 400 years ago, and became especially popular among members of the Spanish and French aristocracy. Support for the breed declined during the 19th century, however, and it became associated with organ-grinders, who relied on its attractive appearance to induce generous support from onlookers.

In the circus ring, its intelligence endeared it to another audience, but it was to be World War I that began the welcome rise in popularity of these dogs. Soldiers returning home with the Bichons meant that attention became focused on the breed in Britain. A standard was first established in

France in 1933, and the breed was exported to the USA by a Monsieur Picault and his wife in 1956.

The coat color of the Bichon Frisé is pure white, with the hairs being naturally curly. Unfortunately, to retain the immaculate appearance of these little dogs, a considerable amount of time must be devoted to grooming. Its white coat can become muddy on even a short walk. In such cases, it is best to let the mud dry and then brush it out of the coat, rather than washing the legs frequently. It is usual for puppies to have a less elaborate coat than older dogs. The Bichon Frisé should prove to be a relatively easy breed to train and makes a good companion.

BOSTON TERRIER

This American breed was developed during the latter part of the last century, with various strains of Bulldog, Bull Terrier, and Boxer all contributing to its ancestry. Indeed, these dogs were originally called American Bull Terriers for a period, until objection from Bull Terrier owners forced a change of name. The breed was finally recognized in 1890 by the American Kennel Club as the Boston Terrier.

Since then, it has become widely known throughout the world. They have proved easy dogs to train and make delightful companions. Boston Terriers are quite at home even in urban surroundings, and will walk happily on a leash if it is not possible to give them a daily run. Nevertheless, they do enjoy a period of freedom, to explore in the company of their owner.

The short coat of this breed is easy to groom and is never shed profusely, which makes housework easier. Boston Terriers may snuffle because of their compact noses, while their relatively prominent eyes are prone to injury, especially if they charge off through undergrowth. However, the most significant problem associated with these terriers is only apparent during the whelping period. The relatively large head, coupled with a narrow pelvis, often causes problems when a bitch is giving birth. A Caesarean section may be required if a puppy's head becomes stuck in the birth canal. Particular care is therefore necessary when breeding Boston Terriers.

Character sprightly and entertaining but thoughtful and considerate with quirky good looks.

Exercise needs moderate exercise.

Grooming easy to groom because of its short, smooth coat.

Feeding an average sized appetite.

Longevity about 13 years.

Characteristics difficult to breed a show specimen with the right markings—ideally a white blaze over the head and down the collar, breast, and forelegs below the elbows.

ORIGIN

USA

49

GIANT SCHNAUZER

ORIGIN

Germany

Character robust, good with children, playful, yet a fine guard.

Exercise likes plenty. Will follow horses. Useful obedience dog.

Grooming use wire brush daily. Comb whiskers. Coat needs stripping twice a year.

Feeding 2½ cans (14½ oz size) of a branded meaty product, with biscuit added in equal parts by volume.

Longevity good.

Characteristics include any white markings on head, chest, and legs.

Another German breed, the Giant Schnauzer arose in the south of the country and was used in the UK for herding cattle. They have also been used as police dogs. Giant Schnauzers are now often less popular than the Miniature and Standard forms, which they otherwise resemble in terms of care. These dogs are frequently pure black in color, but may also be seen in shades of pepper and salt, in equal proportions in the case of a show dog.

Coat care of Schnauzers may prove quite demanding, with their whiskers and mustache requiring to be combed each day. In addition, stripping the coat will also be necessary at regular intervals, although you can have this varied out professionally at a grooming parlor if so desired.

JAPANESE SPITZ

ORIGIN

Japan

Character affectionate and companionable,
but tends to be wary of strangers.
Exercise a natural herder, enjoys freedom,
but will adapt to its owner's requirements.
Grooming daily with a stiff brush.
Feeding 1 can (14½ oz size) of a branded
meaty product, with biscuit added in equal
parts by volume.
Longevity 12 years.
Characteristics makes a good house
protector and guard.

The Japanese Spitz is a comparative newcomer outside its
native land as both family pet and show dog, and is fast
gaining a band of devotees.

To discuss the background of the Japanese Spitz one must
look to its close relative the Nordic or Norbotten Spitz, as they
have the same origins.

The breed's ancestor, the Norbotten Spitz, is also little
known outside its native Sweden. It was in fact declared
extinct in 1948 but there was renewed interest in the 1980s,
resulting in sufficient registrations for the breed to become

re-established. These Spitz varieties no doubt derived from
Finnish Spitz or Norwegian Buhund ancestry.

The Japanese Spitz was developed as a separate breed in
Japan, and is not unlike the Pomeranian (another Spitz variety)
but in a larger frame.

The Japanese stands 12–14 in (30–36 cm), bitches slightly
less, and the only allowable color is pure white. It has a
pointed muzzle, triangular ears standing erect, and a bushy tail
curled over its back, characteristic of the Spitz breeds.

BULLDOG

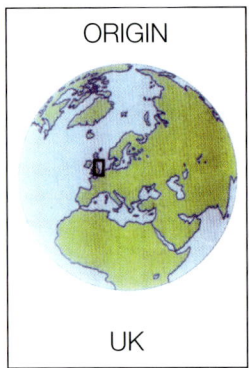

ORIGIN

UK

Character gentle and good natured.

Exercise does not need a lot of
exercise, must not be exerted in hot
weather.

Grooming daily run through with a
stiff brush and a rub-down.

Feeding moderate appetite.

Longevity short to average.

Characteristics uniform color with a
black mask or muzzle, red brindle,
piebald. Black is undesirable.

The Bulldog has undergone a dramatic change in
appearance during its long history, particularly since the
development of show standards over the past century. In
their early years, Bulldogs were used for bull-baiting, and
tended to be a longer-legged breed than those seen today.
After bull-baiting was banned in 1835 in the UK, it was also
involved in dog-fighting, but Bulldogs proved less popular for
this purpose than the Bull Terrier. The breed could then have
slipped into obscurity but was rescued to become a popular
show dog.

Today, the Bulldog has evolved into a placid and
phlegmatic dog with a somewhat comical appearance.

However, it is a solid, muscular animal with powerful jaws.
Criticisms of the breed have been made because of its
respiratory and reproductive problems, Caesarean section
births being common because of its relatively large head.

Bulldogs suffer badly from heat stress and should not be
exercised during the warmest part of the day. In addition,
they must never be kept enclosed in a car on their own in the
summer. Dogs are vulnerable to heat stress in such
surroundings, but Bulldogs in particular are liable to die very
rapidly under these conditions. They tend not to want a lot of
exercise, but should be given a daily walk, as this will help to
prevent them becoming obese.

CHOW CHOW

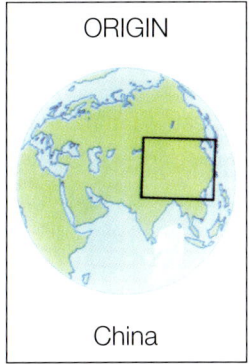

ORIGIN

China

Character beautiful and aloof, this companion and guard reserves its affection for the family.

Exercise appreciates a fair amount of exercise.

Grooming use a wire brush, a few minutes daily. An hour-long grooming at weekends works wonders.

Feeding approximately 1–1½ cans (14½ oz size) of a branded meaty product, with biscuit added in equal parts by volume.

Longevity average.

Characteristics include an artificial shortening of the coat which alters the natural outline or expression.

This ancient Chinese breed has served a variety of purposes since its development many thousands of years ago. Its history is said to date back to the 11th century BC, and in these early years Chow Chows were kept for hunting purposes. One Chinese emperor is said to have maintained a kennel of 5,000 of these dogs, cared for by 10,000 people! Subsequently, the breed was kept as a source of food, with young dogs being reared solely for this purpose on a diet comprised mainly of grain. The Chow Chow has also been used as a means of transporting goods and pulling sleds, and its fur has been made into clothing.

Chow Chows were first seen in the UK during the latter part of the 18th century, and were originally exhibited as wild dogs. They later gained more widespread acceptability when kept by Queen Victoria. Unfortunately, in spite of their close association with people, Chow Chows are not always the best tempered of dogs. They can also be very difficult to train, compared with other breeds. Yet the Chow Chow often develops into a loyal companion, preferring to live with an individual person rather than as a family dog.

A good brushing is required to keep its coat in good condition, especially in the case of a long-coated dog. Regular exercise, preferably away from other dogs, is essential as well. As show dogs, Chow Chows often reign supreme, and a member of this breed holds the record out of all breeds for the greatest number of Challenge Certificates ever won.

SHIH TZU

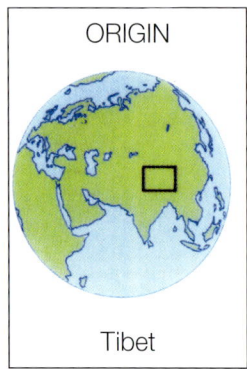

ORIGIN

Tibet

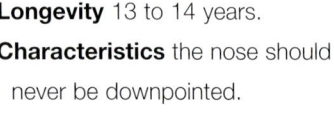

Character courageous, playful, happy, and hardy. Alert and independent.

Exercise gentle exercise.

Grooming good daily grooming with a bristle brush; the topknot is tied with a bow.

Feeding relatively small appetite.

Longevity 13 to 14 years.

Characteristics the nose should never be downpointed.

The unusual name of this breed, which is pronounced "Shiszoo," actually means "lion." The Shih Tzu was originally bred in Tibet, and then developed further in China. It is closely related to both the Tibetan Terrier and the Lhasa Apso, and has become smaller in size through selective breeding. The Pekingese may also have played a part in the development of this ancient breed. It remained unknown in the West until the early years of the 20th century, and much of today's stock can be traced back to a number of dogs obtained from China during 1930s.

The Shih Tzu is a true companion breed, being naturally affectionate and friendly toward people of all ages. It is intelligent and will not thrive on its own, rapidly becoming bored under these circumstances. A wide range of colors has been bred, and, in view of its long coat, daily grooming is absolutely essential in all cases, otherwise the hair will become badly tangled and will then be painful to unravel. You may prefer to keep the long top-knot of hair away from the eyes by means of a bow.

You must ensure that you check the ears regularly for any signs of infection. The hair around the mouth will also have to be cleaned should it become soiled with food. Shih Tzus do not need long runs. Instead, they are perfectly content with regular short walks, and are unlikely to stray far away when off the leash.

STANDARD POODLE

ORIGIN

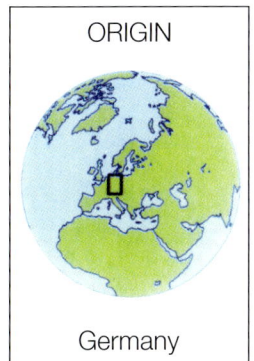

Germany

Known in France as the Caniche, the Poodle was certainly favored by the French Queen Marie Antoinette (1755–93). However, it originated in Germany as a water retriever, or Pudel in German. It resembles the Irish Water Spaniel, and both share common ancestors in the French Barbet.

The Standard Poodle still retains its ability as a gundog and swims well. Its intelligence and eagerness to learn mean that it is popular in obedience trials and as a circus dog.

This happy, good tempered, lively dog makes a good family pet, enjoying a fair amount of exercise. It is also a fine show dog, provided you have the time for intricate preparation. While it is shown in the lion clip, many pet owners prefer the lamb clip (with hair uniform length). Whatever style you choose, you will need to use a wire-pin pneumatic brush and a wire-toothed metal comb for daily grooming. Even the pet Poodle must attend the canine beauty parlor every six weeks or so.

Character high spirited and good natured. Excellent show dog.

Exercise varies with size. The standard is particularly active. Miniatures and Toys are suitable for town-dwellers.

Grooming need regular clipping. The lion clip is obligatory for showing. Preparation takes time.

Feeding the Standard would require approximately 1½ cans (14½ oz size) of a branded meaty product, with biscuit added in equal parts by volume. (Toy and Miniature ¼–½ can respectively.) But all dogs are individuals.

Longevity many Poodles live well into their teens.

Characteristics include eyes set quite close together, tail curled, or carried over back.

DALMATIAN

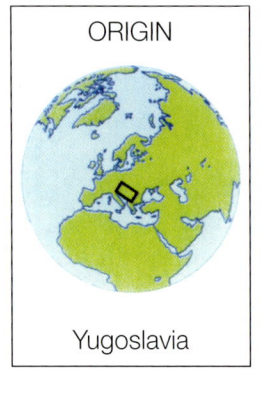

ORIGIN

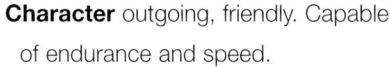

Yugoslavia

Character outgoing, friendly. Capable of endurance and speed.

Exercise a traditional coach dog needing plenty of exercise.

Grooming daily brush and rub down. Easy to care for but beware: neglect grooming and this pet will deposit white hairs on the carpet.

Feeding 1½–2 cans (14½ oz size) of a branded meaty product, with biscuit added in equal parts by volume.

Longevity good.

Characteristics include patches, tricolors and lemon spots. Also

This elegant breed was originally developed in Serbia and Montenegro (formerly Yugoslavia) and subsequently brought to the UK where it became popular as a carriage dog during the 18th century, although its original function was probably to protect travelers against highwaymen. Dalmatians were also known for a time as "firehouse dogs," because they used to accompany horse-drawn fire wagons through the streets of London.

These are very good house dogs and make dependable guardians. They are unlikely to bark unless there is a stranger in the vicinity. You must be willing to allow them a good run every day, however, which may not always be easy in a town. Dalmatians are energetic dogs by nature. Interestingly, their

puppies are born pure white in color and only develop their characteristic spots during the first few weeks of life. The short coat itself requires very little attention, even during a molt.

Check that any puppy that you are thinking of purchasing has normal hearing, as some individuals can prove deaf. In a good exhibition dog, the spots should be clearly defined and circular in shape. Although black-spotted Dalmatians are most common, there is also a variety with spots that are liver-brown in color. The coat itself needs the minimum of grooming to stay in good condition, but, particularly during a molt, brushing should be carried out in the garden to save loose hairs from being shed around the home.

FINNISH SPITZ

Acknowledged as the national dog of Finland, the Finnish Spitz shows the unmistakable characteristics of this northern group of dog. Its alert demeanor, with pricked ears and the curly tail that extends forward over the back, reflects a breed that has evolved to flush game birds such as the capercaillie from cover for waiting guns. Its tracking skills have also been used to pursue bear and elk. The appearance of the Finnish Spitz, in terms of an official standard, was first established back in 1812.

Only quite recently, however, has it become popular elsewhere. In the UK, Lady Kitty Ritson did much to draw attention to the breed during the 1920s and 1930s. The Finnish Spitz is a hardy yet home-loving breed, with plenty of stamina. It will thrive in a family environment and also makes an alert guard dog in these surroundings. However, a possible drawback associated with the breed can be its tendency to bark repeatedly. This behavior is related to its hunting technique, the dog having been encouraged to bark to indicate the presence of a bird in a tree. This breed is still judged on its barking abilities in working trials held in its country of origin.

Character hard-working, vigilant, cautious yet lively.
Exercise requires plenty of exercise .
Grooming daily brushing.
Feeding moderate appetite.
Longevity long life expectancy.
Characteristics tail curves vigorously from root forward and down.

ORIGIN

Finland

MINIATURE POODLE

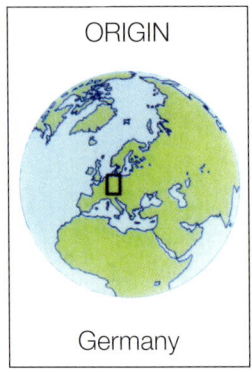

ORIGIN

Germany

Character high spirited and good
natured. Excellent show dog.

Exercise varies with size. The standard is
particularly active. Miniatures and Toys
are suitable for town-dwellers.

Grooming needs regular clipping. The lion
clip is obligatory for showing. Preparation
takes time.

Feeding the standard would require
approximately 1½ cans (14½ oz size) of
a branded meaty product, with biscuit
added in equal parts by volume (Toy and
Miniature ¼–½ can respectively). But all
dogs are individuals.

Longevity many poodles live well into
their teens.

Characteristics include eyes set very close
together, tail curled, or carried over back.

The Miniature Poodle was bred down from the Standard, presumably by using the smaller specimens, and in turn played its part in producing the even smaller Toy Poodle. During the 1950s the Miniature Poodle became the most popular breed in many countries because it was believed, wrongly, that as more people migrated to the towns, interest in working breeds would lessen. This did not prove to be the case, and while there are those who say that it is not a proper dog at all—no doubt blissfully unaware of its origins as a gundog and water retriever—the Miniature Poodle remains a favorite.

The Miniature Poodle has the same show standard as the larger and smaller breeds, except in the matter of size, and has similar characteristics. It requires frequent regular visits to the canine beauty parlor, even if it is not the intention to exhibit. Use a wire-pin pneumatic brush and a wire-toothed metal comb for daily grooming.

MINIATURE SCHNAUZER

The Miniature Schnauzer, known in its native Germany as the Zwergschnauzer, was derived from crossing the Standard Schnauzer with smaller dogs—probably Affenpinschers. The breed was exhibited for the first time in 1899, and was established in Germany by the early 1920s. W.D. Geoff is credited with taking the first breed member to the USA in 1923, while the first imports to the UK were made by a Mr. W.H. Hancock in 1928.

In the USA and Canada, the Miniature Schnauzer is classed as a terrier and was at one time the most popular terrier there. In the UK, where it is regarded as a member of the utility group rather than a terrier, it is a popular family pet, and also does well in the obedience and show rings.

The Miniature Schnauzer is a delightful small dog, which makes an excellent family pet and children's companion. Like its larger contemporaries, it needs a fair amount of exercise and its coat should be periodically stripped and plucked. The coat may also be clipped but this will spoil it for the show ring, so it is best to discuss grooming with the breeder at the time of purchase.

Character robust, good with children, playful, yet a fine guard.

Exercise likes plenty. Will follow horses. Useful obedience dog.

Grooming use wire brush daily. Comb whiskers. Coat needs stripping twice a year.

Feeding ½–¾ can (14½ oz size) of a branded meaty product, with biscuit added in equal parts by volume.

Longevity good.

Characteristics include any white markings on head, chest, and legs.

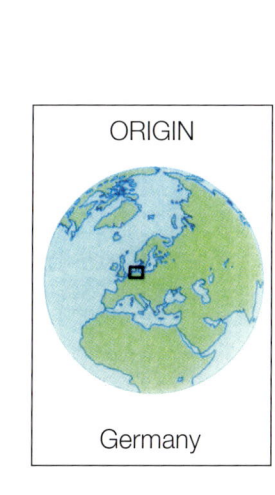

ORIGIN

Germany

FRENCH BULLDOG

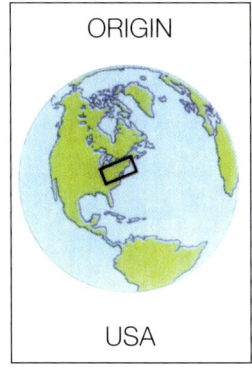

ORIGIN

USA

Character full of courage, yet with clown-like qualities. Devoted. Intelligent.

Exercise moderate. Not in very hot weather.

Grooming use fairly stiff brush daily. Rub down with hound glove or towel. Lubricate facial features.

Feeding approximately ¾ can (14½ oz size) of a branded meaty product, with biscuit added in equal parts by volume.

Longevity short to moderate.

Characteristics include showing white of eye when looking straight ahead.

In the middle of the 19th century, bulldogs were among the most popular dogs in the UK, especially in urban areas. Various strains were available and among these were miniature forms, which appear to have been common in the Midlands. These appealed particularly to French breeders and a number were in all likelihood exported to France during this period.

From France these dogs were taken to the USA. While European breeders tended to favor the floppy or "rose" ear characteristic of the Bulldog itself, American enthusiasts preferred to breed these smaller bulldogs with upright, bat-type ears. These dogs were brought to the UK in about 1900, and a dispute promptly broke out over their name because it

was felt in some quarters that the term "bull-dog" could only be associated with a British breed.

Agreement was finally reached, however, and today the French Bulldog is highly appreciated both as a pet and by breeders. Its facial changes are less extreme than those presently associated with the Bulldog. It does not snuffle to the same extent, nor is it as susceptible to heat exhaustion. Even so, it is not a great lover of exercise, and will be content with a short walk each day, broken by a brief period off the leash. You may need to watch for occasional signs of localized infection in its facial creases, but this can be dealt with effectively through treatment by your veterinarian.

GERMAN SPITZ

ORIGIN

Scandinavia

Character refined, elegant, and confident. Independent but devoted.

Exercise an average amount of exercise is required.

Grooming vigorous daily brushing will prevent it becoming matted.

Feeding about 1 can (14½ oz size) of a branded meaty product, with biscuit added in equal parts by volume.

Longevity average to long.

Characteristics is elegant in the show ring, and when trained, makes an equable companion.

The only difference between the Small German Spitz (Kleinspitz) and Standard German Spitz (Mittelspitz) is size. Both are smaller versions of the Great German Spitz (Großspitz) or Wolfspitz. There are many varieties of spitz and, although it is difficult to pinpoint their origin, they were probably brought from Scandinavia by the Vikings. Spitz dogs were known as early as 1700 when white specimens were said to be kept in Pomerania and black ones in Würrtemberg. Some of the smaller varieties of the white spitz bred in Pomerania became known and established in the UK under the name Pomeranian. In 1899, the German Spitz Club was formed, and standards were issued for the separate varieties.

This active, intelligent, and alert dog is independent, yet devotion to its human family is a breed characteristic. The German Spitz can adapt to life in the town or country, and needs vigorous daily brushing and an average amount of exercise. If unchecked, the breed does have a tendency to yap.

SCHIPPERKE

ORIGIN

Belgium

Character affectionate, resilient, good with children, an excellent watchdog.
Exercise can walk up to 6 miles (10km) a day but will make do with far less.
Grooming coat needs very little attention.
Feeding smaller than average appetite.
Longevity short to average.
Characteristics resilient and conveniently sized, makes an ideal household companion.

The Schipperke originated in Belgium but is often thought to be a Dutch dog, a confusion which may have arisen because the Netherlands and Belgium are relatively modern countries. The breed is thought by some to be 200 years old, although no records exist to prove this. It may have been established as long ago as the mid-1500s, based on a story that two black dogs without tails rescued Prince William of Orange (1533–84) from an assassin. Differences of opinion also exist on the breed's ancestry. Some think it arose from early northern spitz dogs, while others consider it is a descendant of a now-extinct Belgian Sheepdog.

The Schipperke was once the most popular house pet and watchdog in Belgium. Traditionally its job there was to guard canal barges when they were tied up for the night, and it was this task that earned the breed its name. Schipperke is Flemish for "little captain," and has also been translated as "little

skipper," "little boatman" and even "little corporal."

This breed was first exhibited in 1880. It was recognized by the Royal Schipperke Club of Brussels in 1886, and given an official standard in 1904. The Schipperke Club of England was formed in 1905 and the Schipperke Club of America in 1929. Miss F. Isabel Ormiston of Kelso Kennels is credited with being the greatest pioneer of the breed in the USA.

The Schipperke is an affectionate dog which is good with children, usually very long lived, and an excellent watchdog. It is said to be able to walk up to 6 miles (10km) a day without tiring, but will make do with considerably less exercise. It should be housed indoors rather than in a kennel, and its coat needs very little attention.

SCHNAUZER

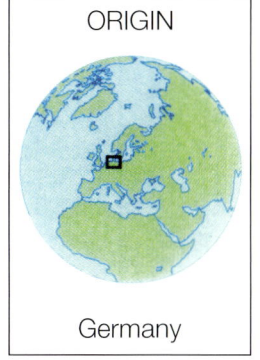

ORIGIN

Germany

Character robust, good with
children, playful, yet a fine guard.
Exercise likes plenty. Will follow
horses. Useful obedience dogs.
Grooming use wire brush daily.
Comb whiskers. Coat needs
stripping twice a year.
Feeding ½–¾ cans (14½ oz size) of a
branded meaty product, with biscuit
added in equal parts by volume.
Longevity good.
Characteristics include any white
markings on head, chest, and legs.

The Schnauzer or Standard Schnauzer is the oldest of three
varieties of Schnauzer, the others being the Miniature and
Giant. It has been depicted through the ages by artists,
including Albrecht Dürer (1471–1528), Rembrandt (1606–69),
and Sir Joshua Reynolds (1723–92). The earliest likeness of
the breed is probably that in Dürer's painting, *Madonna with
the Many Animals*, 1492.

Despite its many representations over the centuries, the
Schnauzer's origin remains obscure. Some say that it was a
cross between two now extinct breeds, the Beaver Dog of the
Middle Ages and a rough-coated dog, perhaps a terrier, which
was kept to dispel vermin. Others think that it evolved from
the extinct Schafer Pudel and the Wire-haired German
Pinscher. Still other researchers believe that the Schnauzer is

descended entirely from drovers' dogs, including the Bouvier
des Flandres to which it certainly bears a close resemblance.
It was originally used as an all-purpose farm dog, and was a
good ratter. It is also an excellent companion. The breed
standard was first published in Germany in 1880. In 1918 the
Bavarian Schnauzer Club united with the Pinscher Club of
Cologne.

The Schnauzer is an attractive, robust, intelligent, and
playful dog, which makes a good companion and is generally
good with children. It enjoys plenty of exercise, and its hardy,
harsh, wiry coat needs a certain amount of stripping and
plucking. Pet dogs can be clipped but this will spoil the coat
for showing, so owners wishing to exhibit are advised to
discuss grooming with the breeder at the time of purchase.

KEESHOND

ORIGIN

Netherlands

Character sensible, smart,
good-natured, devoted.

Exercise a moderate amount of exercise
is required.

Grooming daily grooming with a stiff
brush.

Feeding average appetite.

Longevity long lived.

Characteristics feet are very small and
cat-like, with thick hair between toes.

Descended from Spitz stock, the ancestors of this breed
were a common sight on barges traveling along the River
Rhine. They are believed to be named after two leaders of the
Dutch Patriot Party, who adopted the breed as a symbol
during the 18th century. Both these men had the Christian
name of Kees, but this link ultimately had an adverse effect
on the popularity of the Keeshond (pronounced "Kayshond")
when the Prince of Orange took power in the Netherlands.

During the present century, however, Keeshonden (the
plural form) have attracted increasing attention from dog-
lovers, with a member of this breed winning the top award at

Crufts in 1957. They are wolf-gray in color, with an attractive
fluffy coat. The ruff around the neck is more prominent in
adult dogs than puppies. Avoid using a choke chain of any
kind when training a Keeshond, as this may damage its ruff.
A thorough daily grooming will be necessary to keep the coat
in top condition, while proper training is required because
these dogs can prove to be independent and strong willed.
Keeshonden are quite at home in the domestic environment,
and can be relied upon as keen guards. Their bell-like bark is
characteristic of the breed.

LHASA APSO

Another of the ancient Tibetan breeds, the Lhasa Apso used to be given as a gift to the Chinese court by the Dalai Lama who ruled Tibet. The unusual name of these dogs translates as "goat-like," and it may have been that their ancestors were actually kept as guardians for herds of goats before they acquired regal status. Traditionally, they lived inside homes, with the Tibetan Mastiff being kept as a guard outside. Lhasa Apsos first reached the West in the early years of the last century, and there was initially some confusion between these dogs and the larger Tibetan Terrier. By the 1930s, however, the Lhasa was established in its own right, and has since become the most commonly seen of the four Tibetan breeds.

They are attractive, affectionate dogs, but their long, flowing coats obviously need careful grooming on a daily basis, otherwise the hair will become badly tangled and, in extreme cases, the dog may have to be anaesthetized to have the mats removed painlessly. As companions, there are few dogs as long lived, with Lhasa Apsos frequently living into their late teens and beyond—up to 29 years in one astonishing case!

Character happy, adaptable, and good with children.

Exercise reasonable amount of exercise.

Grooming a great deal of careful daily grooming is required to maintain its long coat.

Feeding small appetite.

Longevity particularly long lived.

Characteristics its bark is the basis for its name, "hairy barking dog."

ORIGIN

Tibet

A capable worker, the Bernese Mountain Dog may also be kept as a loyal and affectionate pet.

WORKING BREEDS

ESKIMO DOG

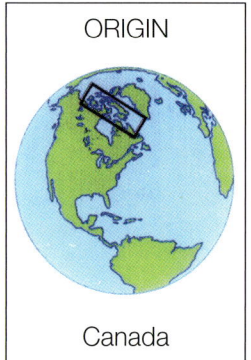

ORIGIN

Canada

Character energetic, independent, will make
an affectionate pet but most suitable for
working. Rarely lives indoors but prefers a
kennel.

Exercise needs as much excercise as
possible.

Grooming will benefit from regular brushing.

Feeding huge appetite, will scavenge for
food whenever it can.

Longevity 12 to 13 years.

Characteristics dense coat that protects
dog from temperatures far below freezing.

This hardy, strong spitz dog was developed to haul sleds in
and around the Arctic Circle. The American polar explorer
Robert Peary (1856–1920) considered that there was only
one breed of sled-dog with regional variations, but now a
number of breeds are recognized. The beautiful Eskimo Dog
probably originated in eastern Siberia, and shared common
ancestry with the Alaskan Malamute, Siberian Husky, and
Samoyed. It bears a considerable resemblance to the

Greenland Dog (which is not, at the time of writing,
recognized in the UK), but the Eskimo Dog is shorter in the
back and weightier.

The Eskimo Dog is an excellent sled dog of remarkable
endurance. It is a fine guard, which rarely lives indoors with its
owners. It relishes vigorous outdoor exercise and a job of
work, and benefits from regular brushing.

ESTRELA MOUNTAIN DOG

The Estrela Mountain Dog, also known as the Portuguese Mountain Dog or Cao da Serra da Estrela, originated many centuries ago in the Estrêla mountains of central Portugal. It was bred as a herding dog and has in its make-up something of the Mastiff, and of the Saint Bernard, to which it bears some resemblance.

It has always been popular in its native Portugal, where it is still used as a guard dog. The breed standard was first published there in 1933. The breed was first introduced into the UK in 1974, and it is shown there at larger shows.

The Estrela Mountain Dog is an excellent guard, with immense stamina. It is very loyal and affectionate to its owners but indifferent to other humans. This intelligent dog is said to need a great deal of love and firm, kindly handling. It requires plenty of exercise, regular brushing, and a light diet, which should be discussed with the breeder at time of purchase.

Character loyal, affectionate, and full of stamina. Will make an excellent guard for humans or animals.

Exercise requires plenty of exercise and is not suitable for urban, towerblock living.

Grooming regular brushing.

Feeding light diet.

Longevity 11 to 13 years.

Characteristics abundant topcoat is darker than equally thick undercoat.

ORIGIN

Portugal

SAINT BERNARD

The Saint Bernard is a gentle giant, despite being descended from the fierce Molossus dogs of ancient Rome. It is named after the medieval Hospice of St. Bernard in the Swiss Alps, to which it was introduced between 1660 and 1670. It became famous for rescuing travelers and climbers on the Swiss Alps. One dog, Barry, saved 40 lives during the period 1800–10.

Prior to 1830, all Saint Bernards were short-coated, but in that year Newfoundland blood was introduced in an attempt to give the breed added size and vitality. As a result the modern Saint Bernard may be long-or-short-haired. In 1810, a Saint Bernard called "Lion" was introduced into the UK and the breed was first exhibited ithere in 1863. An international standard for the Saint Bernard was drawn up in Berne in 1887.

True to its past, the Saint Bernard is intelligent, eminently trainable, loves children, and is a kindly dog. Because of this, it is, unfortunately, sometimes kept in conditions which do not allow it nearly enough space. Like many heavyweights, the breed should not be given too much exercise in the first year of life, short regular walks being better than long ones. It needs daily brushing and requires generous quantities of food. It also slobbers. Sadly, like the Great Dane, this lovable, large dog has only a limited lifespan.

Character calm, sensible, trustworthy, and courageous mountain rescue dog.

Exercise plenty. However, not too much before adulthood.

Grooming regular combing and brushing to keep coat in good condition and avoid shedding.

Feeding at least 2½ cans (14½ oz size) of a branded meaty product, with biscuit added in equal parts by volume.

Longevity not long lived.

Characteristics chest should never project below elbows. Subject to hip deformities.

ORIGIN

Switzerland

SAMOYED

Character independent but devoted, obedient, and good with children.
Exercise needs as much exercise as an owner can give it.
Grooming requires daily brushing and combing.
Feeding average appetite.
Longevity average.
Characteristics an exceptionally good natured and friendly dog, particularly enjoys human companionship.

The Samoyed or Smiling Sammy takes its name from the Siberian tribe of Samoyedes. This beautiful and devoted spitz variety has great powers of endurance and was one of the breeds used by Fridtjof Nansen and Ernest Shackleton on their expeditions to the North Pole. It has also been used as a guard and to hunt reindeer. The Samoyed was introduced into the UK in 1889 by a Mr. Kilburn-Scott, who returned from the north coast of Russia with a pup. He subsequently mated a bitch "Whitey Pechora," said to have been obtained from a sailor in London, to a dog named "Musti" owned by

Lady Sitwell, and many present-day Samoyeds descend from this pair. The standard originally drawn up by the Kilburn-Scotts has changed little over the years and British stock has been exported all over the world.

Unlike many sled dogs, the Sammy lives in the homes of its owners in its native land. It is a devoted dog, which is good with children and makes an obedient, if slightly independent, housepet. Some breed members have excelled in obedience work. It revels in exercise, and its thick, water-resistant coat needs regular brushing and combing.

PINSCHER

ORIGIN

Germany

Character high spirited and self possessed, lively but docile, makes an efficient and fearless guard dog and is suitable for urban living.

Exercise will welcome a lot of exercise.

Grooming a good brush every few days.

Feeding has an average appetite.

Longevity average 12 to 14 yrs.

Characteristics has a tendency to fight with other dogs, requires the firm handling of an experienced trainer.

The Pinscher ("biter," in German) originated in Germany, where it has existed for several hundred years, as proved by likenesses in various works of art. The old Black and Tan Terrier may have contributed to its development at some stage.

Resembling the larger Doberman, to which it contributed, the Pinscher was officially recognized by the German Kennel Club as long ago as 1879. At the beginning of the 20th century, both smooth and coarse-haired puppies appeared in litters. However, the Pinscher Club ruled that a short-haired Pinscher would not be registered unless short-haired ancestors could be proved for three generations. However, it is only since 1988 that an interim breed standard has been set up for it by the British Kennel Club, and it will be interesting to see whether this good sporting and show breed makes an impact on the international show scene.

The Pinscher's temperament has been described as high spirited and self possessed. It is a good natured, playful dog which is good with children and makes a fine guard, being alert, loyal, watchful, and fearless. It needs exercise and grooming and can cope with life in an apartment.

PORTUGUESE WATER DOG

The Portuguese Water Dog (Cão d'Agua) was once a familiar sight throughout the fishing ports of the Iberian Peninsula, and is still commonly found in the Algarve region of Portugal. It is a fisherman's dog, a fine swimmer with great powers of endurance, and undertakes a wide variety of tasks. It will guard the catch, swim between boats, and dive and retrieve fish or objects lost overboard. It is also a good rabbiter.

There are two distinct varieties of the breed, one with a long glossy, wavy coat and the other with a shorter, thicker, curlier coat, but conformation is identical. Although the Portuguese Water Dog was once a comparative rarity outside its native land, it is now a regular contender in the ring in the UK and elsewhere, and makes an attractive show dog.

This intelligent and energetic dog is said to be self-willed but obedient to its owner, and somewhat apprehensive of strangers. It is a superlative swimmer and diver, needs ample exercise and regular brushing and combing. For exhibition purposes, the hindquarters are clipped from the last rib, and two-thirds of the tail are clipped.

Character strong, independent and alert, obedient and loyal, makes an excellent guard for humans due to a naturally suspicious nature.

Exercise needs a lot of exercis, ,ideally near water, enjoys swimming and diving.

Grooming will benefit from regular brushing and combing

Feeding large appetite.

Longevity 12 to 14 years.

Characteristics uncomfortable with strangers.

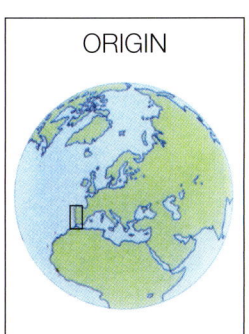

ORIGIN

Portugal

73

ALASKAN MALAMUTE

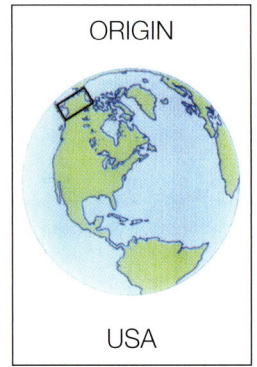

ORIGIN

USA

This is one of the native
North American spitz breeds,
developed by a tribe called the Mahlemuts, after which they
are named. Alaskan Malamutes are used in sleigh teams, and
six harnessed together can cover a distance of 50 miles
(80 km) in a day, pulling loads of 100 lb (355 kg) or more.
Their rather vulpine appearance belies an affectionate nature.
They tend to be a combination of gray or black and white,
with distinctive facial patterning forming a mask or cap, or
combination of both.

As may be anticipated from their origins, these are active
dogs, not suited to apartment living. At present, the Alaskan
Malamute may be less common than other similar breeds
such as the Siberian Husky, but it appears to be growing in
popularity, especially in the USA and Canada. Coat care
presents no particular problems and they are, in addition, very
hardy dogs, able to live outdoors in kennels if required,
although they do delight in human companionship.

Character social, gentle, affectionate, active,
devoted to humans but not very good with
other canines.
Exercise needs as much exercise as
possible.
Grooming daily brushing.
Feeding good size appetite.
Longevity average.
Characteristics heavily muscled, strong-
boned legs are ideal for traction and weight
pulling.

BERNESE MOUNTAIN DOG

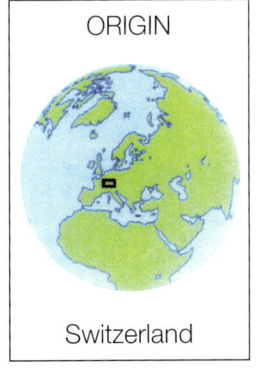

ORIGIN

Switzerland

Character a multi-purpose farm dog, capable of draft work. An ideal family pet in the right environment.

Exercise this is not a town dog. It needs plenty of exercise.

Grooming regular brushing or coat will shed.

Feeding Approximately 2 cans (14½ oz size) of a branded meaty product, with biscuit added in equal parts by volume.

Longevity average.

Characteristics may show sign of aggression, which must not be tolerated.

This beautiful animal is the best known of the four Swiss mountain dogs. The others are the Great Swiss Sennenhund, the Appenzell Sennenhund, and the Entlebuch Sennenhund.

In Switzerland, Bernese Mountain Dogs are extensively used for draft purposes, and it is not unusual to see a Bernese Mountain dog pulling milk churns up the mountain side. In some countries (in the UK, for instance) it is illegal to use dogs in this way, but owners get great enjoyment from harnessing up their pets for off-highway events, such as local fêtes, where they frequently raise money for charity.

A large dog—25–27½ in (64–70 cm), bitches 23–26 in (58–66 cm)—the Bernese is not all that dissimilar to a very large Border Collie. In fact, however, its origins lie in ancient Rome.

Two thousands years ago when Roman legions crossed the Alps into northern Europe they were accompanied by war and guard dogs. From survivors of the latter, four large Alpine breeds evolved, three as sheep herders, the fourth as a draft dog, the Bernese Mountain Dog. It takes its name from Berne from where the inhabitants, many of them weavers, would drive their wares.

The Bernese makes an excellent family pet in the right environment. It needs space and exercise. It would be cruel to keep it in an apartment. It also prefers cold weather and while many breed members do live indoors they come to no harm being kenneled outside.

The breed tends to devote itself to one person, but will adapt to share its tremendous loyalty with the family.

The coat of the Bernese should be jet black, with rich reddish brown on cheeks, over the eyes, and on all four legs and chest. There is a slight to medium sized symmetrical white head marking (blaze) and white chest marking (cross) which are essential. White paws are preferred, but not essential.

MASTIFF

ORIGIN

UK

Character brave, intelligent, and loyal.

Exercise needs plenty. Best kept on a farm or estate.

Grooming daily brushing.

Feeding 2½–4 cans (14½ oz size) of a branded meaty product, with biscuit added in equal parts by volume.

Longevity average.

Characteristics include a tendency to lameness. Check with veterinarian for soundness.

The Mastiff is among the most ancient breeds of dog. Mastiff-like dogs were treasured by the Babylonians over 4,000 years ago, and the Mastiff has been resident in the UK since the time of Julius Caesar. The breed has proved its worth as a formidable guard and as a hunter. The Mastiff was depicted on the 12th century Bayeux Tapestry and in a painting by Van Dyck (1599–1641) of the children of King Charles I. Shakespeare's play Henry V mentions "…*mastiffs of unmatchable courage.*"

In the 19th century Saint Bernard blood was introduced. There were less than a dozen Mastiffs left in the UK after World War II because many kennels had been disbanded, and numbers declined in America as well. The situation is gradually improving.

The Mastiff is large and dignified. It is usually devoted to its owner. It needs regular walking to build up its muscles. Many do not complete growth until their second year.

NEAPOLITAN MASTIFF

ORIGIN

Italy

Character majestic with an air of ferocity, generally friendly and affectionate with the right training from an experienced dog handler.

Exercise requires plenty of exercise, but must be kept on a leash at all times.

Grooming needs a good brush every few days.

Feeding this dog has an immense appetite.

Longevity quite short. 10 to 11 years.

Characteristics not suitable for children or first time owners.

The origins of this Italian dog stretch right back to the fierce Molossus dogs of ancient Rome. These Mastiffs have particularly large heads, supported by equally powerful bodies. They used to be concentrated largely in their Italian homeland, but are now being seen in greater numbers elsewhere. Neapolitan Mastiffs are bred in shades of gray and black. Although used for dog-fighting in the past, they retain strong territorial instincts and will prove determined guards.

BOXER

For the family with young children, the boxer is an excellent choice. It is fairly exuberant, and takes a long time to grow up, but generally fits in well with the average family, particularly if there is someone able to take it for long country walks. However, in summer it should not be taken for walks in the heat of the day. Boxers can also be trained for obedience and have been used by the police, in the armed forces, and as guide dogs for the blind.

The boxer's ancestry goes back to the "holding" dogs of Molossus (Mastiff) type, taken into battle against the wild Cumbrians by the Romans. The jaw, like that of the Bulldog, is undershot—a common trait in bull-baiters. The Barbant bull-baiter, from which the English Bulldog evolved, also had a hand in the evolution of the Boxer.

The Boxer stands 22½–25 in (57–63 cm), bitches 21–23 in (53–59 cm) and comes in fawn or brindle. The all-white Boxer, which makes an attractive pet, is unacceptable in the show ring. The ears are cropped in many countries.

ORIGIN

Germany

Character brave, clownish, marvelous with children. Not averse to a scrap with other dogs.

Exercise enjoys unleashing its boundless energy.

Grooming daily brushing.

Feeding 1½–2½ cans (14½ oz size) of a branded meaty product, with biscuit added in equal parts by volume.

Longevity fairly good.

Characteristics include enjoying a scrap: it goes in with its stumpy tail wagging.

BULLMASTIFF

There have been bull-dogs in the UK since the 13th century, but the Bullmastiff was developed some 200–300 years ago. It is the result of a cross between the Mastiff, an ancient breed which fought in the arenas of ancient Rome, and the British Bulldog. It was used in bull-baiting until this "sport" was outlawed, and was a brave fighting dog, which could bear pain without flinching. It also had a considerable reputation for ferocity.

Later breeders worked toward a type which was 60 percent Mastiff and 40 percent Bulldog. The resultant Bullmastiff was registered by the Kennel Club in the UK in 1924. Despite its ferocious past, the Bullmastiff of today is a playful, loyal, and gentle animal, and excellent guard and usually very dependable with children. However, it is too powerful for a child or slight adult to control, and should only be kept by experienced dog owners. It needs grooming every few days.

Character brave, intelligent and loyal.

Exercise needs plenty. Best kept on a farm or estate.

Grooming daily brushing.

Feeding 2½ cans (14½ oz size) of a branded meaty product, with biscuit added in equal parts by volume.

Longevity average.

Characteristics include a tendency to lameness. Check with veterinarian for soundness.

ORIGIN

UK

KOMONDOR

ORIGIN

Hungary

The Komondor was known as early as 1555, and has been used for centuries to guard flocks and property from predators and thieves on the Hungarian plains. It has worked with and without other dogs, first herding the semi-wild Hungarian sheep, and later protecting whatever required a large and commanding dog as guard. The breed was recognized in the USA in 1937, but is still comparatively rare in western Europe and has made its mark in the British show ring only over the last ten years.

Very strong and agile for its size, the Komondor is hardy, healthy, and tolerant of changing temperatures. It is a breed that can never be mistaken for any other because of its full white coat falling in tassels, or cords, which is thought by some to resemble an old-fashioned string mop. The cords of the coat form a kind of controlled matting which feels felty to the touch.

The Komondor is a natural protector and will guard with its life sheep and cattle, or children and other pets if it is cast in the role of family companion. While it is utterly devoted to its human family, it is wary of strangers, does not take kindly to teasing and if a warning growl goes unheeded, may attack without warning.

This breed needs plenty of exercise and meticulous grooming.

Character excellent guard, wary of strangers. Not for the inexperienced, but immensely loyal to owner.

Exercise puppies are particularly active. Adults need a good amount of exercise, which must be on a leash if in town.

Grooming the Komondor has a thick double coat. The undercoat is soft and woolly, the outer coat long, coarse, and wavy. The coat forms in tassel-like cords which are never brushed and combed, although matting has to be avoided.

Feeding at least 2½ cans (14½ oz size) of a branded meaty product, with biscuit added in equal parts by volume.

Longevity good.

Characteristics strong heavy cords of coat feel like felt when touched.

LEONBERGER

A German breed, the Leonberger is generally thought to have come about through the crossing of a Landseer and a Pyrenean Mountain Dog. However, some people believe that it is a descendant of the Tibetan Mastiff, while others consider it to be the product of selective breeding by Herr Essig of Leonberg. He is said to have used the Newfoundland, Saint Bernard, and Pyrenean Mountain Dog to develop the breed. The breed was devastated by both World Wars and is considered a rare breed.

It was not until 1949 that a recognized standard for the breed clearly defined the differences between the Leonberger and the Saint Bernard. The Leonberger has worked in Germany, France, the Netherlands, and Belgium as a watchdog, a protector of livestock, and as a draft dog, but has only become known outside these countries fairly recently.

Good natured, intelligent, and lively, the Leonberger is a fine-looking watchdog, produced from breeds of sound temperament. It is essentially a country dog, and needs daily brushing, regular exercise, and plenty of space. It is very good with children, and has a great love of water.

Character intelligent, active with a good temperament, great with children and other dogs.

Exercise needs lots of exercise and plenty of space. Unsuitable for urban living.

Grooming daily brushing.

Feeding needs plenty of food.

Longevity quite short. 11 years.

Characteristics this breed tends to suffer from hip dysplasia.

ORIGIN

Germany

81

CANAAN DOG

ORIGIN

Israel

Character alert, homeloving, aloof, but loving and loyal to its family. The Canaan Dog makes an excellent guard dog for humans and animals alike.

Exercise needs plenty of exercise.

Grooming needs regular grooming with a brush and comb.

Feeding large appetite.

Longevity 12 to 13 years.

Characteristics used for mine detection during the war, even used as guide dogs.

The Canaan Dog is an indigenous breed of Israel, which is said to have been developed through the selective breeding of the semi-wild Pariah dogs of the Middle East. A fine guard and protector of livestock, the Canaan has also proved its worth as a guard dog and as a messenger in the Israeli army. Other uses have been as a guide dog for the blind and as a search and rescue dog.

There are two varieties of Canaan Dog, one collie-like and the other Dingo-like, the latter being more heavily built.

The Canaan is alert, home loving, and loyal to its family. It has a distrust of strangers and will faithfully guard the humans and animals entrusted to its care, standing its ground if called upon to do so. It needs regular grooming with a brush and comb.

DOBERMAN

The Doberman was developed in the 1880s by Louis Dobermann of Apolda in Thuringia, Germany, who happened to be the keeper of the local dog pound. He wanted a ferocious, short-coated, medium-to-large-sized dog with courage and stamina and developed his stock around the German Pinscher, which was both alert and aggressive. To this he introduced the Rottweiler with its stamina and tracking ability, the Manchester Terrier, then a much larger animal, from which the Doberman inherited its markings, and possibly also the Pointer.

The German National Doberman Pinscher Club was launched by Otto Göller in 1899, and the breed was given official recognition and a breed standard there in 1900. It was not until 1948 that the Doberman Pinscher Club was formed in the UK, and shortly afterward the breed received recognition from the British Kennel Club.

The Doberman is a fine obedience and show dog and can make a good family pet, but it needs knowledgeable handling and training, being wary of strangers and constantly "on guard." It needs a lot of exercise, and should be groomed every couple of days.

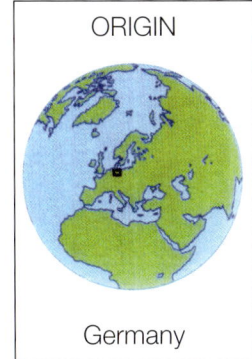

ORIGIN

Germany

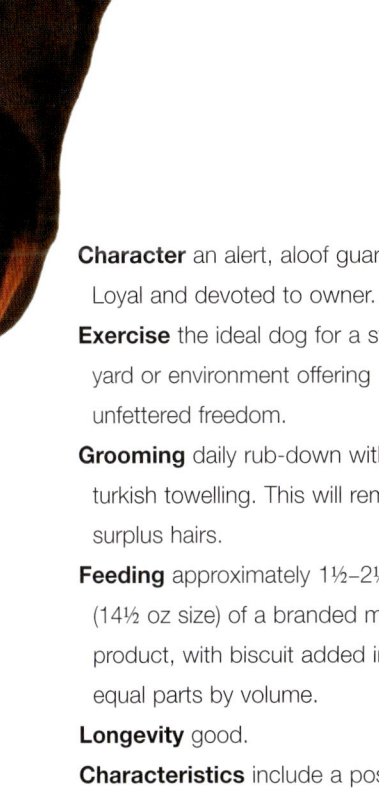

Character an alert, aloof guard. Loyal and devoted to owner.

Exercise the ideal dog for a stable yard or environment offering unfettered freedom.

Grooming daily rub-down with turkish towelling. This will remove surplus hairs.

Feeding approximately 1½–2½ cans (14½ oz size) of a branded meaty product, with biscuit added in equal parts by volume.

Longevity good.

Characteristics include a possible tendency to overguard.

SIBERIAN HUSKY

Few dogs have more stamina than the Siberian Husky, which was developed as a sled dog by the Chukchi tribe who lived in north-east Asia. From here, some of these dogs were taken to Alaska just after the turn of the last century, where they won the gruelling 400 mile (644 km) All Alaska Sweepstake Race. The popularity of these dogs spread, helped by their appealing temperament.

In addition to being kept just as active companions or show dogs, however, they have also been used in recent years to develop the sport of sled racing. This is now a popular pursuit among owners of these Huskies, both in the USA and in parts of Europe, including the UK. There are no restrictions on the coloration of the Siberian Husky, and some individuals are most attractively marked. They are also known under the alternative name of Arctic Husky.

Character reliable, medium-sized working sled dog.

Exercise this dog has considerable endurance and a great turn of speed. Not suitable for the suburban semi.

Grooming daily brushing and combing. Toweling after coat has got wet. Coat sheds once a year, when surplus hair will need combing out.

Feeding 1½– 2½ cans (14½ oz size) of a branded meaty product, with biscuit added in equal parts by volume.

Longevity 11 to 13 years.

Characteristics include a tendency to wander. Can be destructive.

ORIGIN

Siberia

SWEDISH VALLHUND

ORIGIN

Sweden

Character friendly, loyal, and affectionate, active, and eager to please. Makes an excellent farm dog.

Exercise needs planty of exercise.

Grooming will benefit from daily brushing.

Feeding average appetite.

Longevity 12 to 14 years.

Characteristics can be boisterous with other dogs. Has a tendency to nip on occasion.

The Swedish Vallhund is known in its native land as Vastgotaspets, which means "Spitz of the West Goths." It closely resembles the Welsh Corgi, although the Vallhund is somewhat higher in the leg and shorter in the back. Undoubtedly there is a connection between the breeds but whether Corgis taken by the Vikings to Sweden developed into the Vallhund or Swedish dogs brought to the UK developed into Corgis is not known. Like the Corgi, the Vallhund is a splendid cattle dog. Much credit for the development of the modern breed must go to the Swedish fancier, Bjorn van Rosen. Despite its antiquity, the Vallhund did not win recognition by any kennel club until 1950, but it is now gaining popularity in the international show ring.

The Swedish Vallhund is a friendly, loyal, affectionate little dog, described in its standard as active and eager to please. It makes a good family pet and needs plenty of exercise.

GREAT DANE

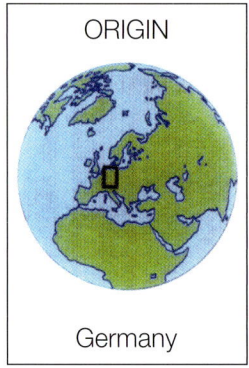

ORIGIN

Germany

Character devoted, good natured, and easy to train—but not cheap to feed!

Exercise ideally miles of walking on hard ground every day, if you haven't the land to give it freedom.

Grooming daily grooming with a body brush.

Feeding feeding up to 4 cans (14½ oz size) of a branded meaty product, with biscuit added in equal parts by volume.

Longevity short. Average eight or nine years.

Characteristics a little boisterous when young, and has greater-than-average incidence of hip and elbow arthritis and bone tumors.

This is the tallest of the various mastiff breeds, and has been known for over 400 years. Its modern ancestry can be traced back to Germany, where these dogs were originally used for hunting wild boar. Here they are known as Deutsche Dogge and the original German standard for the breed has since received virtually universal acceptance. Brindle, fawn, blue, and black varieties are all recognized, as well as harlequin form. This is basically white with the body coloration broken by either black or blue patches, although the former coloration is favored.

The short coat of the Great Dane is easy to keep in good condition by using a body brush. Although they require plenty of exercise, do not be tempted to allow young puppies to run excessively before the age of six months or so, as this can cause lasting damage to the tendons and joints in the limbs.

Bigger dogs in general tend to have a faster growth rate than the toy breeds, which can leave them more susceptible to problems of this type. Naturally, the Great Dane's appetite is in proportion to its size.

You may need to rearrange your house with a Great Dane puppy around, as they tend to be rather clumsy and bang into things. They are not the best choice for a home with young children, although this breed is generally good natured.

JAPANESE AKITA

The Akita (or Akita Inu or Shishi Inu) is the largest and most well known internationally of the Japanese breeds. It originated in the Polar regions and has a history tracing back more than 300 years. The Akita was bred to hunt deer and wild boar, and has also, on occasion, hunted the Japanese black bear. It is an extremely swift-moving dog, which can work in deep snow. It also has webbed feet and is a strong swimmer, with the ability to retrieve wildfowl and to drive fish into fishermen's nets.

The Akita is revered in Japan, where it was officially appointed a national monument in 1931 in order to preserve the breed, and more recently was featured on a series of commemorative postage stamps. It is the recipient of a Japanese Dog Federation's "National Treasure" award, given under the auspices of the Japanese Government. Indeed, at one time this classic breed could only be owned by members of the Japanese nobility. The international popularity of the breed began when American servicemen took the Akita back to their homeland, after World War II.

The powerful but very trainable Akita is a versatile hunter and retriever, and a first class guard. It has a good temperament for a show dog and is now being kept widely as a pet. However, this alert and energetic dog should not be kept in confined conditions. It can be formidable if its hunting instincts become aroused and needs a good outlet, such as obedience classes, for its undoubted abilities. It also requires daily brushing and a reasonable amount of exercise.

Character alert and energetic with a good temperament and huge training potential.

Exercise needs a reasonable amount of exercise and should not be kept in confined conditions.

Grooming daily brushing with a body brush.

Feeding average appetite.

Longevity average. 10 to 12 years.

Characteristics will require obedience classes.

ORIGIN

Japan

PYRENEAN MOUNTAIN DOG

ORIGIN

The Pyrenees

Character powerful and assertive, patient, noble, and brave. Makes a good watchdog.
Exercise needs lots of regular exercise.
Grooming needs thorough daily brushing.
Feeding fairly large appetite.
Longevity average.
Characteristics can become aggressive if provoked.

Better known in North America simply as the Great Pyrenees, these large shepherd dogs were bred from Mastiff stock and served to protect sheep from wolves, being equipped with fearsome spiked collars to defend themselves. Later they were used to smuggle contraband across the steep mountain paths that separated France and Spain, being fitted with special satchels for this purpose.

The breed had declined sharply by the turn of the last century, and could have died out, but then a breeding program was launched in which emphasis was placed on producing dogs that were good natured, lacking the traditional aggressive traits. This has been successfully achieved, although these dogs still show a marked reluctance to accept strangers and will prove alert guard dogs.

In a show ring, these predominantly white dogs are an impressive sight. They were first recognized by the American Kennel Club in 1933, before being accepted by the British organization 11 years later. The double dew claws on the hindfeet are deemed a breed characteristic and should never be removed in show dogs.

ROTTWEILER

During recent years, the popularity of the Rottweiler has grown at a tremendous rate. Unfortunately, a number of people have been attracted to this dog because of its macho image and, sadly, serious and sometimes fatal injuries have been caused by Rottweilers going berserk, frequently because of poor training. This is actually an intelligent and responsive breed, which has been used for a wide variety of purposes, ranging from police dogs to mountain rescue guides. It is also a prominent contender in many obedience competitions, and a popular entrant in the show ring.

Rottweilers were unknown in the UK until 1936, having been recognized only the previous year by the American Kennel Club. The breed's origins can be traced back to the town of Rottweil in Württemberg, Germany. Their ancestors were used to drive cattle to market and to guard them. In addition, they were trained to pull carts and defend their owners from attacks by highwaymen.

The Rottweiler is not a breed that can be recommended for a home where there are young children. Firm training is also essential, and you must spend sufficient time with these dogs to ensure that they do not become bored, as this can be a recipe for disaster. Exercise is also essential, and it may be worth fitting a muzzle to your pet when it is off the leash, especially in the company of other dogs. Even fellow dog-owners may be nervous about Rottweilers, following the unwelcome publicity that the breed has generated.

Character bold, courageous, and loyal. Working dog and guard. Not recommended for the inexperienced.

Exercise this former wild boar hunter and cattle dog needs an outlet for its energies.

Grooming regular brushing.

Feeding approximately 2–2½ cans (14½ oz size) of a branded meaty product, with biscuit added in equal parts by volume.

Longevity average.

Characteristics fearsome, if provoked.

ORIGIN

Germany

TIBETAN MASTIFF

These large dogs bear some similarity to the Saint Bernard, although they were developed far away in Tibet. In their homeland, Tibetan Mastiffs were used to guard and herd flocks. They may be the closest surviving relative of the original ancestral form of the many Mastiff breeds, which is thought to have been developed in this area.

Unlike some of the small Tibetan dogs, however, this Mastiff has never been well known outside its homeland, although it did have a brief period of popularity in the UK during the 19th century. King George IV (1762–1830) kept two of these dogs, and the Prince of Wales (later King Edward VII) exhibited the breed in 1875. The black and tan or golden forms are best known in the West, but pure black dogs, some showing white markings, have been recorded in Tibet.

There are now signs that Tibetan Mastiffs are becoming more popular. They are hardy and essentially obedient dogs, which can generally be trusted with children in spite of their large size. The American Tibetan Mastiff Association is working hard to encourage the development of this breed along correct lines, ensuring both genetic and temperamental soundness. Interestingly, bitches only come into season once a year rather than twice as most other breeds do.

Character easy going and aloof, hardy, trustworthy, and obedient. Makes an excellent guard of livestock or humans.

Exercise will thrive on plenty of exercise. Needs a good deal of space.

Grooming needs a good daily brushing.

Feeding average appetite.

Longevity not long lived.

Characteristics can be aggressive if territory is threatened.

ORIGIN

Tibet

HERDING BREEDS

SHETLAND SHEEPDOG

ORIGIN

Shetland Islands

Character intelligent, faithful, and obedient. Gets on well with children and adults. Makes an ideal family pet.

Exercise enjoys plenty of exercise.

Grooming daily grooming using a stiff bristled brush and a comb.

Feeding 1–1½ cans (14½ oz size) of a branded meaty product, with biscuit added in equal parts by volume.

Longevity 12 to 14 years.

Characteristics miniaturization has meant an increased risk of fractures to leg bones and a high incidence of inherited digestive problems and eye conditions.

Affectionately known as the Sheltie, this breed is said to have evolved on the Shetland Islands, off the coast of Scotland. Here they were kept by the crofters who scratched a living from this inhospitable terrain. The Shetland Sheepdog probably developed from a range of dogs brought to these islands over the years, but has been established as a pure breed for over a century. It is very similar to the Rough Collie, although smaller in size.

Shelties are intelligent and easily trained, often featuring in obedience competitions. They have been developed in a wide range of colors, with tricolors being among the most striking.

In such cases, the deep tan creates an attractive contrast against their black and white markings. The blue merle is an unusual shade of clear silvery blue, mixed with black and often with tan coloration as well.

The coat of the Sheltie is relatively soft and light and a firm brushing each day should keep it free from tangles. In terms of exercise, Shelties are quite active dogs and need sufficient space for a good run. They are generally quite trustworthy with other dogs, however, and therefore can be allowed off the leash in a suitable area in a park without fear of them provoking any disturbance.

SMOOTH COLLIE

Character tenacious, hardworking sheepdog of great tractability. Not suitable for suburban environment.

Exercise ample if it is not to become bored and snappy.

Grooming brush with an equine dandy brush. Remove dead fur after grooming.

Feeding 1–1½ cans (14½ oz size) of a branded meaty product, with biscuit added in equal parts by volume.

Longevity 12 to 14 years.

Characteristics may have a tendency to coarseness or weediness.

Collies were another of the herding dogs originally bred in Scotland, although their ancestors may have come from Iceland. They first attracted widespread attention when Queen Victoria brought some of these dogs back to her kennels after a visit to Scotland in 1860. The Rough Collie has since become by far the most popular of the two forms, helped perhaps by its involvement in the various *Lassie* films.

Both the Smooth Collie and the Rough Collie are very similar, apart from their coat type, the Rough Collie obviously being the more demanding in this respect. Three color varieties are recognized. These are the sable and white, which can vary from light gold to a rich shade of mahogany, the tri-color, which is a combination of black, white, and tan, especially on the head and legs, and the blue merle, which is silvery-blue, with black mixed in with the colored hairs.

Collies have the typical characteristics of most sheepdogs. they are easy to train and delight in human company. They usually settle well as family pets, provided that they can have a run every day. They are loyal guards and prove wary of strangers.

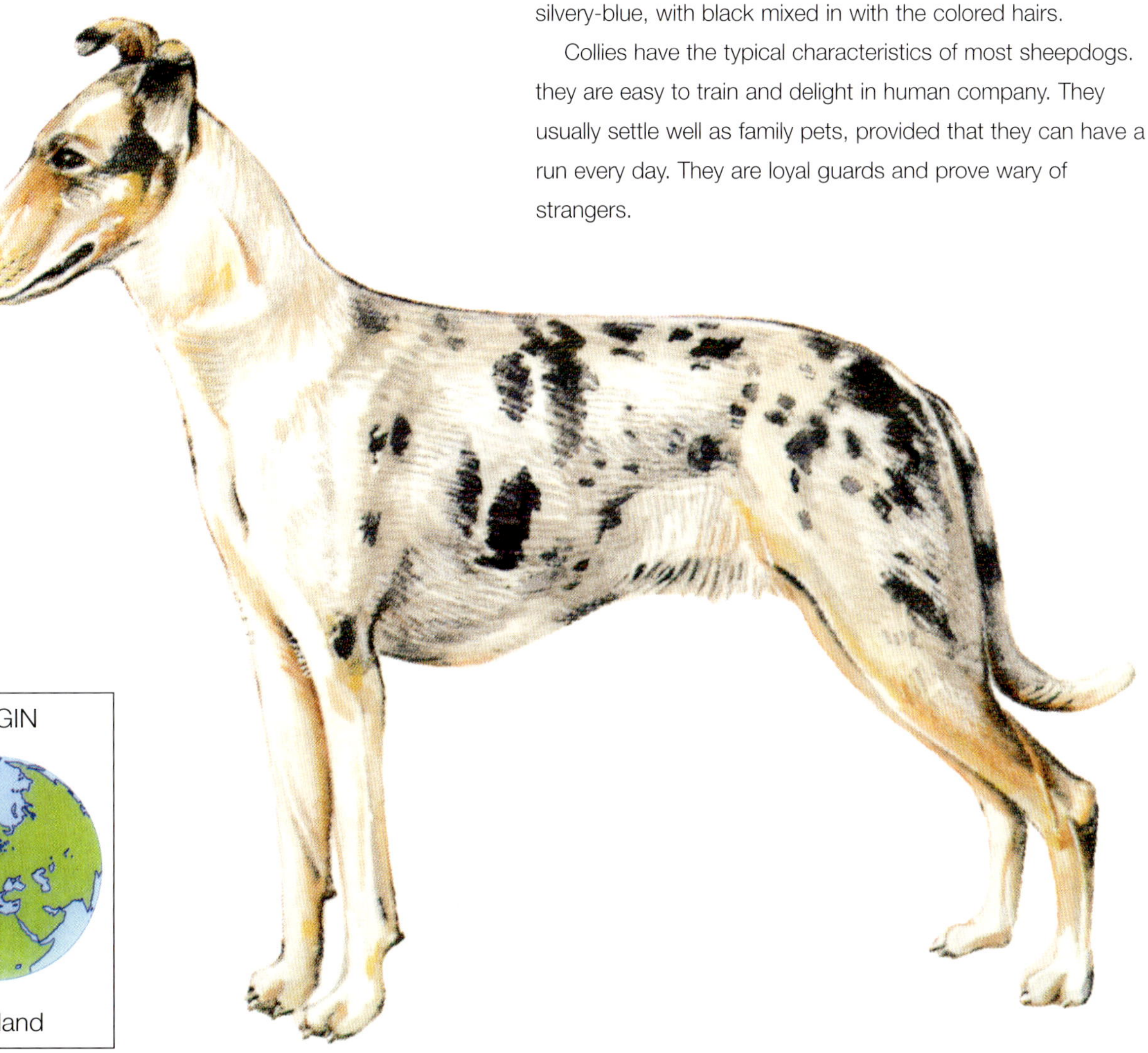

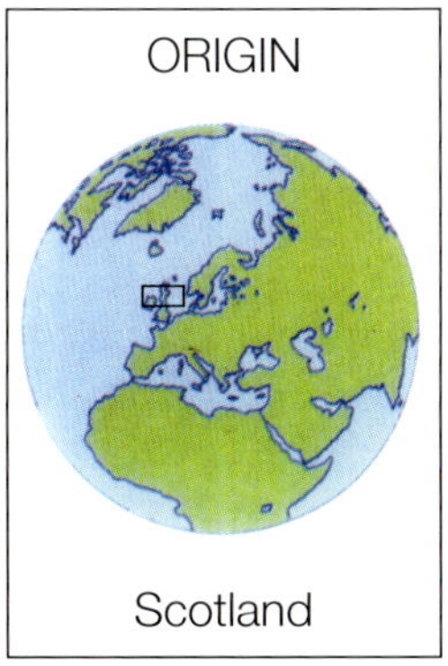

ORIGIN

Scotland

LANCASHIRE HEELER

The Lancashire Heeler has been known in its native country of England for many years as a sporting dog and dispeller of vermin. As its name suggests, it was developed to herd cattle by nipping at their heels, but also has strong terrier instincts and is an excellent rabbiter and ratter. It is a small dog, and its coat is black with tan markings. The breed was little known outside the north of England prior to the 1980s. It was granted an interim standard by the British Kennel Club in 1986, and, happily, breed members are now beginning to appear at dog training classes and in local exemption shows as well as at championship events.

The Lancashire Heeler is a happy, affectionate little dog, which gets on well with humans and other pets. It requires an average amount of exercise and daily brushing.

Character happy, affectionate, gets on well with humans and other animals.

Exercise requires an average amount.

Grooming daily brushing.

Feeding approximately 1½–2½ cans (14½ oz size) of a branded meaty product, with biscuit added in equal parts by volume.

Longevity 12 to 13 years.

Characteristics may show signs of aggression, which must not be tolerated. White spot on fore-chest is permitted but not desirable.

ORIGIN

UK

MAREMMA SHEEPDOG

ORIGIN

Italy

Character strong willed, loyal, and serene.

Exercise needs plenty, unsuitable for urban living.

Grooming regular grooming with a wire dog brush and, occasionally, a good cleansing power .

Feeding approximately 2–2½ cans (14½ oz size) of a branded meaty product with biscuit added in equal parts by volume.

Longevity 11 to 13 years.

Characteristics difficult to obedience train.

The Maremma Sheepdog has two names in its native Italy because for centuries the shepherd dogs spent from June until October in the Abruzzi, where there was good summer grazing, and from October until June in the Maremma. Called both Pastore Abruzzese and Pastore Maremmano, some people thought that they were two different breeds. Then, about 25 years ago at a meeting in Florence, the eminent judge, Professor Giuseppe Solaro, drew up a single breed standard under the name of Pastore Maremmano Abruzzese.

The Maremma has never worked sheep like the Border Collie, but defended the flock against wolves and bears. The first records of a Maremma Sheepdog appeared 2,000 years ago when Columella (c. AD 65) made reference to a white dog and Marcus Varro (127–16 BC) produced a standard for a sheepdog almost identical to that for the Maremma of today. The breed has been known in the UK since 1872.

The Maremma is a natural guard that will never forget a kindness or an injury. To quote an Italian expert, "*If you want obedience and submission keep away from our breed, but if you appreciate friendship given and received, a trace of humor and much teaching of the lore of the wild, a typical Maremmano is the best you can have.*" The Maremma should be regularly groomed using a wire dog brush and, occasionally, a good cleansing powder.

With its rounded head and widely set eyes, the Briard looks out through a dense curtain of hair.

BRIARD

It may be that this breed originated in the French province of Brie as long ago as the 12th century. Here it was valued as a guard dog, protecting sheep from wolves and other dangers, but, as wolves were gradually eliminated, it also served to herd farmstock. The Briard today has retained a brave nature, and will be alert to any intruders around your property. It is easily trained and will settle well in domestic surroundings, provided that is has plenty of opportunity to exercise every day.

The flowing coat of the Briard obviously needs daily brushing. An unusual feature laid down in the breed standard is that the double dew claws present on the hindlegs are retained. Dew claws are normally removed from other breeds because they serve no real purpose for dogs today and there is a risk, especially with the front dew claws, that the dog could become caught up by them, resulting in injury. Where the dew claws are left, however, you may need to trim them regularly, because they will not become worn down in the normal fashion as they are not in contact with the ground. As a result, the claws are likely to become overgrown and will curl back or, even worse, can penetrate the dog's skin.

In spite of its long history, the Briard has only become more widely known outside France during recent years.

Character gentle, good natured, trustworthy, intelligent, and fearless.

Exercise plenty, a big garden is essential.

Grooming daily brushing, comb carefully with a steel comb.

Feeding approximately 2½ cans (14½ oz size) of a branded meaty product, with biscuit added in equal parts by volume.

Longevity average.

Characteristics can nip if provoked.

ORIGIN

France

GERMAN SHEPHERD DOG

It has been suggested that the German Shepherd Dog (Alsatian or Deutscher Schäferhund) may be a descendant of the Bronze Age wolf. Certainly, around the seventh century AD, there existed in Germany a shepherd dog of similar type but with a lighter coat. By the 16th century, the coat is said to have darkened appreciably.

The German Shepherd was first exhibited at a dog show in Hanover in 1882. Credit for the formation of the modern breed is generally attributed to the German fancier, Rittmeister von Stephanitz, who worked tirelessly in the early 1900s to improve its temperament and conformation. The breed won dedicated fanciers in other countries, including the UK and the USA, among those who had seen the breed working in Germany in World War I. It was at that time thought inappropriate to call the breed by a name that included the word "German," and it became known in the UK, and elsewhere, as the Alsatian because it had originated in the Alsace. In 1971, the British Kennel Club finally relented and the name German Shepherd Dog was restored.

The popular German Shepherd is extremely intelligent and makes a first-class companion, show dog, obedience worker, and guard. It is eminently trainable and so works as a police dog, in the armed services, as a guide dog for the blind, and in numerous other capacities. Its superior guarding ability can get it into trouble, because it may misread a sign and spring to its owner's defence. However, with knowledgeable handling and training it is a splendid canine companion. It needs vigorous daily grooming, plenty of exercise and, above all, a job to do, even if this only entails competing in obedience or agility tests. It is unfair and unwise for this intelligent animal to be subjected to a life of boredom.

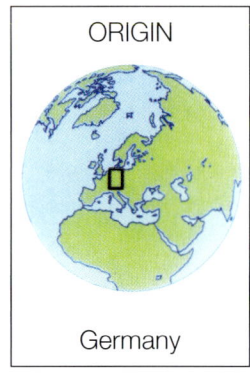

ORIGIN

Germany

Character versatile and alert working dog with keen scenting ability. Excellent guard.

Exercise needs plenty. Best to channel its keen intelligence and exuberance into tasks such as obedience or agility.

Grooming daily brushing.

Feeding 1½–2½ cans (14½ oz size) of a branded meaty product, with biscuit added in equal parts by volume.

Longevity 12 to 13 years.

Characteristics include a tendency to overguard.

GREAT SWISS MOUNTAIN DOG

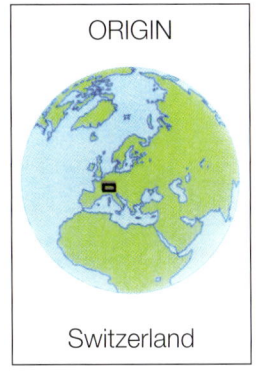

ORIGIN

Switzerland

Character faithful, gentle, and devoted to
children, highly intelligent, an excellent
watchdog.

Exercise needs planty of exercise and thrives
in wide open spaces.

Grooming daily grooming with a bristle brush.

Feeding approximately 2 cans (14½ oz size)
of a branded meaty product, with biscuit
added in equal parts by volume.

Longevity average.

Characteristics may show signs of
aggression, which must not be tolerated.

The Great Swiss Mountain dog or Grosser Schweizer
Sennenhund is the largest of four Swiss mountain dogs, of
which the best known internationally is the Bernese. All are
thought to descend from Molossus dogs, brought north by
ancient Roman armies, and local herding dogs, and they
were used for guarding, herding, and draft work. The Great
Swiss, being an extremely robust dog with very strong hindquarters, is capable of moving quite heavy loads. At the
beginning of this century it was threatened with extinction,
but it revived and today, like the Bernese, is used for pulling
carts loaded with dairy produce. Many members of the breed
have also been used for search and rescue work, particularly
detecting lost people, and objects, in the mountains.

The Great Swiss Mountain Dog is a faithful, gentle animal
that is generally devoted to children. It is alert and highly
intelligent and makes a fine watchdog, willing to protect its
human family with its life. It is essentially a country dog that
thrives in wide open spaces, and needs plenty of exercise. It
requires regular grooming with a bristle brush.

ANATOLIAN SHEPHERD DOG

The Anatolian Shepherd Dog, previously known as the Anatolian Karabash, has existed for centuries, from the Anatolian plateau of Turkey right across Afghanistan. Such large, powerful, and heavy headed dogs have lived in the area since Babylonian times (2800–1800 BC) and were once used as war dogs and to hunt big game such as lions and even horses. However, their more usual job was to guard sheep, and shepherds would crop their ears and fit them with spiked collars to help them defend flocks from predators. They still perform this task today, watching flocks from high ground and then, at the slightest suspicion of trouble, splitting up and converging silently upon the scene at great speed.

This powerful, loyal, and loving dog is good with children, makes a fine watchdog and is eminently trainable. However, it cannot be kept in a confined space, is not suited to town life, and does not take kindly to strangers. It requires considerable exercise and, although the breed has a natural ability to keep itself clean, it should be brushed regularly.

Character strong willed and independent, loyal, and loving. Makes an excellent guard dog.

Exercise needs a lot of exercise.

Grooming will benefit from regular brushing.

Feeding has an ample appetite.

Longevity not long lived.

Characteristics needs very careful socialization, does not take kindly to strangers.

ORIGIN

Turkey

APPENZELL MOUNTAIN DOG

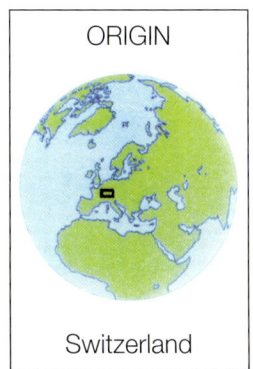

ORIGIN

Switzerland

Character resilient, intelligent, and adaptable. Makes an excellent farm or rescue dog.

Exercise needs plenty of exercise, not a town dog.

Grooming requires daily brushing to prevent coat shedding.

Feeding 2 cans (14½ oz size) of a branded meaty product, with biscuit added in equal parts by volume.

Longevity average.

Characteristics sometimes shows signs of aggression; this should not be tolerated.

The Appenzell (Appenzeller Sennenhund) takes its name from a canton in northern Switzerland. It is one of four varieties of Swiss mountain dog, the others being the Entlebuch, the Great Swiss and, the best known internationally, the Bernese. The Appenzell is similar in appearance to the Bernese but is generally smaller, more rectangular in shape, and smooth coated.

Like all the Swiss mountain dogs, it is thought to descend from the Molossus dogs of ancient Rome, which were brought north with invading Roman soldiers and crossed with herding dogs. The Appenzell was used extensively at one time as a herding dog and to haul carts of produce to market. It is still fairly common in its native land, where there is a thriving Appenzell club, but is rarely seen in other countries.

A resilient, intelligent dog that is easily trained, the adaptable Appenzell makes an excellent farm and rescue dog, companion, and guard. It needs plenty of food and exercise, and a daily brushing.

NEWFOUNDLAND

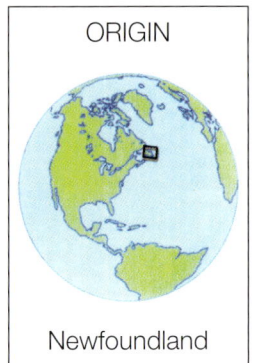

ORIGIN

Newfoundland

Two different forms of the dog developed in Newfoundland, descended from European varieties through breeding by sailors. While the smaller form was to become the ancestor of the Labrador Retriever, the Great Saint John's dog evolved into the breed that is recognized today as the Newfoundland. These dogs took to water readily and, because of their size and strength, were able to save the lives of drowning sailors.

The Newfoundland was first brought to the UK during 1860, but subsequently had nearly died out by the start of World War II. Many of today's bloodlines can be traced back to later imports of American dogs, which maintained the breed's existence in the UK. Both black and brown forms are now recognized, as well as the white and black form that is known as the Landseer after the famous Victorian artist Sir Edwin Landseer (1802–73), who painted these dogs.

Newfoundlands are well-balanced, amenable dogs that will settle well in a household large enough to accommodate them. They have retained their swimming skills, and can also prove valuable as guard dogs. Their size alone is a considerable deterrent, but if threatened they are likely to prove fierce in defence of people around them.

Character excellent guard, fine swimmer, marvelous with children and other animals.

Exercise regular exercise on hard ground.

Grooming daily brushing with a hard brush.

Feeding at least 2½ cans (14½ oz size) of a branded meaty product, with biscuit added in equal parts by volume.

Longevity average.

Characteristics has a tail that sometimes has a kink, or curled over back.

OLD ENGLISH SHEEPDOG

ORIGIN

UK

Character great stamina and sound temperament. Gets on well with children and other animals.

Exercise plenty. Good garden essential for this boisterous breed.

Grooming daily brushing with steel comb. Lengthy show preparation.

Feeding approximately 2½ cans (14½ oz size) of a branded meaty product, with biscuit added in equal parts by volume.

Longevity average.

Characteristics has light eyes.

"Bobtail" or the Old English Sheepdog is thought to have resulted from the crossing of the Briard with the large Russian Owtscharka, which is related to Hungarian sheepdogs. It was once used in the UK as cattle dog and guard. Nowadays it is kept almost solely as a family pet, and while it is a good natured dog, it is not always a good choice for the suburban home because of its sheer bulk and exuberance.

Indeed, over-popularity in the UK following the breed's appearance in a television commercial has resulted in rescue societies being inundated with requests from owners wanting a home found for "Bobtails" which they bought on impulse and found too large to cope with in an apartment, or to exercise alongside a pram. But in the right environment it is a first-rate companion, devoted and sensible, and good with children. Standing 24 in (61 cm) or more, bitches 22 in (56 cm) or more, the "Bobtail" comes in any shade of gray, grizzle, or blue. Body and hindquarters are of solid color with or without white socks.

AUSTRALIAN CATTLE DOG

The Australian Cattle Dog is a superb worker which drives herds by nipping at the cattle's heels. The breed traces back to the now-extinct Black Bobtail, which has been described as large and rather clumsy. In 1840, new blood was introduced, including that of the extinct Smithfield, the native Dingo, the Kelpie, the Dalmatian, and the blue merle Smooth Collie. The Dingo's contributions—its keen sense of smell and hearing, its stealth, speed and stamina, and its tolerance of a dry, hot climate—helped to create this breed, uniquely suited to the Australian outback. The addition of Kelpie made the Australian Cattle Dog an outstanding heeler as well. It has been said that ruthless culling took place during the early years of the breed, but the result has produced one of the most efficient herding dogs in the world.

At the beginning of the last century, the first standard for the breed was drawn up by one Robert Kaleski and published in the Agricultural Gazette of New South Wales. This cattle dog was slow to become known internationally, but was recognized in the USA in 1980 and has made a welcome appearance in the UK show ring over the past five years.

The Australian Cattle Dog is intelligent and good tempered. This superlative working dog is capable of covering immense distances and so requires considerable exercise. It benefits from a vigorous daily brushing.

Character intelligent and good natured with enormous stamina.

Exercise requires considerable exercise.

Grooming will benefit from vigorous daily brushing

Feeding 2–2½ cans of a branded meaty product, with biscuit added in equal parts by volume.

Longevity average.

Characteristics has a tendency to nip if provoked.

ORIGIN

Australia

BEARDED COLLIE

ORIGIN

Border Counties, UK

Character tenacious, hardworking sheepdog of great
tractability. Not suitable for suburban environment.

Exercise ample if it is not to become bored and snappy.

Grooming brush with an equine dandy brush. Remove
dead fur after grooming.

Feeding 1–1½ cans (14½ oz size) of a branded meaty
product, with biscuit added in equal parts by volume.

Longevity 12 to 13 years.

Characteristics has a tendency to coarseness or
weediness.

An old breed, the Bearded Collie appears to have originated
in the border area between Scotland and England; dogs of
similar appearance have been known here since the 18th
century. They were originally working dogs, kept for herding
sheep and cattle. Their origins my be traced back to the
Polish Lowland Sheepdog, which was said to have been
brought to Scotland as long ago as 1514 by sailors who
swapped these dogs for sheep.

By the 1930s, however, the Bearded Collie had declined
dramatically in numbers, almost to the point of extinction. It
was saved largely through the efforts Mrs. Willison, whose
Bothkennar "Beardies" formed the basis of all today's
bloodlines. The breed has since gained in popularity and took
the Best in Show award at Crufts in 1989. These are lovable,
playful dogs, but you must be prepared to give them
adequate exercise, which includes a good daily run, and
spend plenty of time grooming their long and flowing coats. In
addition, they have become a popular breed in the USA
during recent years.

HOVAWART

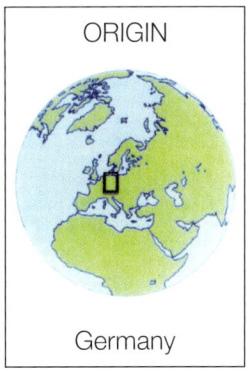

ORIGIN

Germany

Character home loving, reserved, fond of children, and easy to train.

Exercise enjoys regular exercise.

Grooming needs daily brushing.

Feeding approximately 2 cans (14½ oz size) of a branded meaty product, with biscuit added in equal parts by volume.

Longevity 12 to 14 years.

Characteristics may be slow to mature and will respond aggressively when provoked.

The Hovawart has been described as a relative newcomer. In fact, the breed has been recognized by the German Kennel Club since 1936, having appeared in Württemburg toward the end of the 19th century. The name Hovawart comes from the German "Hofewart," meaning "estate of watch dog," but its role, for many years, seems to have been simply that of a companion dog that will rise to the occasion if required to do so. It has appeared on the European show circuit in recent years and is recognized by the Kennel Club in the UK.

An excellent guard dog that is home loving, fond of children, and easy to train, the Hovawart tends to be a one-man dog. It is slow to mature and will respond aggressively when provoked.

HUNGARIAN PULI

ORIGIN

Hungary

Character loyal, devoted, obedient, and good natured.

Exercise requires a good amount.

Grooming separate cords by hand, brush and comb.

Feeding approxiamtely 2 cans (14½ oz size) of a branded meaty product, with biscuit added in equal parts by volume.

Longevity 12 to 13 years.

Characteristics this adaptable dog enjoys working sheep and can easily be trained to retrieve from water.

Although it may appear that a Puli's coat is somehow prepared by artificial means, its dreadlocks are actually quite natural. The breed originated in Hungary, and its name is derived from the words "puli hou." This translates literally as "destroyer Huns," and refers to a tribe of Magyar warriors who invaded Hungary from the East about 1,000 years ago, bringing with them their livestock, which included the ancestors of the Puli. The plural form of their name is Pulix in Hungary, but tends to be Pulik elsewhere. These are herding dogs, originally used to watch over flocks of sheep.

The traditional form of the Puli appears to be black but gray forms are also known. In spite of its rather unkempt appearance, the Puli's coat needs considerable attention. The individual cords, which tend to be thinner in dogs kept in North America and Europe than in Hungary itself, must be carefully groomed by hand. Proper brushing will also be necessary to maintain their distinctive appearance.

The Puli only became known outside Hungary at the end of World War II. Occasionally, in the USA, you may see their coats prepared in a woolly "Afro" style, although the corded appearance is still more typical. They have proved to be both loyal and intelligent companions, as reflected in their working ancestry.

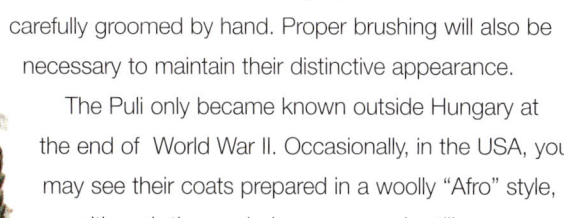

107

PYRENEAN MOUNTAIN DOG

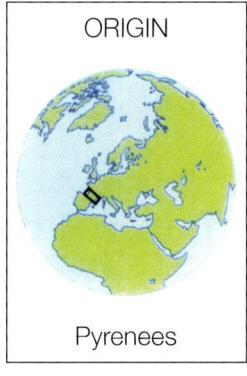

ORIGIN

Pyrenees

Character good natured, though wary with strangers.

Exercise needs plenty.

Grooming requires daily brushing and very little combing.

Feeding approximately 2 cans (14½ oz size) of a branded meaty product, with biscuit added in equal parts by volume.

Longevity 11 to 12 years.

Characteristics include a tendency to over guard and aggression toward strangers which must not be tolerated.

Better known in North America simply as the Great Pyrenees, these large shepherd dogs were bred from mastiff stock and served to protect sheep from wolves, being equipped with fearsome spiked collars to defend themselves. Later they were used to smuggle contraband across the steep mountain paths that separated France and Spain, being fitted with special satchels for this purpose.

The breed had declined sharply by the turn of the century, and could have died out, but then a breeding program was launched n which emphasis was placed on producing dogs that were good natured, lacking the traditional aggressive traits. This has been successfully achieved, althogh these dogs still show a marked reluctance to accept strangers and will prove alert guard dogs.

In a show ring, these predominantly white dogs are an impressive sight. They were first recognized by the American Kennel Club in 1933, before being accepted by the British organization 11 years later. The double dew claws on the hindfeet are deemed a breed characteristic and should never be removed in show dogs.

ROUGH COLLIE

The Rough Collie, sometimes called the Scots or Scottish Collie, is still best known as the star of the *Lassie* films. This breed's ancestors were introduced into the UK from Iceland more than 400 years ago. The word "colley" is a Scottish term for a sheep with a black face and legs, and the breed worked as a sheepdog in the Highlands of Scotland for centuries.

In 1860, Queen Victoria admired the Rough Collie while on a visit to Balmoral, Scotland, and installed some breed members in the royal kennels at Windsor. In that same year, a Rough Collie was exhibited at a show in Birmingham, UK, but its finer points were not agreed upon until some 25 years later. The beauty of the breed was enhanced, perhaps by the introduction of some Borzoi and Gordon Setter blood. The breed is no longer required to work, although it retains its intelligence, hardiness, and keen eyesight.

The Rough Collie makes an excellent guard, being suspicious of strangers. It is supremely loyal and affectionate to its owners, a joy to train, and usually reliable with children. The breed needs a lot of exercise but, despite its thick coat, it is not difficult to groom.

Character tenacious, hardworking sheepdog of great tractability. Not suitable for suburban environment.

Exercise ample if it is not to become bored and snappy.

Grooming brush with an equine dandy brush. Remove dead fur after grooming.

Feeding 1–1½ cans (14½ oz size) of a branded meaty product, with biscuit added in equal parts by volume.

Longevity 12 to14 years.

Characteristics include a tendency to coarseness or weediness.

ORIGIN

Scotland

BELGIAN SHEPHERD DOG

Sometimes known as sheepdogs, these dogs were developed both as guard dogs and for herding purposes. Similar dogs have been kept in Belgium since the Middle Ages, but no serious attempt was made to classify them until 1891. At that stage, eight different breeds were distinguished, but now just four remain.

The Groenendael, with its long black coat, is the form often described in the USA simply as the Belgian Sheepdog. They were introduced here for the first time in 1907, and were also used in World War I, both as messengers and as sentries.

The Tervueren is quite similar to the Groenendael, but can be distinguished by its coloration, which ranges from fawn to mahogany, with the individual hairs themselves being tipped with black. These darker markings are most prominent on the head, forequarters, and at the tip of the tails.

The smooth-coated Malinois is rather reminiscent of a German Shepherd Dog (formerly called Alsatian). It was originally developed in the area around Malines, as a sheep-herder. Like their German counterparts, these dogs are very responsive to training. They are likely to prove protective toward their owners and are reluctant to accept strangers.

The final variety of the Belgian Shepherd is the Laekenois, which was first bred in the vicinity of Boom in Antwerp. Here it served to guard linen that was left to bleach in the sun. The Laakenois is fawn in coloration, with black markings confined to the face.

Character intelligent, agile, attentive, and very protective. Excellent guard.

Exercise needs plenty in order to channel its intelligence and exuberance.

Grooming daily brushing.

Feeding 1½–2½ cans (14½ oz size) of a branded meaty product, with biscuit added in equal parts by volume.

Longevity 13 to 14 years.

Characteristics include a tendency to overguard. Can sometimes suffer from hip dysplasia resulting in chronic lameness in old age.

ORIGIN

Belgium

BORDER COLLIE

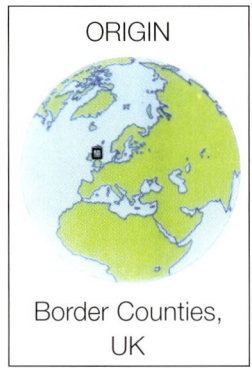
Character tenacious, hardworking
sheepdog of great tractability. Not suitable
for suburban environment.

Exercise ample if it is not to become bored
and snappy.

Grooming brush with an equine dandy
brush. Remove dead fur after grooming.

Feeding 1–1½ cans (14½ oz size) of a
branded meaty product, with biscuit added
in equal parts by volume.

Longevity 12 to 14 years.

Characteristics has a tendency to
coarseness or weediness.

The Border Collie (the term
"Border" refers to the border
counties of England and Scotland)
and has become almost a folk hero
through its television appearances at
sheepdog trials and obedience
competitions. A hardy, working
sheepdog it is also the undoubted
favorite of the obedience trainers
and has, not all that wisely, been
increasingly taken into suburban homes in the role of family
pet. A natural herder (anything from pigs to people), the home
is perhaps not the best environment for this worker which,
while it has a fondness for children, can become bored and
snappy through lack of exercise, freedom, and space.

The present day Border Collies are a modern strain
descended from collies of the Lowland and Border counties of
England and Scotland. They are working sheepdogs of a
distinct, recognizable type and have been exported, often at
great cost, to many countries of the world.

The ideal height of the Border Collie is 21 in (53 cm),
bitches slightly less, and a variety of colors are permissible,
although white should never be the predominant color.

A young Border Collie will crouch instinctively in the
presence of sheep. Farmers generally get an older working
Collie to teach them their paces.

WELSH CORGI

ORIGIN

Wales

Character devoted companion, tireless worker, and fine guard.

Exercise despite its traditional role as worker, will settle for regular walks. Don't neglect these or the Corgi will lose its waistline.

Grooming daily brushing is all that is needed for this breed's water-resistant coat.

Feeding approximately ¾ can (14½ oz size) of a branded meaty product, with biscuit added in equal parts by volume.

Longevity 12 to 14 years.

Characteristics inherent tendency to nip.

Two distinct breeds of Corgi are recognized, named after the old Welsh counties where they first developed. The Pembroke Corgi is the oldest and remains the most popular, possibly because of its links with the British Royal Family. It is characterized by a short, upright tail and pointed ears. In contrast, the Cardigan Corgi has a long tail and more rounded tips to its ears. It is also slightly larger overall, with stockier legs. Temperamentally, the Pembroke tends to be the livelier of the two breeds. Both have a long history in Wales and may trace their ancestry back to the Swedish Vallhund, brought to the region by Viking invaders about a thousand years ago. Even today, there is a clear similarity between these two breeds.

Corgis have traditionally been used as herding dogs, driving cattle by moving in among them and nipping the heels of any animals that were reluctant to move forward. Their short size helped to protect them against being kicked. As companions, Welsh Corgis prove intelligent and are very amenable to training, although occasionally they may be tempted to nip even a royal owner! Their diet needs to be watched carefully, as they can become overweight quite easily, and they must have adequate exercise, although long walks are not considered essential.

GUNDOGS

ENGLISH SPRINGER SPANIEL

ORIGIN

UK

Character a gundog with unlimited stamina
which thrives on physical activity, but is also
an attractive family pet.

Exercise needs plenty of exercise.

Grooming daily brushing and regular checks
to ensure mud does not become lodged in
paws.

Feeding 1–1½ cans (14½ oz size) of a
branded meaty product, with biscuit added
in equal parts by volume.

Longevity 12 to 14 years.

Characteristics good with children.

The English Springer is one of the oldest of the British
Spaniels, with the exception of the Clumber. The Land
Spaniel written about in 1570 by the historian Dr. Caius was
obviously a forerunner of the Springer. It was originally used
for flushing or springing game from cover before shotguns
were in use. For a time it was known as the Norfolk Spaniel,
named after either a Norfolk family that kept a strain of
"springing" spaniels prior to 1900 or the breed's place of
origin in the country of Norfolk in the UK.

Sir Thomas Boughley, who helped establish the modern
breed, had Springers with a pedigree traceable to a bitch that
whelped in 1812. One of her descendants was Field Trials
Champion Velox Powder, bred in 1903, which won 20 field
trial stakes. Sir Thomas's family retained an interest in the
breed until the 1930s and many of today's field trials
champions are descendants of his strain. The English Springer
Spaniel Club was formed in the UK in 1921, but the breed
had found fame as a "bird dog" in the USA long before.

The English Springer Spaniel is an intelligent, loyal, and
popular gundog, which also makes a reliable housepet and is
good with children. The breed needs plenty of exercise, a daily
brushing, and regular checks to ensure that mud does not
become lodged in its paws or its ears. The Springer may not
be a good choice for the houseproud because it tends to
have a good shake when it comes indoors out of the rain!

SUSSEX SPANIEL

This breed of spaniel was developed in the English county of Sussex during the 1790s. Sussex Spaniels have never been especially common, but their placid and hard-working nature made them highly valued both as gun-dogs and companions. The breed nearly vanished into obscurity towards the end of the last century, and it was only in the 1950s that its future became more secure. During recent years, for whatever reason, it has undergone something of a revival.

The Sussex Spaniel is a destinctive shade of golden-liver, with this coloration being broken only by a white chest spot in some individuals. This is considered a show fault, in contrast to the situation in a number of other breeds of spaniel. It has never established a following as a pet dog, as it strongly retains its tough working instincts. For this reason, the Sussex Spaniel is most suited to a rural environment and requires considerable exercise by way of daily walks.

Character has an excellent nose which makes this breed an excellent country dog.

Exercise regular exercise needed.

Grooming requires daily brush and comb, taking care over feet and ears.

Feeding 1–1½ cans (14½ oz size) of a branded meaty product, with biscuit added in equal parts by volume.

Longevity 12 to 13 years.

Characteristics a rich liver-colored coat; due to this dark, dense texture this is not a breed suitable for hot and humid environments.

ORIGIN

UK

115

IRISH RED & WHITE SETTER

The Irish Red and White Setter evolved from spaniels, probably red and white spaniels, that were brought to Ireland from France and crossed with pointers, and by the 18th century, Red and White Setters were being bred to type. Then setter fanciers began to prefer the Red Setter and by the end of the 19th century the Red and White all but disappeared. Since the 1940s the breed has undergone a revival in Ireland. Red and Whites are recognized by the Kennel Club in the UK, have their own breed standard, and have been recognized by the Fédération Cynologique Internationale (FCI).

Fortunately the breed has recently begun to make its mark on the show scene.

The Irish Red and White Setter is a happy, good natured, and affectionate dog, which admirably combines the role of sportsman's dog and family pet. It needs space and plenty of exercise, and requires daily brushing.

Character beautiful, untiring, ready to hunt. Good with children, horses, and other animals.

Exercise an exuberant animal which it would be cruel to keep in a confined environment.

Grooming daily grooming with a stiff brush. You will also need a steel comb to avoid tangles. Ask the breeder about trimming.

Feeding at least 1½ cans (14½ oz size) of a branded meaty product, with biscuit added in equal parts by volume.

Longevity 13 years.

Characteristics far too good natured to be used as a guard dog.

ORIGIN

Ireland

IRISH WATER SPANIEL

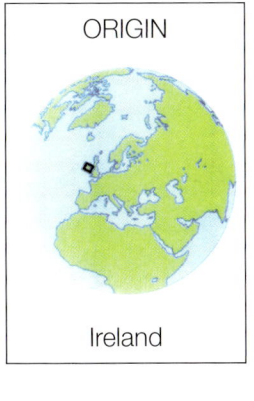

ORIGIN

Ireland

Character gentle, faithful, and attentive companion although has not become a popular house dog.

Exercise needs plenty of exercise.

Grooming regular combing with a steel comb, otherwise its coat will mat.

Feeding approximately 1–1½ cans (14½ oz size) of a branded meaty product, with biscuit added in equal parts.

Longevity 12 to 14 years.

Characteristics immense stamina, excellent swimming ability, a virtually waterproof coat, and muscular power make it an ideal retriever, especially in cold waters.

This traditional Irish breed may have descended originally from stock that originated in Europe. There is a clear relationship between the Standard Poodle and this breed, and there are suggestions that the Portuguese Water Dog might also have played a role in its development. There used to be two forms of water dog in Ireland. The North Water Spaniel was the smaller variety, with a wavy coat that was two-colored (parti-colored), while the southern form had a curly coat and, overall, was more similar to the contemporary Irish Water Spaniel.

The coat of this breed remains a distinctive feature, being dark liver with a slight purplish hue and quite tightly curled over the body. The hair on the legs and also on the top of the head is more open, with the face and tail having conspicuously straight hair.

These spaniels are totally at home in water, being powerful swimmers and able to dive without hesitation. Their coat provides good insulation, and is water-repellent. The Irish Water Spaniel is not a particularly common breed, but is very responsive to training and makes a lively, intelligent companion. You may have to tolerate your pet from time to time plunging into a pond, however, if the opportunity presents itself.

AMERICAN COCKER SPANIEL

Originally bred from English Cocker Spaniels imported to the USA, this American form has been recognized as a separate breed since the 1940s. The American Cocker Spaniel was developed as a gundog, to take smaller game than its English counterpart, such as quail. Although shorter in stature, this should not be viewed principally as a pet dog. You will need to give these spaniels plenty of exercise.

Character the "Merry Cocker" has an ever-wagging tail, is beautiful, intelligent, obedient, and a first-class family pet.

Exercise originally bred for hunting, the Cocker needs and enjoys plenty of exercise, particularly as, with its love of food, it can be in danger of losing its waistline.

Grooming daily brushing and combing to avoid tangles. Mind those ears don't drop into the food bowl and become matted. Many owners peg them back at feed time.

Feeding 1–1½ cans (14½ oz size) of a branded meaty product, with biscuit added in equal parts by volume.

Longevity can live into the teens.

Characteristics include prominent cheek bones.

The coat of the American Cocker is a distinguishing feature, being more profuse compared with the English form of the Cocker Spaniel. As a result, it needs extra care, and will benefit from a regular trim every two months or so. Regular inspection of the ears is also to be recommended, to minimize the risk of infections developing here. The upper part of the ear canal can be wiped over with damp cotton wool, but never be tempted to probe down into the canal itself. If your dog appears to be scratching at its ear repeatedly, your veterinarian will be able to inspect the canal and prescribe appropriate medication.

In terms of temperament, the American Cocker Spaniel usually proves easy to train and makes a good family pet. These spaniels are also available in a wide range of colors, ranging from solid colors such as black, chocolate, or red, to tricolored and mixed parti-colored forms. In the case of the solid colors, it is generally permitted to have a few white markings on the throat and chest, although, preferably, these should not be present. Certainly, small white areas elsewhere on the body will be penalized in the show ring.

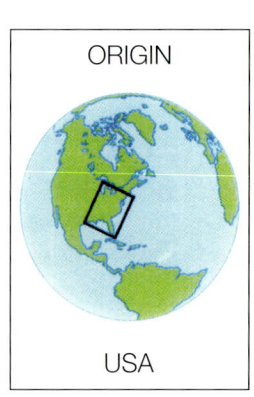

ORIGIN

USA

BOURBONNAIS SETTER

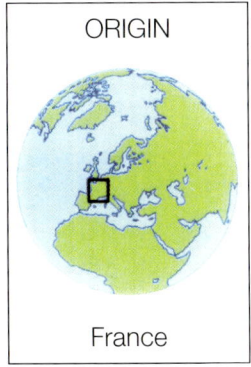

ORIGIN

France

The Bourbonnais Setter or Braque du Bourbonnais is associated with the area of central France after which it is named. However, it seems to derive from the Pyrenees, where a number of other French gundogs also originated. The ancestors of these dogs gradually spread out to other regions, and crossings with local dogs produced varieties which took the name of their new home.

The Bourbonnais is often described as the short-tailed setter because it is almost always born without a tail. It has a striking Dalmatian-like coat pattern on a distinctly thickset body.

The Bourbonnais is a good natured, sporting, and family dog, which is easy to train. Like most gundogs, it requires a fair amount of exercise and needs a brush and rub-down every few days.

Character good natured, loyal, and lively.

Exercise requires a fair amount.

Grooming needs a brush and rub-down every few days.

Feeding aproximately 2 cans (14½ oz size) of a branded meaty product, with biscuit added in equal parts by volume.

Longevity 12 to 14 years.

Characteristics very short tail and set low.

ITALIAN SPINONE

ORIGIN

Italy

The Italian Spinone is an ancient gundog breed. However, it has only recently become a contender in the international show ring and in field trials. Opinions vary, even in Italy, about the dog's origin, as to whether it is of setter descent—climatic conditions alone accounting for its thick coat—or a relative of the coarse-haired Italian Segugio or, indeed, a Griffon cross.

Other authorities believe that this powerful, versatile hunter originated in the French region of Bresse, later finding its way to Piedmont in Italy, and that its evolution is attributable not only to the French Griffon, but also to German Pointers, the Porcelaine, the now extinct Barbet and the Borthals Griffon. Or the Spinone may be the result of a mating between a Coarse-haired Setter and a White Mastiff.

Affectionate, agreeable, and of loyal temperament, the Italian Spinone has a soft mouth and will both point and retrieve. It needs plenty of vigorous exercise, is a fine swimmer, and is best suited to country life.

Character a calm, easygoing, and obedient breed that thrives on work.

Exercise needs plenty of vigorous exercise.

Grooming needs regular brushing.

Feeding 1½–2½ cans (14½ oz size) of a branded meaty product, with biscuit added in equal parts by volume.

Longevity 12 to 13 years.

Characteristics looks dignified and all-knowing with long hair on mustache and beard.

KOOIKERHONDJE

ORIGIN

Netherlands

Character this friendly, even-tempered breed makes a very satisfying companion.

Exercise needs plenty of exercise.

Grooming needs brushing every day.

Feeding 1–1½ cans (14½ oz size) of a branded meaty product, with biscuit added in equal parts by volume.

Longevity 12 to 13 years.

Characteristics initially used to entice ducks because of its lively antics and bushy white tail.

This breed is also known as the Kooiker Dog or Duck-decoy Dog. Its Dutch name means "dog belonging to the Kooiker," the person in charge of the duck decoy. It is a fairly old breed, native to the Netherlands, whose job was to draw ducks out of their cover by walking in and out of low reed fences by the banks of a dyke that was covered with netting. When the ducks investigated, the dyke was closed. Since World War II,

efforts have been made to improve its breeding, and it has recently been introduced into the UK.

The Kooikerhondje is an intelligent, affectionate dog, which is lively but not over-excitable. A good companion dog, it is a handy size for a household pet. It needs plenty of exercise and daily brushing.

ENGLISH COCKER SPANIEL

ORIGIN

UK

Character a gentle and popular pet, as well as
a first-class gundog.

Exercise needs and enjoys plenty of exercise.

Grooming daily brushing and combing to avoid
tangles.

Feeding 1–1½ cans (14½ oz size) of a branded
meaty product, with biscuit added in equal
parts by volume.

Longevity 13 to 14 years.

Characteristics a range of inherited disorders is
not uncommon such as behavioral problems.

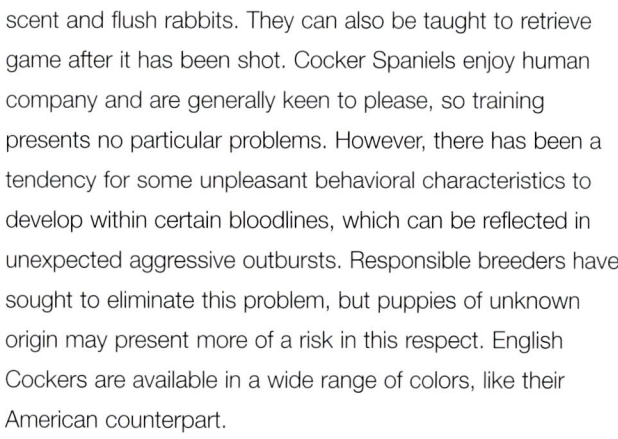

Officially, in the UK, the Kennel Club recognizes this breed just as the Cocker Spaniel, but as American breeders sometimes refer to their breed under the same name, this designation has been made to avoid possible confusion. The description of "cocker" probably originated from the use of these dogs in the hunting of woodcock, which were considered something of a delicacy. Regional differences played a part in the development of the spaniel breeds in the UK, with the Cocker itself evolving in parts of Wales and south-west England.

In spite of their popularity as pets, Cocker Spaniels still retain a strong desire to work and today they are often used to scent and flush rabbits. They can also be taught to retrieve game after it has been shot. Cocker Spaniels enjoy human company and are generally keen to please, so training presents no particular problems. However, there has been a tendency for some unpleasant behavioral characteristics to develop within certain bloodlines, which can be reflected in unexpected aggressive outbursts. Responsible breeders have sought to eliminate this problem, but puppies of unknown origin may present more of a risk in this respect. English Cockers are available in a wide range of colors, like their American counterpart.

ENGLISH SETTER

Setters are superb gundogs and make ideal pets. They are not by any manner of means guard dogs, and would be more likely to persuade a burglar to come and play than repel his entry!

Confusion sometimes exists as to which setter is which. In fact, the Irish (or Red) Setter is the most popular and, if one is frank, the most scatty, especially in youth. It is ideal as a family pet, a gundog, or in stables, where it can run with the horses. It evolved from crossing Irish Water Spaniels, Springer Spaniels, English and Gordon Setters, and the Spanish Pointer.

The Irish Setter began life as a red and white dog and, indeed, Irish Red and White Setters are now making their mark as a separate breed.

The English Setter, again good with children and a first-class gundog, has distinctive black and white, lemon and white, liver and white, or tricolor markings, and is reckoned to have evolved from Spaniels, while the Gordon Setter, which is coal-black with tan markings (described as the color of a ripe horse-chestnut), is the only native Scottish gundog, bred at

Gordon Castle, Banffshire, the seat of the Dukes of Richmond and Gordon and originally known as the Gordon Castle Setter. The Collie and Bloodhound are attributed in its make-up.

Not so frequently seen as the Irish and English variety, the Gordon has possibly the steadiest temperament of the three, being easy-going, calm, and docile. It is also a methodical hunter.

Character beautiful, untiring, ready to hunt. Good with children, horses, and other animals.

Exercise an exuberant animal which it would be cruel to keep in a confined environment.

Grooming daily grooming with a stiff brush. You will also need a steel comb to avoid tangles. Ask the breeder about trimming.

Feeding at least 1½ cans (14½ oz size) of a branded meaty product, with biscuit added in equal parts by volume.

Longevity can live into the teens.

Characteristics they need plenty of freedom, and do not take to being confined in a small area.

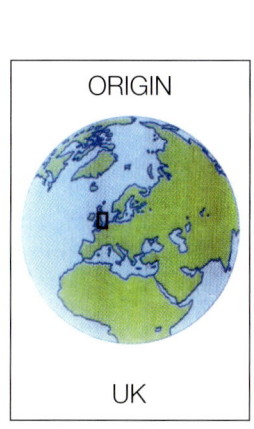

ORIGIN

UK

POINTER

ORIGIN

UK

Character an affectionate, obedient, and easy to train breed, also good with children.

Exercise needs plenty of exercise and is not ideally suited to town life.

Grooming only regular brushing to keep coat in good order.

Feeding 1½–2½ cans (14½ oz size) of branded meaty product, with biscuit added in equal parts by volume.

Longevity 13 to 14 years.

Characteristics the pointer's kindly disposition makes it an ideal family companion.

The original purpose of the Pointer was to find and indicate a "point" where hares were lurking, so that Greyhounds could then be brought in to run them down. The advent of shooting, however, saw the role of the Pointer modified to finding suitable game for the guns. Pointers are therefore essentially working dogs, but can settle in the home if they have plenty of exercise as well.

The influence of the Pointer (its "frozen" stance characteristic of its field work) has extended into many other contemporary gundogs, although its origins are now unclear. It has been suggested that it may first have been bred in Spain, using a combination of Bloodhounds, Greyhounds, and Foxhounds. The Spanish Pointer is a heavier breed today than its English counterpart, which is the form known simply as the Pointer. It is bred in a variety of colors, including lemon, orange and black, and liver, as well as combined forms with white. Tricolored forms are also known.

WEIMARANER

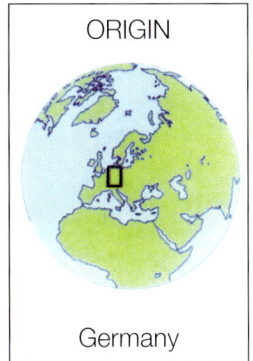

ORIGIN

Germany

This breed has been developed with considerable care. It originated in Germany during the 19th century, from crossings of various breeds, including pointers, and was bred as a gundog. The German breed club insisted on rigorous standards, and only approved matings were permitted. Weimaraners only became more widely known during the 1940s, when the breed was introduced in the USA. Their sleek, silver-gray appearance attracts keen interest, but it is not always appreciated that Weimaraners need proper training to ensure the best development of their working abilities.

These dogs have active natures and must be able to have a good run every day. They have proved obedient and make loyal companions, while their coat needs very little attention to remain immaculate. Occasionally, a long-haired form of the Weimaraner crops up in the litters of normal dogs. These cannot be registered, but are otherwise identical to the true Weimaraner in terms of temperament.

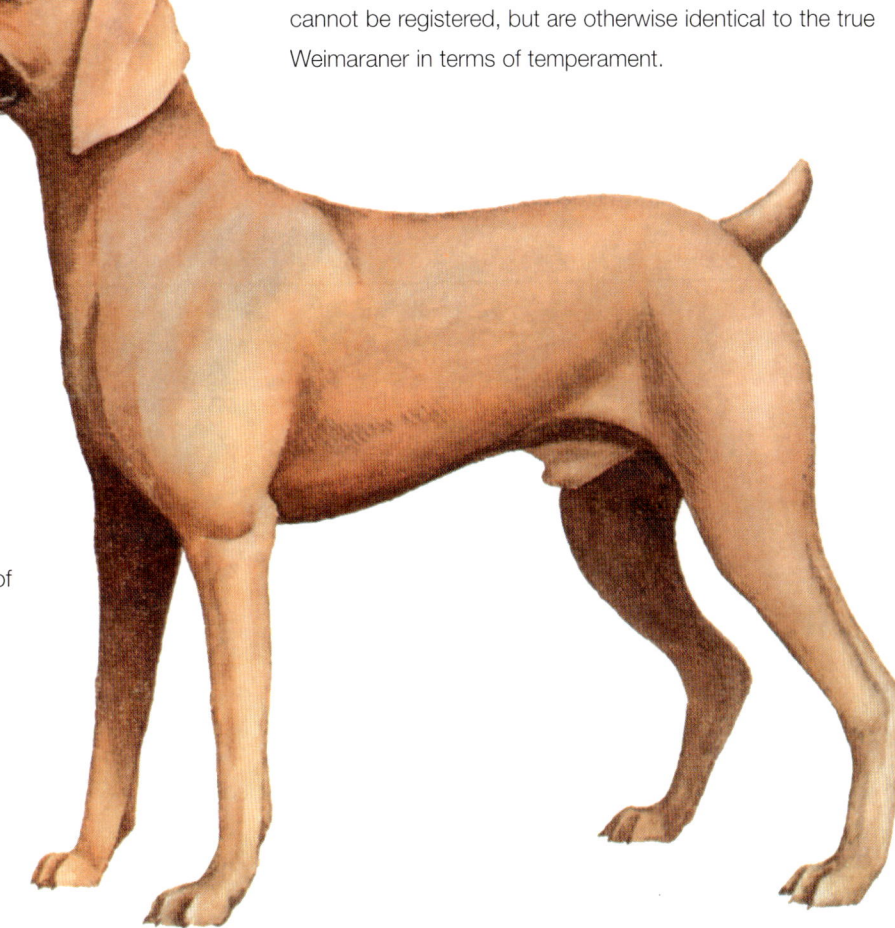

Character good temperament and stamina. Excels at obedience and agility.

Exercise an exuberant dog that needs plenty of exercise and an outlet for keen intelligence.

Grooming daily brushing.

Feeding 1½–2½ cans (14½ oz size) of a branded meaty product, with biscuit added in equal parts by volume.

Longevity 12 to 13 years.

Characteristics has grace, speed, strength and stamina, along with a handsome carriage and shimmering steel coat colour.

LABRADOR RETRIEVER

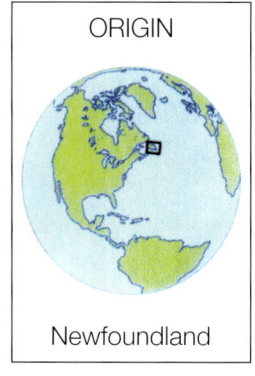

ORIGIN

Newfoundland

The ancestors of this well-known breed were brought originally from Newfoundland by fishermen returning to the UK. In Newfoundland the dogs helped to haul in the nets and took to the water readily. During the 19th century, a tax on dog ownership led to the demise of these dogs in Newfoundland, and UK quarantine laws limited the availability of further stock. They were then interbred with existing retriever breeds such as the Flat-coated until finally, in 1903, a standard was established for the Labrador Retriever itself.

Since then, these dogs have undergone a massive surge in popularity, being kept both as house pets and gundogs. They have retained their affiliation with water and are highly valued by duck hunters. Their scenting skills have also been exploited in other areas of contemporary life, including the search for drugs and explosives at airports. The trustworthy nature of the Labrador Retriever has also seen the breed trained as guide dogs for people with impaired sight.

In terms of coloration, although the black form was best known during the early years of the last century, the yellow variety is now more common. Chocolate individuals may also be seen occasionally as well. It is not unusual for the coat coloration of yellow Labradors to fade somewhat with age, although there is a natural variation to some extent in any event.

In the case of black and chocolate dogs, the development of some white hairs around the muzzle can be anticipated as they become older. These are not sedentary dogs by nature, and you must be prepared to give them plenty of exercise, because otherwise they will rapidly become obese.

Character good tempered, excellent companion, and fine gundog. Adaptable, devoted, and kind with children.

Exercise needs plenty. Has tendency to put on weight if given insufficient exercise, or overfed.

Grooming regular brushing.

Feeding 1½–2½ cans (14½ oz size) of a branded meaty product, with biscuit added in equal parts by volume.

Longevity 12 to 14 years.

Characteristics one of the most loyal and dependable breeds in the world.

NOVA SCOTIA DUCK TOLLING RETRIEVER

ORIGIN

Canada

Character this breed is quiet and easy to train and makes a good family pet.

Exercise needs plenty of regular exercise.

Grooming needs regular grooming with a bristle brush and comb.

Feeding 1–1½ cans (14½ oz size) of a branded meaty product, with biscuit added in equal parts by volume.

Longevity 12 to 14 years.

Characteristics main coloring is red fox, with white markings on the chest, feet, and tip of tail, and sometimes on face.

The Nova Scotia Duck Tolling Retriever originated in the Maritime Provinces of Canada and has only recently become known outside its native area. It is believed to be of Chesapeake Bay and Golden Retriever stock. With the head of the Golden it is well boned down to its strong webbed feet. Although the breed has been set for over 100 years, it only received a breed standard in the 1940s. It was given full international recognition by the Fédération Cynologique Internationale (FCI) in 1982. This dog's job in life is to thrash about at the water's edge in order to attract the attention of wildfowl, a performance known as tolling. Eventually the wildfowl become curious or angry enough to swim within range of the hunter on the bank. The dog will retrieve the fowl shot down.

The Nova Scotia Duck Tolling Retriever is quiet and easy to train. Like many gundogs it makes a good family pet provided that it receives plenty of exercise. It needs regular grooming with a bristle brush and comb.

BRITTANY SPANIEL

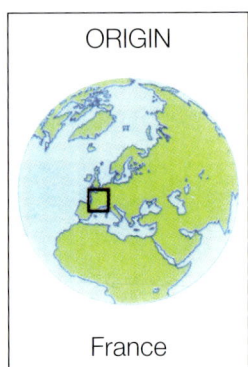

ORIGIN

France

Character an affectionate, trustworthy, reliable, and obedient companion.

Exercise needs plenty of exercise.

Grooming requires daily brushing.

Feeding 1–1½ cans (14½ oz size) of a branded meaty product, with biscuit added in equal parts by volume.

Longevity 13 to 14 years.

Characteristics probably the world's only stumpy-tailed pointer and resembles the features of the setter.

This French breed was effectively re-created at the turn of the last century, having been on the verge of extinction. It is more reminiscent of a setter than a spaniel, in terms both of its appearance and its behavior. As a consequence, the American Kennel Club has recently changed its name simply to the Brittany. As a working dog—commonly seen at field trials rather than shows—it has proved a talented pointer and has a keen scenting nose.

The Brittany Spaniel has a sensitive nature and is correspondingly easy to train, being very responsive to its owner's wishes. In terms of coloration, these dogs can be either orange, maroon, or black combined with white, while tricolored forms are also recognized. You must be prepared to give the Brittany plenty of exercise; although it does make a good pet, it is still a working dog as well and this should be reflected in its surroundings.

CHESAPEAKE BAY RETRIEVER

The ancestry of the Chesapeake Bay Retriever is less obscure than that of many breeds. Indeed, its origins can be pinpointed to 1807, when an English brig was shipwrecked off the coast of Maryland. An American ship, the *Canton*, rescued the English crew and two Newfoundland puppies. One puppy was a male called Sinbad, which has been described as dingy red in color, while the other was a black bitch, which became known as Canton after the rescue ship. The pups were presented to the families that had given shelter to the English sailors and were trained as duck retrievers. In time, they mated with various working breeds in the Chesapeake Bay area. It is likely that the cross bloods added were those of the Otterhound and the Curly-coated and the Flat-coated Retrievers. The matings produced a variety with the swimming ability of the Newfoundland and the duck-retrieving abilities of local dogs.

Until fairly recently, the Chesapeake Bay Retriever was kept strictly as a sporting dog. However, it is now finding its way into the family home and becoming a contender in the show ring.

The Chesapeake is good natured and does well in field trials. It has an oily coat which needs regular brushing and gives off a slight, but not unpleasant, odor. It has yellow-orange eyes. Like all gundogs it needs plenty of exercise and does best in an environment where it has space to roam freely.

Character kindly expression with a temperament to match. Good all-purpose gundog and family pet.

Exercise plenty of exercise to keep this dog fit, happy, and in good shape.

Grooming regular brushing.

Feeding at least 1½ cans (14½ oz size) of a branded meaty product, with biscuit added in equal parts by volume.

Longevity good average.

Characteristics cowhocks are highly undesirable.

ORIGIN

USA

WELSH SPRINGER SPANIEL

ORIGIN

Wales

Character loyal, hardworking, and also makes a good family dog.

Exercise needs lots of exercise.

Grooming needs brushing daily.

Feeding 1–1½ cans (14½ oz size) of a branded meaty product, with biscuit added in equal parts by volume.

Longevity 12 to14 years.

Characteristics with a more tapered head and higher-set ears, the Welsh Springer Spaniel is smaller than the English Springer.

The precise origins of this breed, which resembles the Brittany, are unclear. It may have resulted from the combination of English Springers and Clumber Spaniels, but the only accepted color combination is rich red and white. Welsh Springers were recognized officially by the Kennel Club in 1902, but are not a very common breed, although they are widely known and are accepted by the American Kennel Club. Welsh Springers are quite easy to prepare for showing.

Their coats are relatively soft and any sign of curling is considered a distinct fault.

These spaniels have great stamina and prove diligent workers, not afraid of entering water. As a result, they are not well suited to a purely domestic existence, but will thrive here if they are also kept active. They prove loyal and trustworthy dogs, with a keen scenting ability, like their English counterparts.

WIRE-HIRED POINTING GRIFFON

This breed of gundog was developed originally by a Dutch enthusiast called Edward Korthals, who started his quest in 1874. Unfortunately, a clear picture of its ancestry is not available, although it is known that Korthals began with a gray and brown Griffon bitch and, apart from other Griffons, various setters and pointers may also have been used. For part of the time, Korthals worked in France for the Duke of Penthièvre, and so this country is officially listed as the homeland of the Wire-haired Pointing Griffon.

This new breed was being shown in 1888 in the UK, but has since faded from the scene here, although it is recognized by both the American and Canadian Kennel Clubs. Even so, it is scarce in these countries, being concentrated in the hands of a few breeders and used mainly for working rather than show purposes. The Wire-haired Pointing Griffon is relatively slow in the field, but possesses a keen nose. It is a tough breed, with its hard coat offering good protection in marshy surroundings, and it can also swim if necessary. It is either solid chestnut in color, or chestnut with steel-gray or white markings. These are dogs that need plenty of exercise, and that establish a strong bond with their owners.

Character it is responsive, obedient, good with children, not snappy, and usually easygoing with older dogs.

Exercise requires plenty of exercise.

Grooming its coat should not be groomed too vigorously although it will need trimming.

Feeding 1½–2½ cans (14½ oz size) of a branded meaty product, with biscuit added in equal parts by volume.

Longevity 12 to 13 years.

Characteristics is favored by the one-dog huntsman and can be kennelled out of doors or in the house as a member of the family.

ORIGIN

France

CLUMBER SPANIEL

The stocky Clumber is the heaviest of all the spaniels, with dogs of the breed weighing up to 70 lb (32 kg). Its precise origins are unclear, but it is probably descended from French stock obtained by the Duke of Newcastle over a century ago. The breed was actually named after the Duke's estate, Clumber Park.

Although not ranking as one of the most common spaniels, the Clumber is still highly valued as a sporting companion. It was developed for its scenting skills, but also proves versatile enough to make a good retriever as well. Clumber Spaniels may not be as agile as some breeds, but there is no doubting their stamina. This is not a suitable companion in an urban environment, however, preferring more spacious surroundings where it can have plenty of exercise.

The coat of this breed is somewhat less profuse than in other spaniels and mud will brush out easily once it has dried. In terms of coloration, Clumber Spaniels are invariably lemon and white or orange and white, with paler markings generally being preferred. Their feet are covered with dense hair, and, especially after exercise in the summer months, you must check for grass seeds that may have become tangled up here. These could otherwise penetrate into the feet and track up the leg, causing a painful injury.

Character slow but reliable, a favorite with British Royalty.

Exercise likes plenty of exercise.

Grooming a fair amount of brushing, making sure mud does not get caught between its toes.

Feeding 1–1½ (14½ oz size) of branded meaty product, with biscuit added in equal parts by volume.

Longevity 12 to13 years.

Characteristics massive, square, medium-length head and a long, heavy body close to the ground.

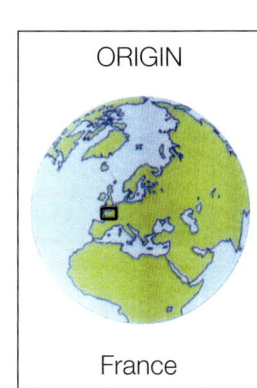

ORIGIN

France

CURLY-COATED RETRIEVER

ORIGIN

UK

Character kindly expression with a
temperament to match. Good all-purpose
gundog and family pet.

Exercise plenty of exercise to keep this
dog fit, happy, and in good shape.

Grooming regular brushing.

Feeding at least 1½ cans (14½ oz size) of a
branded meaty product, with biscuit
added in equal parts by volume.

Longevity 12 to 13 years.

Characteristics cowhocks are highly
undesirable.

Everything about the Curly-coated Retriever points to the Irish
Water Spaniel or the Standard Poodle contributing to its
ancestry. The Labrador Retriever obviously also played some
part in producing this fine breed, of which far too little is seen.

The Curly-coated Retriever was first exhibited at dog shows
in the UK as long ago as 1860, and one of the first breeds to
be used seriously for retrieving purposes in the UK. However,
despite its attractive appearance, stamina, and working ability,
it is now rarely seen outside the show ring. It has been said
that its popularity as a sporting dog declined because of its
reputation of being hard-mouthed, a fault that certainly does

not exist in the breed today.

The Curly-coated Retriever has an excellent nose and a
good memory. It is a better guard than other retrievers, and
while a little anti-social with its canine colleagues in the
shooting field, it generally combines its working life admirably
with that of a reliable family dog. It requires vigorous exercise,
and fares best in a country environment with plenty of
opportunities to run free. Its curly coat does not need to be
brushed or combed, just dampened down and massaged with
circular movements. Advice should be sought on the
necessary trimming if it is the intention to exhibit.

GOLDEN RETRIEVER

ORIGIN

Scotland

These attractive dogs were another of the sporting breeds developed in the second half of the 19th century. They were bred on the Guisachan Estate in Scotland, which was owned by Lord Tweedmouth. Here the Golden Retriever initially evolved from crossing a yellow retriever of Flat-coat ancestry with a local and now extinct breed known as the Tweed Water Spaniel, itself a retriever with a tightly-curled coat. Detailed contemporary records show how the Golden Retriever came into existence over the course of the next two decades. There was introduction of new blood from further Labradors and Wavy-coated Retrievers as well as an Irish Setter. The Yellow or Golden Retriever, as the breed became known, rapidly gained in popularity in late-Victorian England.

At the turn of the last century, the emergent breed was known as the Golden Flat-coated Retriever, and only achieved separate status in 1913. These dogs were already known in the USA by this stage, having been introduced here during the 1890s. There is still variation in the depth of coloration of the Golden Retriever. It can vary from cream to gold, but must not border on red or mahogany.

Golden Retrievers are delightful dogs with an excellent temperament as both a gundog and a family pet. Their natural retrieving instincts mean that they should be given a ball or flying disc to chase when they are being exercised. A good daily run is essential, and they will benefit from being kept in an environment with a large garden.

Character kindly expression with a temperament to match. Good all-purpose gundog and family pet.

Exercise plenty of exercise to keep this dog fit, happy, and in good shape.

Grooming regular brushing.

Feeding at least 1½ cans (14½ oz size) of a branded meaty product, with biscuit added in equal parts by volume.

Longevity good average.

Characteristics is kindly and trustworthy with children.

HUNGARIAN VIZSLA

This is another of the ancient Hungarian breeds, which has become quite well known in the West since the 1930s. Emigrés leaving Hungary brought their dogs with them, and from this base contemporary bloodlines have evolved. The name "Vizsla" under which they are known in the USA, translates as "responsive and alert." These characteristics were essential attributes for a gundog in an area where natural cover was minimal. Vizslas also needed considerable stamina and were used to working in hot conditions, performing effectively as both pointers and retrievers.

The breed is even-tempered and settles well in the home provided that it has adequate opportunity for exercise. Its sleek, short coat creates an elegant appearance, and can range in coloration from sandy-yellow to gold. A more recent introduction has been the Wire-haired form, created during the 1930s by crossings involving the German Wire-haired Pointer. Sometimes referred to by its native name of Drotszoru, this has proved a somewhat hardier dog, happy to retrieve ducks from freezing water. Their affectionate natures make them well worth considering as pets.

Character a versatile, easily trained gundog which also makes a first-class pet and is good with children.

Exercise an exuberant dog that needs plenty of exercise an an outlet for keen intelligence.

Grooming its coat should be brushed regularly.

Feeding 1½–2½ cans (14½ oz size) of a branded meaty product, with biscuit added in equal parts by volume.

Longevity 14 to 15 years.

Characteristics it has a good nose, and follows trails diligently, retrieving either game or thrown tennis balls with enthusiasm.

ORIGIN

Hungary

FLAT-COATED RETRIEVER

Character an intelligent and sound dog with a kindly
temperament.
Exercise needs plenty of exercise.
Grooming needs daily brushing.
Feeding 1½–2½ cans (14½ oz size) of a branded meaty
product with biscuit added in equal parts by volume.
Longevity 12 to 14 years.
Characteristics a gaily-held tail is a hallmark of the alert
Flat-coat, keen to get to work in the field.

ORIGIN

Newfoundland

For many years, following its introduction to the UK in 1860 up until World War I, the Flat-coated was the most popular of all retriever breeds. Subsequently, the essentially more colorful Golden and Labrador Retrievers took over this role, as the great estates with their gamekeepers broke up and the dog fancy developed to cater for the tastes of the exhibitor and pet-seeker. Originally known as the Wavy-coated Retriever, the inclusion of setters in the breeding gave rise to the coat type associated with this breed today.

The breed has undergone something of a revival, however, and achieved the Best in Show award at Crufts in 1980. As could be expected, these are hardy dogs and very responsive to training. They can make good house pets, but require a good period of exercise every day, which is easier to provide in rural surroundings. Their distinctive coat is relatively easy to keep in top condition through brushing. In terms of coloration, the Flat-coated Retriever is either a glossy black or liver, with no white markings being permitted.

GERMAN POINTER

The various breeds of German Pointer are closely related. The Short-haired form is the most common and is considered to be one of the best sporting dogs. It can work both as a pointer, indicating the presence of game, and as a retriever, while it is equally versatile on land or water. This breed has a mixed ancestry, which involved the Spanish Pointer, a number of native hounds and possibly the English form of the Pointer as well.

In turn, the German Short-haired Pointer contributed to the development of the Wire-haired form, known also as the Drahthaar. Its wiry coat affords good protection in undergrowth, while the dense undercoat is shed during the warmer summer months. German Pointers have all the usual attributes of gun-dogs, not least being the fact that they are responsive to training, although the Drahthaar may be slightly more difficult in this respect.

The German Long-haired Pointer or Langhaar has become quite scarce. This breed was used originally for falconry purposes. Its decline has been linked to the rising popularity of the Wire-haired form, and possibly its duller coloration has also counted against it. These pointers are either light brown or a dead-leaf shade, whereas greater variety is seen in the German Wire-haired, with liver and white combinations being common.

Character all excellent companions which make good watchdogs.

Exercise needs plenty of exercise.

Grooming does not require a lot of grooming.

Feeding 1½–2½ cans (14½ oz size) of a branded meaty product, with biscuit added in equal parts by volume.

Longevity 12 to 14 years.

Characteristics they make strong, powerful, and versatile hunting dogs.

ORIGIN

Germany

With its lively intelligence and easygoing nature, the Beagle is as happy in the family home as in the hunt.

HOUNDS

ELKHOUND

ORIGIN

Norway

Character is generally a good natured household pet, which has no doggie odor and is reliable with children.

Exercise needs plenty of exercise.

Grooming requires daily brushing and combing.

Feeding 1½–2 cans (14½ oz size) of a branded meaty product, with biscuit added in equal parts by volume.

Longevity 12 to 13 years.

Characteristics somewhat wilful in youth, this breed is robust, vigorous, and athletic with a strong voice.

Sometimes known also as the Norwegian Elkhound, especially in the USA, these ancient Nordic dogs were originally bred to track elk and other large animals, including bears, wolves, and lynx. Within Scandinavia, there were several slightly different types, some of which were also used to pull sledges. Instead of simply locating quarry, these dogs actually sought to drive it towards the hunter, which called for a considerable degree of courage.

Elkhounds were shown for the first time in 1877, at a gathering organized by the Norwegian Hunters' Association.

They have remained tough, hardy dogs and make devoted companions. An active breed, Elkhounds require plenty of exercise and can be trained quite easily. There is a slight discrepancy in their classification, however, because the European canine authority, known as the Fédération Cynologique Internationale (FCI) distinguishes between the Norwegian Elkhound, which is grey in color, and a slightly smaller form, known as the Black Norwegian Elkhound. Furthermore, a breed called the Jämthund or Swedish Elkhound is also recognized by the same organization.

GREYHOUND

The well-muscled profile of the Greyhound reveals a breed that has been bred for its pace. Illustrations of dogs of this type can be found on ancient Egyptian tombs dating back over 5,000 years. They were certainly known in the UK by the 900s, and were jealously guarded by the nobility here, to prevent poaching activities. In more recent times, Greyhound racing has become a popular sport in many countries. Dogs that are retired from the track, often by four years old, can settle well as household pets, although they should be muzzled when they are first let off the leash, otherwise they may pursue a toy breed or cat with fatal consequences. In terms of temperament, Greyhounds are very gentle dogs and particularly tolerant with children.

A short brisk run will suit them well in terms of exercise, and their short coat is easy to groom. Greyhounds are not guard dogs in any sense, however, and rarely bark in domestic surroundings. An unusual feature of this breed is that it is not troubled by hip dysplasia, unlike most other larger breeds of dog.

Character has remarkable stamina, and is an adaptable, affectionate animal which makes a loyal and gentle pet.

Exercise normal, regular walks are sufficient, but never let a Greyhound (especially an ex-racer) off the leash in a public place or anywhere where there is livestock. Ex-racers need retraining, or they will chase anything that moves.

Grooming use a hound glove every day.

Feeding 1½–2½ cans (14½ oz size) of a branded meaty product, with biscuit added in equal parts by volume. Greyhounds are used to sloppier foods than other breeds, and appreciate a thick slice of brown bread crumbled into milk at breakfast time and another drink of milk with a few biscuits at bedtime (most enjoy bedtime biscuits as a treat).

Longevity 10 to 12 years.

Characteristics does have a tendency to chase anything that moves, but is also a gentle and faithful animal, which is good with children. Even an ex-racer, once retrained, makes a fine and long lived companion.

ORIGIN

Egypt

141

FOXHOUND

Attractive though it may be, the Foxhound is entirely unsuitable as a household pet. Indeed Foxhounds are not exhibited in the show ring in the UK except in a special hound show. It is however a contender in the show ring in the USA.

Foxhounds are invariably the property of a fox hunting pack and are described in couples, for example "fifty couples of hounds," and the nearest they ever get to a domestic environment is in puppyhood, when they may be "puppy walked" by a member of the public.

The Foxhound is a descendant of the former and heavier Saint Hubert Hound, which was brought to the UK by the Norman William the Conqueror, and from another extinct hound, the Talbot. Saint Hubert, or Hubertus, Hounds took their name from the patron saint of hunters, associated in legend with an 18th-century bishop of Liège in Belgium. The American Foxhounds evolved from a pack of Foxhounds taken to the USA by Robert Brooke in 1650. George Washington is also credited with importing Foxhounds from the UK and some fine specimens from France in 1785. We see the result of the cross-breeding of these English and French hounds in the American Foxhound of today.

Hounds stand 23 in (58.5 cm), bitches slightly less. No color is described as bad for a Foxhound.

Character attractive, noisy hunter, which does not fit into a domestic environment.

Exercise it is a hunter—enough said.

Grooming groom with a hound glove.

Feeding Foxhounds are not reared on domestic pet food but trencher-fed with horse flesh and mash comprising oatmeal and known as "pudding."

Longevity 11 years.

Characteristics has a deep girth and long back which allow it to run well over varied terrain.

ORIGIN

UK

BASENJI

ORIGIN

Zaire

These unusual dogs originated in Zaire, in Central Africa. Here they were kept by native tribes, remaining essentially unknown elsewhere until a pair were imported to the UK in 1936. These were exhibited at the famous Crufts Dog Show the following year, and caused a sensation. The breed was seen in the USA shortly afterwards, with the Basenji Club of America being formed here in 1942.

The Basenji is sometimes described as the Barkless Dog, but although it lacks the vocal range of other breeds, it is certainly not mute. It has a variety of calls, including a distinctive yodel, also described as a chortle. Basenjis should be offered green vegetables on a regular basis in addition to their normal diet, and will also eat grass. For this reason you must avoid using potentially harmful chemicals around the garden if you decide to keep this breed. They are very active dogs and need plenty of exercise, otherwise they will soon start to become obese.

In spite of coming from a tropical area, they are quite hardy. Their short coat, which can be red, black, or black and tan, offset against white, is easy to keep in good condition with regular brushing. Alternatively, a hound glove can be used to give a good gloss to the coat. Basenjis will groom themselves rather like cats, licking their coats repeatedly.

Unfortunately, although Basenjis will live well alongside other pets, including cats and horses, they tend to disagree among themselves, and may have to be watched, at least until an order of dominance is established. Their breeding behaviour is different from that of other breeds, because bitches only come into season once rather than twice a year. This is usually between August and November, which means that puppies are only likely to be available in the spring.

Character gentle, quiet, and graceful, good with horses and friendly with children.

Exercise although a dog that essentially should be kept indoors with its owner – and not in an outside kennel – the Basenji was bred as a hunter, and enjoys the open spaces.

Grooming use a hound glove.

Feeding about 1½ cans (14½ oz size) of a branded meaty product, with biscuit added in equal parts by volume.

Longevity 12 years.

Characteristics tan color, rarely barks, only comes into season once a year, and washes itself like a cat.

IBIZAN HOUND

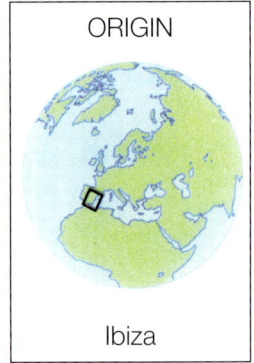

ORIGIN

Ibiza

Character this noble-looking animal has a kindly nature, is good with children, rarely fights and makes a fine gundog or housepet.

Exercise needs a lot of exercise.

Grooming needs only daily brushing.

Feeding 1½–2½ cans (14½ oz size) of a branded meaty product, with biscuit added in equal parts by volume.

Longevity 12 years.

Characteristics this is a fast, silent, and agile hunter, is extremely sensitive with acute hearing, and can jump up to 8 ft (2.5 m) in height from standstill.

This appears to be another ancient breed, which was known to the Egyptians. Its modern name is derived from the island of Ibiza, where the breed is believed to have been maintained in a virtually pure state for several thousand years. Ibizan Hounds are also traditionally popular in nearby Spain, where a wire-haired version is known. These hounds have only become known to a wider audience during recent years, however, first reaching the USA in 1956.

Their sleek, alert demeanour has ensured that they have established a strong following. Their hearing is acute, and they are now valued as gundogs. Ibizan Hounds will settle easily in domestic surroundings, getting along well with children, and are not aggressive by nature. You will need to be prepared to take considerable exercise, however, if you decide to keep one of these lively hounds. They can be either a solid red, white, or lion (tawny), but are more often a combination of these colors.

IRISH WOLFHOUND

The future of the Irish Wolfhound was in doubt during the early years of the 19th century once the wolves themselves had been eliminated from Ireland. The breed had been kept here for as long as 2,000 years, its ancestors being known to the Romans. The survival of these friendly giants was almost entirely due to the efforts of one man, a Scot called Captain George A. Graham. Working with the few Wolfhounds that were still alive in the 1860s, and using judicious crossings with Deerhounds, Graham was able to re-create this ancient breed.

Standing up to 34 in (86 cm) tall, the Irish Wolfhound is the tallest dog in the world but, in spite of its size it makes a trustworthy companion as well as proving an alert guard. The breed is only suitable, however, if you have a large area of land around your home where it can gallop about. As with other large breeds, long walks are not recommended for young Wolfhounds, but they still need plenty of exercise. The wiry coat needs relatively little attention, and a wide range of colors is established, ranging from black through fawn, brindle, and red to pure white. Puppies have to be trained from an early age, as, in view of their size, they can otherwise prove something of a handful in later life.

Character a gentle giant, good with children.

Exercise surprisingly, does not need more than average exercise, but it does need room to spread itself.

Grooming brushing and some plucking, exhibitors aim for the "natural" look with this majestic breed.

Feeding at least 2½ cans (14½ oz size) of a branded meaty product, with biscuit added in equal parts by volume. This is a breed which needs stoking up with food in adolescence, so ask the breeder for a diet chart.

Longevity 11 years.

Characteristics although an enormous animal, this breed is affectionate, loyal, and has a calm temperament.

ORIGIN

Ireland

145

The Afghan – a fearless hunter turned elegant status symbol

AFGHAN HOUND

As a sight hound, this can prove one of the most difficult breeds to train to return to you. Afghans were originally bred to hunt hares, deer, and even wolves in Afghanistan. The Afghan is not a pack hound and is used to working on its own, in conjunction with a horse and rider. Hunting over the inhospitable rocky terrain called for a breed with plenty of stamina and keen eyesight.

The Afghan Hound was first brought to the UK at the end of the 19th century, by soldiers coming home from the Afghan War. Serious interest in these hounds led to the formation of a breed club in 1926. Within Afghanistan, there were several different forms, some of which were bigger and had darker coats than others. These distinctions remained noticeable in the early Afghan bloodlines, but have now essentially disappeared. Their coat does appear to have become more profuse, however, and this aristocratic hound needs thorough daily grooming to prevent its hair from becoming matted. Air-cushioned brushes are often recommended for this purpose.

Sadly, the graceful elegance of the Afghan has attracted owners who have neither the time nor space needed for this breed. These hounds must have a good run off the lead every day, preferably away from areas where other smaller dogs are exercised, otherwise these may be chased. Afghans will amply reward the efforts of their owner, proving both affectionate and devoted, but are soon likely to turn destructive if they are bored.

Character beautiful, loyal, generally good with children, but can have its off moments, so best not to tease.

Exercise need plenty of free running. Afghan racing is becoming a popular sport.

Grooming a Mason Pearson type brush of real bristle is ideal. Daily grooming must not be neglected.

Feeding 1½–2½ cans (14½ oz size) of a branded meaty product, with biscuit added in equal parts by volume.

Longevity 12 to 14 years.

Characteristic has a strong independent streak, and requires extensive obedience training and careful handling from an early age.

ORIGIN

Afghanistan

PHARAOH HOUND

ORIGIN

Malta

Character has a happy, confident personality, likes children, and makes a good family pet.

Exercise does require lots of exercise and is not suited to cramped conditions.

Grooming its coat needs little attention.

Feeding 1½–2½ cans (14½ oz size) of a branded meaty product, with biscuit added in equal parts by volume.

Longevity 12 to 14 years.

Characteristics an elegant and dignified hound, with its rich red or tan color; it is considered the oldest domesticated dog in recorded history.

The Phoenicians are believed to have brought these hounds to the islands of Malta and Gozo over 5,000 years ago, and, since then, the breed has developed largely in isolation. They are popular here for hunting rabbits and, although sight hounds, they can also track their quarry by scent.

There are obvious similarities in appearance between the Pharaoh and Ibizan Hounds, but their coloration is different. Pharaoh Hounds are tan or rich tan, and chestnut forms may also be recognized. A white tip to the tail is encouraged, and a white area on the chest, known as the star, with other white areas on the toes and a narrow blaze down the center of the nose are also allowed for show purposes. The temperament of both breeds is alike, with the Pharaoh Hound benefiting from a good daily run. The rise in popularity of the Pharaoh Hound has been quite staggering. Back in 1970, none were registered with the Kennel Club, yet within five years, they were given championship status. A similar occurrence took place in North America.

RHODESIAN RIDGEBACK

The unusual name of this breed is derived from the raised line of hair along its back, which forms two whorls or crowns just behind the shoulders. The Rhodesian Ridgeback evolved in South Africa, and this characteristic pattern reflects an ancestry that extends back to an old breed known as the African Hottentot Hunting Dog. The Ridgeback was bred by European settlers who were seeking a dog that could survive in the harsh and often inhospitable African climate. For a period, they were used to hunt lions, and so became known as the African Lion Hound.

Rhodesian Ridgebacks enjoy human company and are affectionate by nature, but they will not tolerate trespassers on their property. Although not common, the breed still enjoys a dedicated following. These are truly unusual dogs with an interesting history, and while they may sleep longer than other breeds, Rhodesian Ridgebacks will spark into life when out for a run. They are an attractive shade of wheaten color, and may also show traces of white on their chest and toes.

Character is obedient, good with children, and will guard its owners with its life.

Exercise needs plenty of exercise.

Grooming needs daily grooming with a hound glove.

Feeding 1½–2½ cans (14½ oz size) of a branded meaty product, with biscuit added in equal parts by volume.

Longevity 12 years.

Characteristics attractive animal with a distinctive ridge of hair growing in the reverse direction along its back in light wheaten to red wheaten. Has a gentle temperament and can move with great speed.

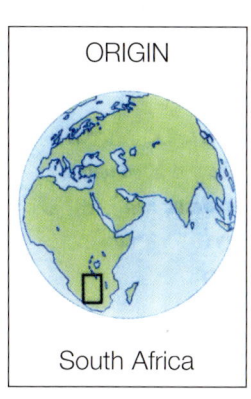

ORIGIN

South Africa

149

BASSET HOUND

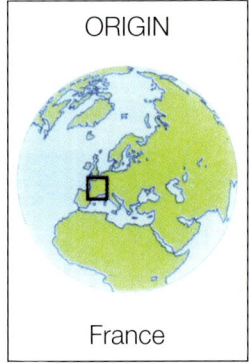

ORIGIN

France

Character often stubborn, but usually gentle and
benign, was once a superb hunting dog.
Exercise needs lots of exercise.
Grooming requires daily grooming with a hound
glove.
Feeding 1–2 cans (14½ oz size) of a branded
meaty product, with biscuit added in equal parts
by volume.
Longevity 12 years.
Characteristics mainly kept as a companion now,
although makes a good tracker; the typical
Basset is heavy, long and slow.

The term "Basset" first appeared in a book on hunting that
was published in 1585 in France. Various different breeds of
Basset were developed here, and the term itself appears to
have come from the French word "bas," meaning "low." All
Bassets are short-legged dogs, being bred initially from taller
hounds. The Basset Hound itself is of relatively recent origin,
derived from crosses involving the Basset Artesian Normand
and the Bloodhound. It first achieved prominence in the UK
at the end of the 1800s. Here the breed has been used to
hunt rabbits, but in the USA it has been pitted against a wide
range of game, including opossums.

As pack animals, Basset Hounds tend to be greedy by
nature, and particular care needs to be taken with pet

Bassets, to ensure that they do not become overweight,
otherwise male dogs can suffer direct trauma to their penis
from the ground. Regular daily walks are particularly vital with
this breed. Typical Basset colors are lemon and white or a
tricolored combination of black, white, and tan.

Especially in the countryside, Basset Hounds will often set
off in pursuit, regardless of their owner's instructions, if they
pick up a scent. Like other hounds, they can be stubborn and
relatively difficult to train, but Bassets are generally good
natured, and make lively companions, their loud, baritone bark
carrying over a considerable distance. They do not suffer any
inconvenience from their shortened legs, although it is probably
best to choose the puppy with the straightest legs in the litter.

BEAGLE

This is another popular hound that is somewhat similar to the Basset, both in terms of appearance and temperament. It, too, is usually either lemon and white or a tricolored combination of black, white, and tan, but its ears are much shorter than those of a Basset Hound. The origins of the Beagle are relatively obscure, although it is an old breed that has been kept for 500 years or so. These dogs were developed in the UK, and here, early in their history, wire-coated individuals were sometimes known, although today all Beagles are smooth-coated. There is still some variation in size, although the original small "Pocket" Beagle, which faded out during the early years of the 19th century, is smaller than those seen today. It stood up to 25cm (10in) at the shoulder, whereas the smallest Beagles today are rarely less than 12 in (30 cm).

Beagles have proved highly adaptable by nature, and packs have been used to hunt a wide variety of game, ranging from rabbits in the UK to wild pigs in Sri Lanka. They may be accompanied on foot or horseback, and must have regular exercise if they are kept as pets. Persistent training is to be recommended from an early age, so as to ensure they will return when called, if they are running off the leash. Their short coats are easy to keep in top condition with very little grooming.

Character happy, lovable, "naughty" little dog that possibly shouldn't be kept as a pet, but often is.

Exercise revels in it.

Grooming the Beagle's weatherproof coat requires little or no grooming.

Feeding 1–1½ cans (14½ oz size) of a branded meaty product, with biscuit added in equal parts by volume.

Longevity 13 years.

Characteristics independent, with a strong tendency to wander off, has affectionate nature and a low degree of aggression.

ORIGIN

UK

SALUKI

ORIGIN

Middle East

Character elegant, somewhat
aloof breed, is loyal,
affectionate, and trustworthy.

Exercise requires plenty of
exercise.

Grooming the coat should be
groomed daily, using a soft
brush and a hound glove.

Feeding 1½–2½ cans (14½ oz
size) of a branded meaty
product, with biscuit added in
equal parts by volume.

Longevity 12 years.

Characteristics sought after
both as a pet and a show dog
and care should be taken in
the countryside that its hunting
instincts are kept under control.

These athletic sight hounds were originally developed in the
Middle East and are of ancient lineage. Dogs of similar
appearance were being kept in this region over 2,000 years
ago, and were used to hunt gazelles, which rank among the
fastest of all antelope. When they were first seen in the UK,
about 1840, they were described as Persian Greyhounds,
having originated from Persia (modern-day Iran). They only
became widely available at the turn of the last century, and
were recognized by the Kennel Club in 1922, and by the

American Kennel Club five years later.

These hounds make loyal companions, but should only be
kept if you can give them plenty of exercise. Salukis may need
to be supervised closely when they are off the leash, because
they have not lost their hunting instincts. Available in a good
choice of colors, daily brushing of the Saluki's coat is essential
to maintain its sleek appearance. You may need to comb the
longer hair on the ears and tail.

WHIPPET

Developed for its speed in the north of England, the Whippet used to be known as the poor man's racehorse. These dogs were raced over straight tracks, which were typically 183m (200yd) long, being thrown into the course by their owners. The fastest individuals could reach the finish within 11.5 seconds, and even today the Greyhound is not a match for a Whippet in terms of pace over such distances.

A combination of small Greyhounds and terriers contributed to its ancestry, with a later contribution from the Italian Greyhound. The breed was introduced to the USA by emigrants from the UK during the early years of the 19th century. Although no longer kept primarily for their pace, Whippets have now found a new following in show circles and as a household pet. They are very trustworthy with children, but can sometimes prove nervous in unfamiliar surroundings.

No restriction is imposed on their coloration by either the Kennel Club or the American Kennel Club (which did not recognize the breed until 1976), and as grooming of their short coats is straightforward this breed makes an ideal introduction to the show ring. Whippets are adaptable dogs. Although they may chase hares in the country, they will settle well in the town, provided they can have a short, brisk run off the leash every day. In cold or wet weather, they should be fitted with a coat to protect them against the elements when they are out of doors, as they are not a particularly hardy breed.

Character this is a gentle dog, which is good with children and makes a fine pet and show dog, and a splendid watchdog.

Exercise this powerful runner needs plenty of exercise.

Grooming requires very little grooming, just a regular brush and rub-down.

Feeding 1–1½ cans (14½ oz size) of a branded meaty product, with biscuit added in equal parts by volume.

Longevity 13 to 14 years.

Characteristics may look like a delicate breed, but in the field its personality changes to that of a robust, fearless, and successful hunter.

ORIGIN

UK

DACHSHUND

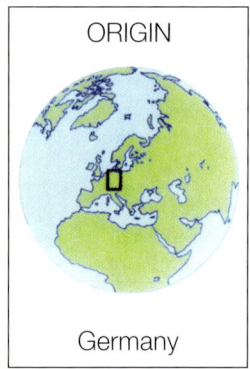

ORIGIN

Germany

Character intelligent, lively, courageous, obedient and affectionate.

Exercise short, frequent walks help preserve the Dachshund's waistline.

Grooming use a hound glove and rub down with a soft brush. A stiff brush and a comb need to be used on the long and wire-haired varieties.

Feeding about ½ can (14½ oz size) of a branded meaty product for the Miniature, ¾–1 can maximum for the Standard, with biscuit added in equal parts by volume.

Longevity 14 to 17 years.

Characteristics makes an excellent family pet and a good watchdog too as this breed has a surprisingly loud bark for its size.

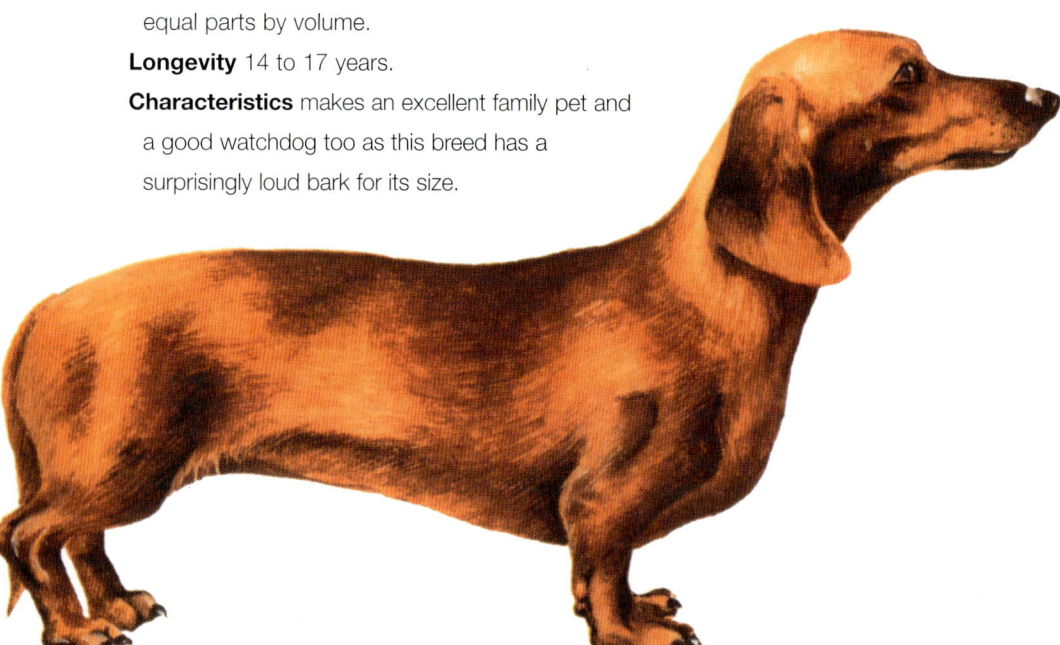

A number of different types of Dachshund are now recognized, descended from short-legged hunting dogs that have been popular since the Middle Ages in parts of Germany. Here they were used primarily for badger-hunting, with the traditional form of the Dachshund, or Teckel as it is better known in its homeland, being the standard short-haired form. Aside from their appearance, however, it is also generally accepted that there is a difference in temperament between these lively dogs and the somewhat shyer Long-haired Dachshund, which will require more grooming. The Wire-haired Dachshund, produced by crosses involving the Dandie Dinmont Terrier and other similar breeds, is the third member of this group. Selective breeding has meant that there are now miniature versions of all

three types of Dachshund as well.

As companions, Dachshunds prove loyal to their owners, and possess a bark suggestive of a larger dog. Their elongated body shape, which has led to them being nicknamed "sausage dogs," has made them susceptible to inter-vertebral disc problems, particularly if they are overweight. As a rough guide, like most of the other dogs covered in this section, they need about half a can of standard complete dog food (7 oz), with a similar volume of biscuit meal, which can be measured out using a clean can. As a further precaution against disc injuries, take pains to discourage these dogs from running up the stairs or jumping up onto furniture.

DEERHOUND

Better known in North America as the Scottish Deerhound, these hounds were bred before the advent of the gun, to assist in the capture of red deer for the table. Pace and stamina were essential characteristics, and Greyhounds appear to have been involved in their early development. Changes in hunting techniques contributed to the decline of the Deerhound, but Queen Victoria helped to ensure the survival of the breed, which was immortalized in paintings by the artist Sir Edwin Landseer.

It is not a common breed today but retains support from a dedicated group of owners. Deerhounds are good natured dogs and settle well in spacious domestic surroundings. They need plenty of exercise, and will still chase game if the opportunity presents itself. Although the Deerhound may appear somewhat similar to the Irish Wolfhound, it can be distinguished by its overall sleeker appearance. A good brushing of its harsh wiry hair will be adequate. Dark bluish-grey is the favoured coat color.

Character a good natured breed, gets on well with other dogs and can be kennelled out of doors, does not like intense heat.

Exercise needs lots of exercise.

Grooming minimum of grooming—just the removal of stray hairs for showing.

Feeding at least 2½ cans (14½ oz size) of a branded meaty product, with biscuit added in equal parts by volume.

Longevity 11 to 12 years.

Characteristics although gentle in the home, this breed needs careful training around livestock, for it can kill when its hunting instincts are roused.

ORIGIN

Scotland

155

BLOODHOUND

ORIGIN

Belgium

Character superlative tracker, good with children, and makes a good pet if you have room to accommodate it.

Exercise a great deal.

Grooming use a hound glove daily.

Feeding about 2–2½ cans (14½ oz size) of a branded meaty product, with biscuit added in equal parts by volume.

Longevity 10 to 12 years.

Characteristics long, drooping ears, wrinkles, and dewlaps give this breed an expression of inconsolable sadness, also prone to torsion – a build up of stomach gasses. Be aware of this, and contact a veterinarian immediately if hound is in trouble.

Known for its scenting skills, the Bloodhound was probably developed from an old breed known as the Saint Hubert Hound, which was brought to Europe by soldiers returning from the Crusades before the Middle Ages. It was introduced to the UK by the Normans after the Battle of Hastings in 1066. As a result of the careful breeding of these hounds, they became known as "blooded hounds," which, in turn, was presumably shortened simply to Bloodhound.

In spite of their name, these are not aggressive dogs and make good family pets. They will need long walks, however, where their scenting skills will soon become apparent.

Bloodhounds are surprisingly sensitive by nature and respond best to encouragement rather than criticism. You will need to watch their pendulous ears, as these are easily damaged. Their eyes, too, can suffer from problems, while the wrinkled skin on their head may provide a focus for local infections. Bloodhounds usually prove hardy and tenacious by nature. They are bred in several colors, notably combinations of black and tan and liver and tan, as well as red. Small areas of white on the chest, feet, and at the tip of the tail will not be penalized for show purposes.

BORZOI

Another member of the sight hounds, the Borzoi evolved in Russia to hunt wolves, and is sometimes also known as the Russian Wolfhound. It has an elegant, aristocratic appearance – long legs, a gracefully curving back with a long neck and tapering head – and appears to have changed little since it was developed in the middle of the 17th century. Borzois hunted in couples, approaching a wolf simultaneously from each side. They then wrestled it to the ground and held it for the huntsman so that it could be killed.

Borzois were first exhibited in the UK by the Prince of Wales at the end of the 19th century, and also became known in the USA at about the same time. In 1903 the Russian Wolfhound Club of America was founded and did much to popularize the breed. They can be bred in any color, although white is generally prominent in their coat, which needs careful grooming to preserve its appearance.

Borzois can prove rather remote by nature, being far less playful than many other breeds. It is important that they be kept in an environment where they can use their speed regularly. There are few sights more graceful than these dogs running together.

Character an elegant, intelligent, and faithful, albeit somewhat aloof, pet and a reasonably popular show dog.

Exercise requires a considerable amount of space and exercise.

Grooming regular amount of brushing.

Feeding 1½–2½ cans (14½ oz size) of a branded meaty product, with biscuit added in equal parts by volume.

Longevity 11 to 13 years.

Characteristics not ideally suited to being a child's pet as it does not take kindly to teasing, and care must be taken that it does not, true to its hunting instincts, worry livestock when out exercising.

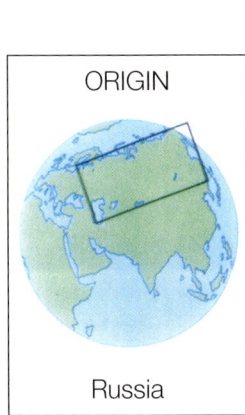

ORIGIN

Russia

Bright eyes, erect ears and a short muzzle help give the Cairn Terrier its attitude of keenness.

TERRIERS

JACK RUSSELL TERRIER

ORIGIN

UK

Character feisty, exuberant, fun-loving, and affectionate.
Exercise likes plenty.
Grooming requires little grooming.
Feeding ½–1 can (14½ oz size) of a branded meaty product, with biscuit added in equal parts by volume.
Longevity good.
Characteristics can be snappy and aggressive with people and pets.

One of the most widely recognized terriers, the Jack Russell has a long ancestry, dating back over a century. It is named after the Revd. Jack Russell, who was popularly described as the "Hunting Parson" because of his keen interest in fox hunting. Russell lived in Devon, UK, and here, during the latter part of the 19th century, he began to create a strain of versatile hunting terriers. He wanted dogs that would be able to hunt alongside hounds, and were also capable of going to earth and driving out a fox.

An influential member of the Kennel Club during its formative years, the Revd. Russell nevertheless vehemently opposed the creation of an official standard for this breed. He feared that this would actually weaken its character. As a result, the Jack Russell has remained a breed in everything but name. Moves are now afoot to change this situation in various countries, however, and widespread formal recognition is likely to take place before long.

In terms of temperament, the Jack Russell is a lively and rather excitable dog. It can sometimes prove snappy, but this is the exception rather than the rule. In addition to its original hunting skills, the Jack Russell has proved to be a dedicated ratter, although it does not appear that its creator used these dogs for this task. As a result, they can be particularly vulnerable to leptospirosis as this infection is often spread by rats. As with all dogs, Jack Russells should be routinely vaccinated against this serious bacterial disease.

NORFOLK AND NORWICH TERRIERS

In the eastern counties of England, a breed of hunting terrier that was rather similar to the Border Terrier in many ways, including coloration, was bred during the early 1800s. However, it was only toward the end of the 19th century that these terriers started to attract attention, becoming popular with students at Cambridge University. Subsequent crosses involving Glen of Imaal Terriers, Dandie Dinmonts, and others saw the emergence of the type of dog that has since become know as the Norfolk Terrier.

These terriers were taken to the USA at an early stage in their history, and used in a traditional manner to drive out a fox that had gone to earth. Here they were originally known as Jones Terriers. However, in 1964 a decision was taken by the Kennel Club in the UK, which split the breed on the basis of ear carriage, and the American Kennel Club also agreed to follow this precedent in 1979. Now Norfolk Terriers are deemed to have folded ears in both countries, whereas Norwich Terriers have ears that are held erect.

In terms of temperament, neither breed is quarrelsome by nature, although they are strong, active dogs for their size. Their coat is wiry to the touch and needs little grooming. The dense thickness of the undercoat provides good insulation, even against water. Norfolk and Norwich Terriers show a loyal and trustworthy nature toward people whom they know well, and settle happily in a home with children. They should not be considered as typical toy dogs.

Character lovable, hardy, and active. Good family pet.

Exercise like most terriers, these little dogs like nothing better than a good scamper in the country, but will adapt to town life.

Grooming routine brushing and combing. Some trimming.

Feeding ½–1 can (14½ oz size) of a branded meaty product, with biscuit added in equal parts by volume.

Longevity good lifespan.

Characteristics include a tendency to chase small livestock, if unchecked. (They love farm life and can be taught to guard rather than chase stock).

ORIGIN

UK

161

GLEN OF IMAAL TERRIER

One of the more unusual terrier breeds that is now attracting increasing interest, the Glen of Imaal Terrier is actually an old breed, developed in the vicinity of County Wicklow, Ireland. Here it was used to hunt badgers and, for a period, as a fighting dog. This rather anti-social side to the Glen of Imaal Terrier is still apparent to some extent today; although they agree well with people, these terriers do not relish the company of other dogs.

The Glen of Imaal Terrier is a tough and hardy breed, with a brave nature. It also has a playful side to its character, and enjoys a good chase after a ball. These terriers are best kept in fairly rural surroundings, but will adapt to urban life provided that they can be exercised away from other dogs. Glen of Imaal Terriers are bred in either brindle, blue, or wheaten colors, and their harsh coats need a thorough brushing each day. Although, at the present time, the breed is not recognized by the American Kennel Club, many American fanciers, as elsewhere, are falling under the charm of these courageous terriers.

Character affectionate, brave, good with children, and very playful.

Exercise requires a moderate amount of exercise.

Grooming maintaining its charming, dishevelled appearance requires only a good daily brushing.

Feeding 1–1½ cans (14½ oz size) of a meaty branded product, with biscuit added in equal parts by volume.

Longevity good.

Characteristics makes a devoted family pet, but it won't back down from a fight.

ORIGIN

Ireland

KERRY BLUE TERRIER

ORIGIN

Ireland

Character lively and affectionate, good with children but can be fierce.

Exercise needs plenty of exercise.

Grooming a difficult dog to prepare for show, it needs daily groming with a stiff brush and a metal-toothed comb.

Feeding 1½–2 cans (14½ oz size) of a branded meaty product, with biscuit added in equal parts by volume.

Longevity very good.

Characteristics displays a fiery temper against dogs and other pets when roused.

Developed in the vicinity of County Kerry in southern Ireland well over a hundred years ago, this breed shows a clear resemblance to the Bedlington Terrier, which contributed to its ancestry. The Irish Terrier was also used in the development of the Kerry Blue Terrier, as is clearly evident from the shape of the ears, which fall forward onto the forehead. These terriers were used originally to hunt a variety of creatures, notably foxes, badgers, and otters, but since then, and especially in the 1920s, they became fashionable show dogs.

The coat of the Kerry Blue tends to be soft and wavy.

Puppies are born black and their coats will lighten to blue by 18 months old, although they may still retain black points. Interestingly, those puppies whose coloration changes relatively late often have an adult coat that is a more desirable, darker shade of blue.

The Kerry Blue Terrier is a lively breed that does not always agree well with other dogs, although it should develop into an affectionate pet. It will also prove an alert guard dog and a keen rat-catcher. In Eire itself the breed is shown without any trimming, whereas elsewhere the coat is carefully groomed for the show ring.

BORDER TERRIER

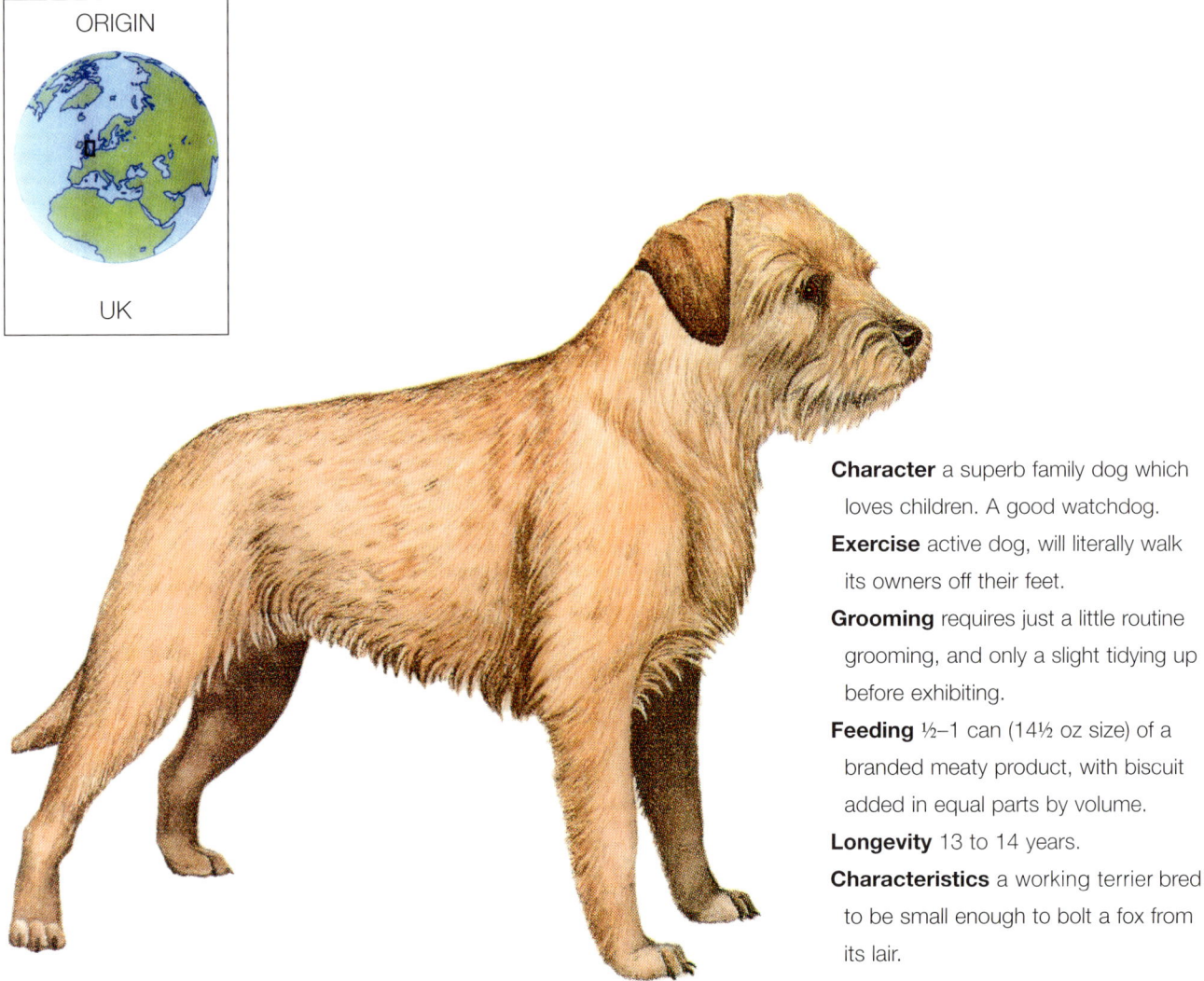

ORIGIN

UK

Character a superb family dog which loves children. A good watchdog.

Exercise active dog, will literally walk its owners off their feet.

Grooming requires just a little routine grooming, and only a slight tidying up before exhibiting.

Feeding ½–1 can (14½ oz size) of a branded meaty product, with biscuit added in equal parts by volume.

Longevity 13 to 14 years.

Characteristics a working terrier bred to be small enough to bolt a fox from its lair.

Originating in the Cheviot Hills that separate England from Scotland, the Border Terrier is the smallest of the working terrier breeds. It was first known as the Reedwater Terrier, a localized name, before being recognized under its present name in 1880. A tough and hardy breed, the Border was used originally to drive foxes from their earths. Indeed, Border Terriers are still kept for working purposes in their homeland today, although their precise ancestry now appears unknown. They are probably related to other terriers from this region, such as the Lakeland and Dandie Dinmont breeds. They probably acquired the name of Border Terrier as a result of working alongside the Border Foxhounds. In spite of their

size, these terriers have the tremendous stamina required for hunting in this terrain, accompanying riders on horseback.

For this reason, you should only acquire one of these terriers if you can give it a long walk on a regular daily basis. Their short coats are easy to keep in good condition, and a range of colors, from wheaten to red and both blue and tan, and grizzle and tan are all permissible for show purposes. The coat does not need stripping to remove dead hair, and possibly only a brief trim will be required if you wish to show a Border Terrier. They have probably altered less in appearance down the years than other terrier breeds, and are particularly responsive to training.

BULL TERRIER

It is believed that the English White Terrier, which has now vanished, was the main ancestor of this sturdy breed. Crossings involving Bulldogs, Dalmatians, and others also played a part in its development. A dog dealer called James Hinks was instrumental in the early stages of its evolution, which took place in and around Birmingham, UK. There was initial opposition from breeders of Staffordshire Bull Terriers, until one of Hinks's dogs beat a Staffordshire in a challenge dog-fight so clearly, that it then won a dog show prize on the next day!

A miniature form, under 35cm (14in) in height, has since been developed, and both types are powerful, energetic dogs. They need firm training from an early age, especially to ensure that they will not fight with other dogs. The sheer power of the Bull Terrier makes it a formidable opponent, capable of inflicting serious injury. Nevertheless, they are normally quite trustworthy with people, although they will not tolerate intruders. It is best to avoid this breed if you have young children because these dogs are sometimes rather short-tempered.

Character described as the gladiator of the canine race. Super pet for the devotee, but not for beginners.

Exercise active dog that needs a great deal of exercise.

Grooming brushing and rub-down will keep coat in good condition.

Feeding approximately 1½ cans (14½ oz size) of a branded meaty product, with biscuit added in equal parts by volume.

Longevity average.

Characteristics include obstinacy, and blue or partly blue eyes.

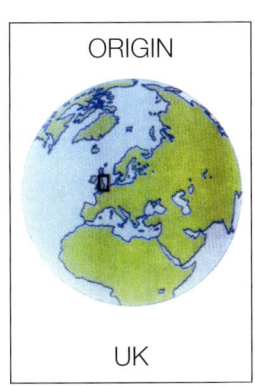

ORIGIN

UK

SKYE TERRIER

ORIGIN

Isle of Skye

Character loyal, hardy, and protective.

Exercise will benefit from plenty of exercise.

Grooming long coat requires a considerable amount of careful grooming.

Feeding ½–1 can (14½ oz size) of a branded meaty product, with biscuit added in equal parts by volume.

Longevity good.

Characteristics inclined to be snappy when provoked, and perhaps not ideal for children, the Skye is intensely loyal but dislikes strangers.

This long-coated terrier breed was developed on the Isle of Skye off the west coast of Scotland. As befits a small breed developed for hunting animals such as foxes and badger, it has a fearless nature. Skye Terriers are also very loyal to their owners, but are reluctant to accept strangers. This may need to be borne in mind when you are looking at adult dogs of this breed. There is a famous story concerning the devotion of one Skye Terrier called Greyfriars Bobby. After his owner's death, Bobby visited the grave every day for a decade, until he himself finally died. A statue commemorating the terrier's loyalty was subsequently erected in Greyfriars Churchyard near Edinburgh.

Puppies do not have such an elegant coat as an adult dog, but, even so, you should be prepared to spend time each day grooming it. At the same time, as with all dogs, it is a good idea to open the puppy's mouth, so that, in the future it will not resent this treatment. This is particularly important with a Skye Terrier, as this breed may be reluctant to allow a stranger such as a veterinarian to undertake this task without attempting to bite.

In spite of their rather manicured appearance, these terriers have remained hardy, working dogs. They will benefit from plenty of exercise off the leash, following up scents, and investigating their surroundings. The Skye Terrier is a breed probably best suited to a rural environment, rather than an urban lifestyle. The breed has gone into decline during recent years.

STAFFORDSHIRE BULL TERRIER

Crossings of terriers with Bulldogs during the early years of the 19th century gave rise to origins of this breed. It was developed for dog-fighting purposes in England, but when this activity was made illegal, breeders sought to remove aggressive traits from its nature. Recognition was slow in coming, however, the Kennel Club of Great Britain only acknowledging the Staffordshire Bull Terrier in 1935.

These are relatively stubborn dogs by nature, and still retain a tendency to scrap with other dogs that cross their path. Firm training is therefore essential from the outset, especially if you keep one of these terriers in an urban area, where it is more likely to come into contact with other dogs. They tend to make loyal house pets, however, and prove determined guards of property.

The Staffordshire Bull Terrier was recognized by the American Kennel Club in 1974. A slightly different form is also popular here, classified as the

American Staffordshire Terrier, often abbreviated to AmStaffs. These are not the same as the fearsome American Pit Bull Terrier, but resemble their English ancestor in temperament. A good choice of color is available in the case of both Staffordshire breeds.

Character courageous, intelligent, affectionate. Super pet, wonderful with children, but has a liking for fights.

Exercise boundless energy. Like the Bull Terrrier, best in a controlled country situation.

Grooming a brush and rub-down will keep the coat gleaming.

Feeding approximately 1 can (14½ oz size) of a branded meaty product, with biscuit added in equal parts by volume.

Longevity good.

Characteristics include a nose that projects forward, light colored eyes.

ORIGIN

UK

CAIRN TERRIER

ORIGIN

Scotland

Character an intelligent, lively, and affectionate dog. Adaptable, attentive, and hardy.

Exercise enjoys plenty of exercise.

Grooming daily brushing and combing, remove any excess feathering.

Feeding approximately 1 can (14½ oz size) of a branded meaty product, with biscuit added in equal parts by volume.

Longevity good.

Characteristics an excellent vermin controller.

One of a number of localized Scottish breeds of terrier that have become known to dog-lovers throughout the world, the Cairn's history dates back over 500 years. It evolved in the west of the country and also on the Isle of Skye, whence the Skye Terrier also originated. Indeed, when they were first exhibited in 1909, Cairns were described as Short-haired Skye Terriers, but objections from Skye breeders led to the adoption of their current name. Cairn Terriers, so-called after the Gaelic word for a pyramid of stones, would often hunt vermin in the vicinity of such stones, and this name now has universal acceptance. The Cairn was introduced in the USA in 1913.

These terriers are very even-tempered and affectionate,

making them an ideal choice for a home where there are children. They will readily take part in ball-games and other family activities. Their shaggy coat provides adequate protection against the elements. If the opportunity presents itself, Cairn Terriers will instinctively hunt vermin—still an advantageous trait, especially in rural areas.

One possible drawback of their tendency to go to ground is their desire to dig, and they may have to be taught not to use flowerbeds for this purpose. However, this is a small problem that can usually be overcome without difficulty. You can purchase special chemical deterrents for this purpose from pet shops; these simply need to be applied around the flowerbeds.

FOX TERRIER WIRE & SMOOTH

Both the Wire and Smooth-coated Fox Terriers share a common ancestry and are thought to be the descendants of some of the old terrier breeds of England, crossed with hounds. They were used for hunting purposes, and have remained active dogs best suited to a country environment today.

In an earlier stage in their history, it was usual to cross both coat types together, but they are now recognized as separate breeds. Undoubtedly, the Smooth Fox Terrier is the easier form to care for, its short coat needing just an occasional brushing to remain in good condition. The Wire Fox Terrier will need stripping, to remove dead hairs from the coat.

This can be carried out by hand, but will prove to be a time-consuming process, so pet owners may resort to having their dogs trimmed instead. Nevertheless, the Wire Fox Terrier has become a very popular breed internationally, a well-manicured show dog looking both impressive and appealing. In terms of temperament, these are typical terriers, with inquisitive and lively natures.

Character affectionate, inquisitive, and trainable, an ideal companion for small children.

Exercise appreciates plenty.

Grooming The Smooth needs daily grooming with a stiff brush, the Wire needs to be hand stripped three times a year, and to be groomed regularly.

Feeding 1–2 cans (14½ oz size) of a meaty branded product, with biscuit added in equal parts by volume.

Longevity good to average.

Characteristics a descendant of terriers from the English counties of Cheshire and Shropshire with some Beagle blood added.

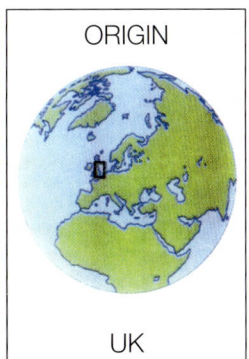

ORIGIN

UK

SCOTTISH TERRIER

ORIGIN

Scotland

Character faithful, sporty, loving, and independent.

Exercise requires a moderate amount of exercise.

Grooming needs daily brushing, its beard needs gentle brushing and combing and its coat should be trimmed twice a year.

Feeding 1–1½ cans (14½ oz size) of a branded meaty product, with biscuit added in equal parts by volume.

Longevity good.

Characteristics has a reliable temperament but does not welcome interlopers and has no interest in anyone outside its own family group.

Known affectionately simply as the Scottie, this breed of terrier came into fashion during the middle of the 19th century. It was originally called the Aberdeen Terrier, after the town where the breed first became prominent. Many people assume that the Scottish Terrier is invariably black, but it is also bred in a variety of other colors, including wheaten, which is whitish-brown, and also brindle. When grooming these terriers, particular care should be given to the beard; this may even need to be washed from time to time if it becomes soiled with sloppy food.

Scottish Terriers are brave little dogs and make alert guards around the home. They are not a particularly patient breed, however, and so not ideally suited to a home where there are young children. These terriers thrive on exercise, but you will need to take care to ensure that they do not come into conflict with other dogs once they are off the leash. Scotties are perhaps best suited to rural areas where they can live largely on their own. Even so, firm training is to be recommended, in view of their naturally dominant natures. However, if you are having trouble with rodents, few dogs will prove more effective or dedicated in dealing with them.

WEST HIGHLAND TERRIER

ORIGIN

Scotland

This breed was originally known as the Poltalloch Terrier, being named after the area where it was first bred, in Argyllshire, Scotland. Its development here occurred by chance, when a dark-colored terrier owned by one Colonel Malcolm was accidentally shot and killed by its owner in 1860. He then decided to breed only white terriers, and so the Westie came into existence, although prior to this, odd white terriers had been recorded.

As with other similar breeds from this region, the West Highland Terrier was used to hunt vermin. Its rough, wiry coat reflects its hardy ancestry, with mud soon falling off the hairs once they dry. Regular grooming is essential, however, to keep these dogs looking their best, and stripping about twice a year on average will be required. In terms of temperament, West Highland Whites are typically lively, jaunty terriers. They prove alert guards at home, and need firm training from an early age, because, in spite of their small size, they can have rather dominant natures.

Westies enjoy a good run off the leash, especially if you have a ball for them to chase. It may be advisable to avoid areas where a number of other dogs are also being exercised, however, as these terriers are likely to prove rather possessive, and will not appreciate the involvement of others in their game.

Character game, hardy, adaptable, and attractive pet that gets on with children and other pets.

Exercise a born ratter and hunter, this keen terrier will adapt to suburban living, but do ensure that it gets the exercise it deserves.

Grooming daily brushing and combing. However, like the Airedale, this fellow needs twice-yearly hand stripping and constant work on its coat if you aspire to the show ring.

Feeding approximately 1–1½ cans (14½ oz size) of a branded meaty product, with biscuit added in equal parts by volume.

Longevity good average.

Characteristics slightly domed head; eyes set wide apart; small, erect ears, carried firmly.

AIREDALE TERRIER

ORIGIN

UK

Character friendly, courageous, and intelligent. Good with children.

Exercise needs plenty, particularly if kept in town.

Grooming daily brushing with a stiff brush. Professional stripping twice a year.

Feeding approximately 1–1½ cans (14½ oz size) of a branded meaty product, with biscuit added in equal parts by volume.

Longevity 13 years.

Characteristics a born watchdog, has a stubborn streak and a tendency to get into street brawls with other dogs.

The largest of the terrier breeds, the Airedale is named after the River Aire in Yorkshire, UK, where it was first bred. Here it was originally known by a variety of local names, such as the Bingley and the Waterside Terrier. Its present name was established at the Airedale Agricultural Show in 1879.

Airedale Terriers are thought to be descended from the now extinct Black and Tan Terrier, with crossings involving Otterhounds also playing a part in its ancestry. The Airedale has been used for hunting a variety of game, ranging from rats to foxes and badgers. Its intelligent and alert nature has led to its involvement in police work, and the breed was a popular choice as a messenger dog, working in the trenches during World War I.

Today, these terriers are a frequent sight at dog shows around the world, although for show purposes their coat has to be stripped by hand, which is an onerous task. Airedales are tough dogs and may occasionally become embroiled in a fight with another dog, but they are not aggressive by nature. They will prove formidable guards, however, being very loyal to their owner. In terms of exercise, they do need a good run every day, otherwise they may become bored and destructive.

BEDLINGTON TERRIER

The rather manicured appearance of this breed belies a true terrier temperament. Its origins date back to the 1820s when Joseph Ainsley began the development of these terriers, naming them after the town in Northumbria, UK, where he was living. Subsequent crosses involving Whippets gave the emerging breed a more streamlined appearance, with the sloping or "roach" back still being evident in Bedlington Terriers today. The Dandie Dinmont Terrier was also used during its evolution, and is credited with contributing the characteristic top-knot of the breed.

The Bedlington has been used to hunt rats, its pace also proving useful against other animals, especially rabbits and hares. Their natural intelligence, coupled with a willingness to swim if necessary, meant that these terriers were popular companions for poachers. The tenacious nature of the Bedlington was also utilized in dog-fighting circles.

The coat of the Bedlington Terrier does not molt like that of most breeds, and so regular daily combing is needed to remove dead hairs. Trimming will also be necessary on occasion, to prevent the coat from becoming tangled, while for exhibition purposes scissoring by hand is required, rather than stripping as with other terriers. Bedlingtons are active dogs and quite playful, but they may not always agree with other dogs. They generally become a loyal, affectionate member of a family, however, and are quite patient with children, although this obviously depends to some extent on the individual dog. Bedlington Terriers are relatively easy to train.

Character lovable, full of fun, and a terror when its temper is provoked.

Exercise requires an average amount of exercise.

Grooming needs regular trimming; a good grooming every day using a stiff brush will normally keep it tidy.

Feeding approximately 1 can (14½ oz size) of a branded meaty product, with biscuit added in equal parts by volume.

Longevity 14 to 15 years.

Characteristics this breed looks like a shorn lamb with its distinctive thick and linty coat standing well out from the skin.

ORIGIN

UK

This toy breed owes its name to the affection King Charles II developed for its ancestors.

TOYS

CHIHUAHUA

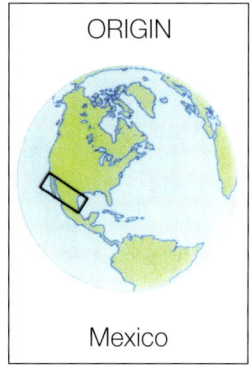

ORIGIN

Mexico

Character devoted, clannish, keenly intelligent. Splendid miniature guard.

Exercise don't be misled into thinking that Chihuahuas are just for carrying. They can be, but you would be surprised how much they enjoy a good walk.

Grooming brush with a soft brush and rub down with a velvet pad or chamois leather to make the coat gleam. Don't neglect tear stains around eyes.

Feeding ⅓–½ can (14½ oz size) of a branded meaty product, with biscuit added in equal parts by volume.

Longevity can live well into the teens, but the particularly tiny specimens rarely do so.

Characteristics include tipped or broken-down ears.

Named after the Mexican state where they were first obtained, these dogs are the likely descendants of a very old breed, known as the Techichi, which was kept here by the Toltec Indians as far back as the 9th century AD.

Recognized by the American Kennel Club in 1904, the original Chihuahuas were smooth-coated, but through crossing these with other dog breeds it was possible for breeders in the USA to produce long-coated forms. Obviously, these dogs require more grooming to keep their coats in top condition.

Chihuahuas are very loyal by nature, and live well in reasonably confined surroundings, although they do have quite a penetrating and persistent bark for their size. They

dislike the cold, and are surprisingly social by nature, so if you find that you have to be out at times, consider a companion for your dog. This can also help to overcome the rather finicky eating habits of some Chihuahuas, as will offering small quantities of food three or four times during the day.

This is not a breed recommended for children as Chihuahuas can prove short-tempered and many then snap, while they can also be fatally injured by a blow on the head. Instead of having a solid casing to the skull, as is normal, Chihuahuas generally have an opening here, known as the molera, like that of a new-born human baby. This never ossifies, leaving the brain vulnerable as a result.

CHINESE CRESTED DOG

The Chinese Crested Dog was almost extinct until, in 1966, Mrs. Ruth Harris of Gloucestershire in the UK contacted an elderly lady in the USA who owned the only remaining examples of the breed. Mrs. Harris imported several of these. The breed is kept both for the show ring and as household pets.

Happy and scatty, the Chinese Crested is an extremely active little dog which simply cannot resist the temptation to use a room as a race circuit. It is, however, lovable, reasonably intelligent, good natured, and usually fairly easy to train to the leash. Strange but true is that haired examples of the breed, known as "Powder Puffs," appear in almost every litter, and are thought to be nature's way of keeping the other, hairless pups warm.

The Chinese Crested comes in two distinct body types: the Deer, which is racy and fine-boned, and the Cobby, which is heavier in body and bone. It stands 11–13 in (28–33 cm) at withers, bitches 9–12 in (23–30 cm). Weight varies considerably but should not be over 12 lb (5.5 kg).

Character happy, never vicious, extremely energetic, and affectionate.

Exercise enjoys a walk but tends to exercise itself rushing about in the home.

Grooming bathing about every three weeks, and skin treated with baby cream. Crest and tail plume brushed. Shave off any stray hairs for show.

Feeding rapacious appetite but averagely ½–¾ can (14½ oz size) of a branded meaty product, with biscuit added in equal parts by volume.

Longevity 12 to 13 years.

Characteristics lively and affectionate, makes an affable companion, but needs to be protected from both hot and cold weather.

ORIGIN

China

177

TOY POODLE

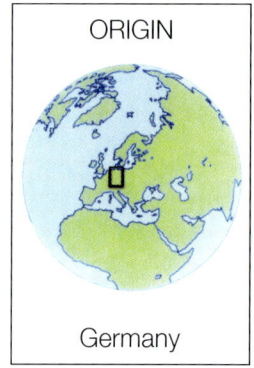
Character happy, hardy, and devoted. Thinks it is a much bigger dog.

Exercise some Poodles are exercised in the garden or park, others go for long walks in the countryside with their owners.

Grooming need regular clipping. The lion clip is obligatory for showing, preparation takes time.

Feeding approximately ½ can (14½ oz size) of a branded meaty product, with biscuit added in equal parts by volume.

Longevity many live well into the teens.

Characteristics exceptionally responsive, trainable, and thoughtful.

The Toy version of the Poodle is recognized as a separate breed, in spite of the fact that it shares a common ancestry with both the Miniature and the larger Standard Poodle. These particular dogs are descended from working stock, in spite of their often elaborate appearance, which may be more suggestive of a cosseted and delicate breed. In fact, Poodles were originally used to guard sheep, and, being descended from the Irish Water Spaniel, would also readily enter water as retrievers.

Interest in the Poodle as a lap dog meant that the smaller individuals were favored, and certainly the Toy form appears to have been established by the 18th century, according to contemporary Spanish portraits. Poodles do not molt their hair in a similar way to other breeds, and, certainly for show purposes, coat care is very time-consuming. In the case of a pet dog, however, this can be carried out at a grooming parlor. Ask the breeder for a recommendation, or, alternatively, you can contact a professional groomer through the telephone directory.

Although show dogs have more elaborate clips, the simple lamb clip, which merely keeps the hair at an even length, can be recommended for a Poodle kept just as a companion. This will need to be carried out about every six weeks or so, and will add to the cost of keeping your dog unless you decide to undertake the task yourself. When purchasing a puppy of this breed, it is especially important to ensure that it is sound. Like some other smaller dogs, Toy Poodles can suffer from a problem affecting the knee-caps. Known as luxation of the patella, this problem can lead to lameness.

YORKSHIRE TERRIER

So popular has the Yorkshire Terrier become that there are many specimens about in varying sizes. The unknowledgeable will tell you that their pet is, or isn't a "miniature." In fact the standard for the breed calls for a dog up to 7 lb (3 kg) in weight, that is only 1 lb (450 g) more than the standard for the world's smallest dog, the Chihuahua. However, there is no doubt that some of the bigger Yorkies one sees around do make happy, hardy pets.

With its keen terrier temperament in a small frame, the Yorkie makes a first-rate companion, and will live happily whether in an apartment or on a farm. However, the show specimen tends to live a sedate life, spending most of its time done up in rag-like paper curlers.

The origin of this little dog is fairly new. Its ancestry traces back only about 100 years to the crossing of a Skye Terrier with the old Black and Tan Terrier. Rumor has it that the Maltese Terrier and even the Dandie Dinmont may also have played a part.

The Yorkie, whose coat should hang quite straight and evenly down each side, with a parting extending from nose to end of tail, should be dark steel blue in color (not silver-blue), extending from occiput to roof of tail, never mingled with fawn, bronze, or dark hairs. The hair on its chest should be rich, bright tan, and all tan hair must be darker at the roots than in the middle, shading still lighter at the tips.

Character alert, intelligent terrier in a small frame.

Exercise will walk its owner literally off his/her feet in the country, or settle for a walk in the park.

Grooming daily brushing and combing for the pet owner. Continuous work for the show aspirant.

Feeding approximately ½ can (14½ oz size) of a branded meaty product, with biscuit added in equal parts by volume.

Longevity the 16-year-old Yorkie is not a rarity, but there is no hard and fast rule.

Characteristics described as the tyrant of the dog world, it may well take you over, with your household, if unchecked.

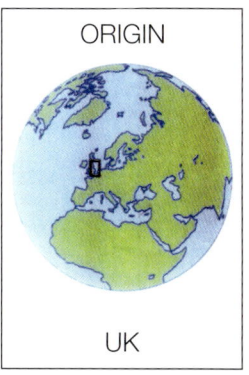

ORIGIN

UK

GRIFFON: BRUXELLOIS & BRABANÇON

The Griffon comes in two varieties: the rough (Griffon Bruxellois) and the smooth, more correctly known as the Griffon Brabançon. In the USA the breed is referred to as the Brussels Griffon.

The Griffon is an affectionate, intelligent, happy little dog, with an almost human expression. It revels in being with its owner and will follow for miles, whether picking up driftwood on a beach, or walking sedately in the park. However, while they have the facility to follow, they are not the easiest of breeds to leash-train. Perseverance is the key.

Generally good natured with children and other pets, the Griffon is an excellent house dog, but does have the tendency to yap if unchecked. Like other short-nosed breeds, great care must be taken that it does not become overheated in warm weather, that there is adequate ventilation and drinking water.

Whether to choose the rough or smooth-coated variety is a matter of personal inclination. Roughs seem to come away with more prizes in the show ring, perhaps because of their sheer numbers, but their coats do need a fair amount of attention.

Sometimes referred to as "the mongrel of the pure-bred world" the Griffon is said to derive from the Affenpinscher, while the smooth-coat undoubtedly owes much to the Pug.

Once used in stables to kill vermin, the Griffon was first exhibited at the Brussels Exhibition in 1880. Later it found immense popularity when the much loved Queen Astrid of the Belgians took a fancy to the breed, though numbers were severely reduced during the war years (1939–45).

Today the Griffon is loved and exhibited in many countries. The Griffon weighs from 5–11 lb (2.2–5 kg), most desirable 6–10 lb (2.7–4.5 kg), and comes in clear red, black, or black-and-rich-tan, without white markings.

Character hardy, happy, intelligent and devoted.

Exercise adaptable. Not too keen on leash. Will follow for miles, or settle for a walk in the park.

Grooming rough coat needs stripping, smooth coat needs brushing, towelling and rubbing down with chamois leather.

Feeding approximately ½ can (14½ oz size) of a branded meaty product, with biscuit added in equal parts by volume.

Longevity long lived.

Characteristics include high stepping front movement.

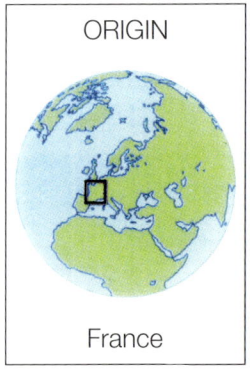

ORIGIN

France

CAVALIER KING CHARLES SPANIEL

Character sporting, affectionate, and fearless. Ideal pet, good with children.

Exercise should not be kennelled out of doors, but the Cavalier enjoys a good walk with its owner.

Grooming daily brushing with bristle brush. Eyes should be kept clear of tear streaks.

Feeding approximately ¾ can (14½ oz size) of a branded meaty product, with biscuit added in equal parts by volume.

Longevity good.

Characteristics include possible over-popularity resulting in some poor stock—so choose your breeder with care.

A larger toy breed, the Cavalier is immensely popular because of its good temperament and attractive appearance. It is a faithful, loving companion, reliable with children, and draws enormous entries in dog show classes.

Alas, there must be many who set out to get either a Cavalier or a King Charles Spaniel and come home with the other simply because they do not know the difference. In fact, the Cavalier is larger, unlike the King Charles' well-domed skull, the Cavalier's is almost flat between the ears, and its stop is much shallower. It is a matter of choice, for they both share the same characteristics.

The Cavalier and the King Charles both trace back to common stock. The King Charles can trace its ancestry to Japan 2,000 years ago and became popular at the Stuart court in 16th-century England. It has often been related how King Charles II of England spent more time playing with his spaniels in council chambers than attending to affairs of state and how he would take his pets into the bedchamber.

In fact, the King Charles was more like the Cavalier, having a longer nose. It was when shorter nosed dogs became fashionable that the King Charles as we know it came about, the old type almost disappearing, until in the late 1920s when a group of devotees determined to bring back the older type—which they wisely prefixed with the word "Cavalier."

The Cavalier weighs 12–18 lb (5.4–8 kg) and comes in a number of attractive colors: black and tan, ruby (whole-colored rich red), Blenheim (rich chestnut markings well broken up on a pearly white ground), and tricolor (black-and-white well spaced, broken up).

AFFENPINSCHER

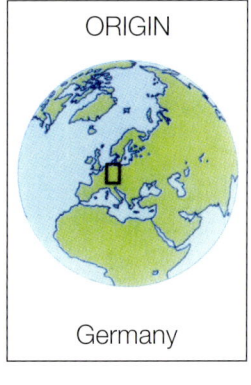

ORIGIN

Germany

Character lively, loving, and self-confident. Carries itself with comic seriousness.
Exercise adaptable to town or country. Enjoys a walk.
Grooming regular trimming, daily brushing.
Feeding approximately ½ can (14½ oz size) of a branded meaty product, with biscuit added in equal parts by volume.
Longevity good.
Characteristics include hackneyed action.

An old breed whose history dates back over 300 years, the Affenpinscher is probably descended from a combination of small wire-haired and pug-like dogs. It originated in Germany and is sometimes known as the "Monkey Dog," because of its facial features, which resemble those of certain primates. The bushy area of hair above the mouth, and the flattish nose, have led the French to refer to this breed less flatteringly as the "Diabletin Mustache"—the mustached little devil.

In terms of personality, however, the Affenpinscher has all the best qualities of the terrier breeds. These dogs are lively, loyal, and affectionate, although they may prove stubborn on occasions. The coat is wiry in texture and relatively long, but grooming is quite straightforward, a daily brushing usually proving adequate. The preferred coloration for the coat is black, but gray, black, and tan, and red individuals may be encountered on occasions as well.

Affenpinschers require a daily walk, although this need not be a lengthy period of exercise. They also enjoy a run off the leash in suitably safe surroundings.

The breed was first recognized by the American Kennel Club in 1936, and then by the Kennel Club in the UK during the 1980s.

In the Affenpinscher, the lower jaw may be slightly larger than the upper; although this undershot arrangement is often considered a fault in other breeds, it is not regarded as a weakness in this case.

AUSTRALIAN SILKY TERRIER

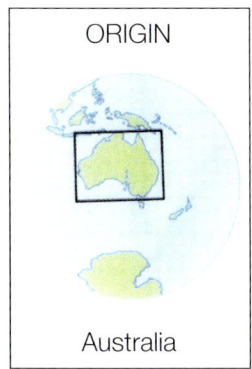

ORIGIN

Australia

Character affectionate and energetic, independent, and possessive of its own territory.

Exercise likes a moderate amount of exercise, needs a good walk each day.

Grooming a thorough daily brushing is enough.

Feeding ½–1 can (14½ oz size) of a branded meaty product, with biscuit added in equal parts by volume.

Longevity good.

Characteristics a strong willed breed which can be intolerant of handling and strangers. Obedience training is necessary.

As its name suggests, this breed originated in Australia, in tandem with its close relative, simply known as the Australian Terrier. Both breeds are descended from imported British terriers, and bear an obvious similarity in appearance to the Yorkshire Terrier. In the USA, to avoid possible confusion over the names of these two terriers, they are now described as the Silky and Australian Terriers, respectively.

It is likely that the Australian Silky Terrier is the combined result of three separate British breeds which were involved in its development. The Dandie Dinmont Terrier probably contributed toward the breed's relatively long body, as well as its silky coat. Skye Terriers may also have emphasized this characteristic, while its blue coloration probably came from the Yorkshire Terrier.

The coat of the Australian Silky Terrier, which is straight and silky to the touch, is usually parted over the head and down the center of the back. It is not as long as that of the Yorkshire Terrier, although there is a top-knot on the top of the head.

Today, their ears are held erect, although, formerly, drop ears were also possible, suggesting a close relationship with the Skye Terrier.

In terms of care, the Australian Silky Terrier is probably less demanding than its appearance may suggest, daily brushing being adequate to keep its coat in top condition. It is a lively breed, but will adapt well to apartment-living if it can have a good walk each day.

POMERANIAN

ORIGIN

Germany

Character adores lots of attention, is a lively and robust little dog, is also good with children.

Exercise needs regular exercise in the garden or park.

Grooming must be groomed with a stiff brush every day and be regularly trimmed.

Feeding approximately ½ can (14½ oz size) of a branded meaty product, with biscuit added in equal parts by volume.

Longevity about 15 years.

Characteristics it will bark unchecked, making it a superb watchdog that will also challenge larger dogs, also makes an excellent companion.

This is the smallest member of the group of spitz dogs, distinguished by their curly tails and upright ears. It appears to have been developed in the German province of Pomerania, and attracted the attention of Queen Victoria. She exhibited the breed at the Crufts Show in 1891, and this immediately led to an upsurge of interest in these dogs. Originally, Pomeranians were much larger than they are today, weighing as much as 30 lb (13.6 kg), but now members of this breed are lighter than 8 lb (3.6 kg). Nevertheless, they have retained the typical temperament of a spitz dog, being lively and loyal, and generally prove easy to train. Pomeranians are available in a wide range of colors, and will live quite contentedly in a home where there is a small garden, with a park in the neighborhood for more prolonged periods of exercise.

Grooming is more time consuming than with some breeds, as the Pomeranian has a dense undercoat and a long, straight outer coat. Trimming will also be necessary on occasion to ensure that the coat remains immaculate. They are very alert dogs and will indicate the presence of strangers by yapping loudly. Although this can be advantageous under certain circumstances, you may need to dissuade a Pomeranian from barking unnecessarily at the slightest sound. Nevertheless, as small guard dogs they can give great reassurance, especially to elderly owners who are living on their own.

PUG

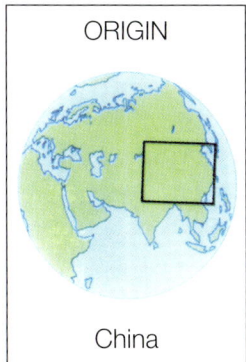

ORIGIN

China

Character pugnacious and individualistic, this vibrant breed is extremely tough and opinionated.

Exercise requires only a modest amount of exercise.

Grooming daily with a brush and a rub-down with a silk handkerchief which will make its coat shine.

Feeding ½–⅓ can (14½ oz size) of a branded meaty product, with biscuit added in equal parts by volume.

Longevity 13 to15 years.

Characteristics affectionate with its human family, this breed makes an amusing and rewarding companion.

It is believed that the ancestors of this breed were obtained in China by the Dutch East India Company, who brought these dogs back to Holland. Here they obtained royal patronage and were adopted as the symbol of the House of Orange. They were brought to the UK when William of Orange became King of England in 1689. This is another breed whose face is said to resemble that of a monkey, in this case a marmoset. These small New World primates were popular during the 18th century, and were themselves referred to as "pugs" for a period, the name then being transferred to the dogs.

With its thick-set appearance and wrinkled face, the Pug would seem to be a miniature mastiff. It is an energetic breed, with a matching appetite, and if spoilt it will soon become obese. This will almost certainly shorten its lifespan, and will worsen any tendency toward difficulty in breathing resulting from the compact face of the breed. Exercise during the warmest part of the day is inadvisable, particularly in hot climates.

Pugs become loyal companions and are easy to care for, their short coat needing only regular grooming to remain in good condition. You can monitor the weight of a Pug quite easily, by holding it in your arms and weighing yourself. Then stand on the scales on your own, and subtract your own weight from the previous figure. Pugs should weigh between 14–18 lb (6.4–8.2 kg). If a dog appears to be putting on weight, not only should you review its diet, cutting back on biscuits in particular, but you must also give your pet more exercise.

ITALIAN GREYHOUND

ORIGIN

Italy

Character intelligent, graceful, gentle, and
obedient.

Exercise enjoys plenty of freedom. But
beware, those slender legs so easily break.

Grooming brush and rub-down with
chamois leather or toweling.

Feeding approximately ½ can (14½ oz size)
of a branded meaty product, with biscuit
added in equal parts by volume.

Longevity 13 to 14 years.

Characteristics include black or blue dogs
with tan markings—or, especially, brindled.

The graceful Italian Greyhound is a Greyhound in miniature,
but more slender in proportions. It is a very loving, sensitive
house-pet which nonetheless enjoys plenty of exercise.
However, it is frightening that it was recently publicized as the
"ideal pet:" remember that it is a pet for extra-careful people
who understand that clumsiness could lead to broken legs,
that the little Italian feels the cold and always needs a coat in
chilly weather, and that harsh words cause this dainty pet
very much pain.

An obvious descendant of the Greyhound, it has been
around in its present form for a very long time. At one time
there were disastrous attempts to miniaturize the breed further
with an infusion of English Toy Terrier blood and it was not
until the early 1970s, following the import from Italy of fresh
stock, that the breed really got on its feet again.

This keen little rabbiter weighs only 6–10 lb (2.7–4.5 kg)
and comes in black, blue, cream, fawn, red, or white or any of
these colors broken with white.

JAPANESE CHIN

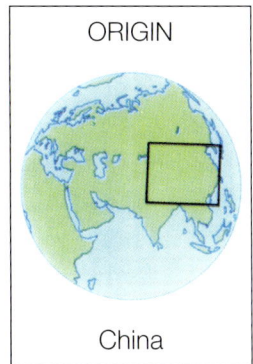

ORIGIN

China

Character independent, majestic, and robust.

Exercise requires a moderate amount of exercise.

Grooming daily brushing with a soft-bristled brush. Best to tackle the under-side with the dog lying on its back.

Feeding ½ a can (14½ oz size) of a branded meaty product, with biscuit added in equal parts by volume.

Longevity good, can live well into its teens.

Characteristics extremely forceful characters whose affection has to be earned by its owner.

In spite of its name, the Japanese Chin was first bred in China, and is one of the oldest of all toy breeds. It is thought that similar dogs were brought to Japan about AD 520 by Buddhist monks emigrating from China. In terms of appearance, the Japanese Chin has similarities to both the Pekingese and the Pug, and may share a common ancestry with them. They were accorded divine status by one Japanese emperor, and kept exclusively by members of the nobility. It is believed that the first pair of these dogs released from Japan to the West was given to one Commodore Perry in 1853, in return for establishing trade links with Japan. Queen Victoria, who was a keen dog-lover herself, soon acquired the breed, and Japanese Chins were first seen in the USA in 1882.

Although some of the original stock did not settle well after the long journey by sea from Japan, today's examples of the breed are hardy and long lived dogs. They have an attractive silky coat, which can only be kept in top condition by careful grooming every day with a bristle brush. The Japanese Chin is either black and white or red and white, with the red in this case being variable and encompassing shades of lemon, orange, brindle, and sable. An even distribution of the colored areas across the body is deemed preferable, with the tail curling down over the back. Puppies tend to have a less profuse coat than adults.

PAPILLON & PHALENE

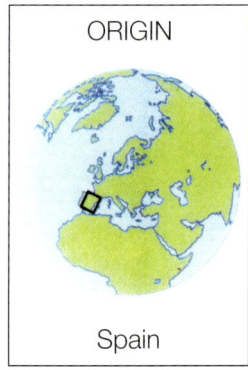

ORIGIN

Spain

Character this breed is intelligent, usually healthy, and has proved an able contender in obedience competitions.
Exercise needs daily walks.
Grooming needs only a daily brushing to keep the coat shining.
Feeding ½ a can (14½ oz size) of a branded meaty product, with biscuit added in equal parts by volume.
Longevity 13 to 15 years.
Characteristics there is a physical tendency to suffer from slipping kneecaps and a psychological tendency to be possessive toward its owner.

The name of this breed refers to the positioning and shape of its ears, and is derived from the French word "papillon" meaning butterfly. The raised ears are said to resemble a butterfly's wings, while in the case of the closely related continental toy spaniel, known as the Phalene, they hang downward over the sides of the head.

The precise origins of these dogs are unclear, although, bearing in mind their popularity among the nobility of mainland Europe during the 17th century, crosses involving the Bichon Frise and small spaniels may have contributed to their ancestry. The dainty movements of the Papillon belie its robust constitution. Whereas some toy breeds, such as the Chihuahua, may encounter difficulties when whelping, this type of problem is distinctly uncommon in the Papillon. They

are easy dogs to care for, and will live quite happily in an apartment, if they can have daily exercise.

Papillons are intelligent and invariably keen to please their owners, which in turn makes them relatively easy dogs to train successfully. However, you will need to ensure that they do not become too demanding and possessive, which can be a fault associated with the breed. Try to involve other members of the family as much as possible in the dog's care, so as to prevent the occurrence of this problem. Both the Papillon and the Phalene have been bred in a wide range of colors, with only liver and white outlawed for show purposes, so you should find a good choice of colors available if you decide to purchase a puppy.

PEKINGESE

Another of the ancient Oriental breeds, whose ancestry can be traced back to the T'ang dynasty, about 1,200 years ago, the Pekingese was finally brought to Europe for the first time in 1860, following the seizure of Peking by British troops. Prior to this, these dogs had been closely associated with the Chinese imperial court, and could only be kept by the nobility. They were known as sleeve dogs, because their small size enabled them to be carried within the flowing robes of the emperor.

One of the first Pekingese obtained from China was presented to Queen Victoria in England, and this helped to gain the breed immediate popularity. These small dogs are available in a wide range of colors and color combinations, all of which are acceptable for show purposes except for liver and albino. They enjoy being lavished with affection, as befits their royal ancestry, but they are quite hardy little dogs as well.

Take care when exercising them during periods of hot weather, as Pekingese can suffer from heat stroke. Their prominent eyes are also vulnerable to injury, and they should certainly be discouraged from running through undergrowth once off the leash. You must be prepared to groom the flowing coat every day in order to prevent it from becoming tangled. The Pekingese is an ideal breed for people who are at home on their own throughout the day, as it will form a strong bond with its owner. Left alone to their own devices for long, however, the intelligent and mischievous side to their nature will soon become apparent, and they are likely to prove destructive.

Character aloof, dignified, small well-balanced dog of quality.

Exercise despite its glamorous appearance in the show ring, the Pekingese enjoys nothing better than a good long scamper in the mud. Park walks will, however, suffice.

Grooming daily brushing with a soft-bristled brush. Best to tackle the under-side with the Peke lying on its back.

Feeding approximately ½ can (400g size) of a branded meaty product, with biscuit added in equal parts by volume.

Longevity can live well into the teens.

Characteristics include domed skull.

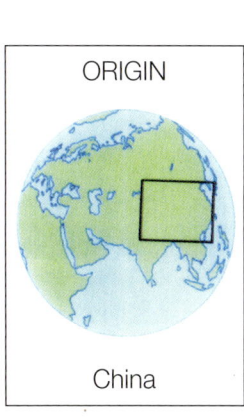

ORIGIN

China

KING CHARLES SPANIEL

ORIGIN

UK

Character affectionate, sporting, and brave.

Exercise enjoys a good walk with its owner.

Grooming daily brushing with bristle brush, eyes should be kepy clear of tear streaks.

Feeding ¾–1 can (14½ oz size) of a branded meaty product, with biscuit added in equal parts by volume.

Longevity 12 years.

Characteristics over-popularity can result in poor stock, choose your breeder with care.

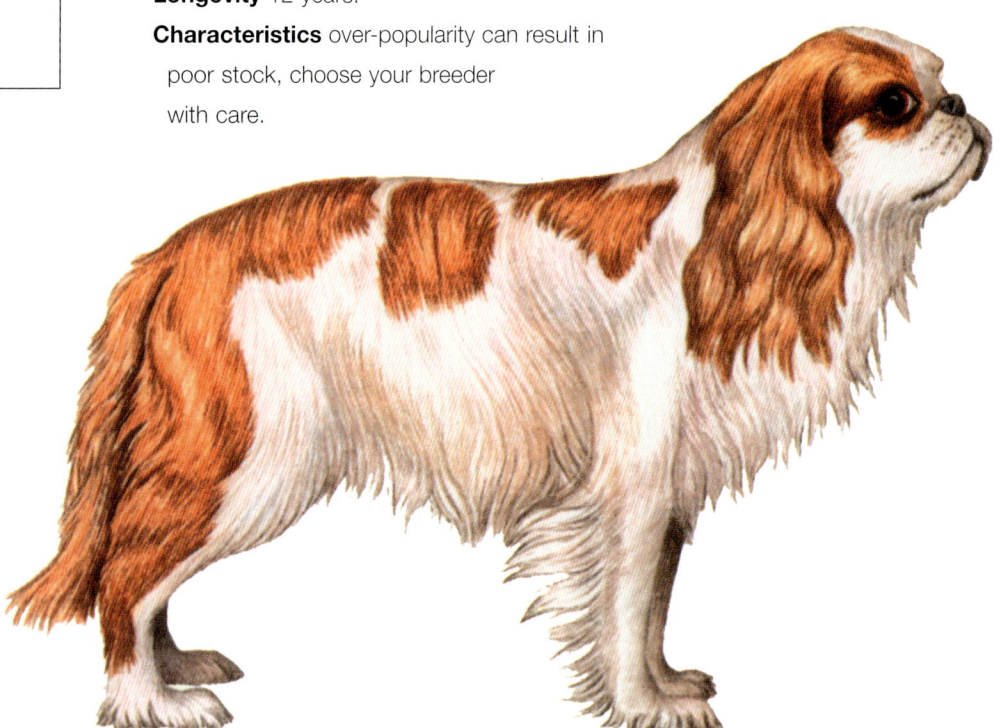

Although closely related to the Cavalier King Charles Spaniel, this particular breed is significantly smaller, and, to avoid confusion, is better known in the USA as the English Toy Spaniel. These dogs were apparently great favorites of King Charles II (1660–85), who used to exercise his pets personally in Saint James's Park in London. Four distinct varieties are recognized today, on the basis of their coloration, the traditional form being black and tan. The others are the Prince Charles, which is tricolored, the Ruby, which is chestnut-red, and the Blenheim, a combination of ruby and white markings, initially bred by the First Duke of Marlborough and named after his palace.

The nose of this breed is much shorter than that of the Cavalier, and the flattened face may make the prominent eyes more prone to injury as a result. You will need to check the ears regularly in this breed, as they are both pendulous and heavy. As a consequence, infections can develop quite easily within the ear canal, with persistent scratching being an early sign of irritation. Seek veterinary assistance without delay, as some infections of this type can be difficult to cure successfully, especially if treatment is delayed.

These spaniels, which vary considerably in size, are usually friendly dogs and should settle well in the company of other pets, notably cats, without problems. You must be prepared to groom the coat each day, and the eyes may also benefit from being wiped over at the corners with moist cotton wool, to remove any build-up of dirt.

MINIATURE PINSCHER

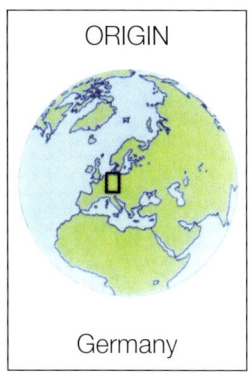

ORIGIN

Germany

Character fearless, self possessed, and spirited. Intelligent and easy to look after.

Exercise suitable for town and country and will adapt to its owner's needs.

Grooming daily brush and rub down with a chamois leather.

Feeding approximately ½ can (14½ oz size) of a branded meaty product, with biscuit added in equal parts by volume.

Longevity 13 to 14 years.

Characteristics the Min Pin has an attractive hackney (high-stepping) gait. It makes an ideal pet for town or country.

The delightful Miniature Pinscher (commonly known as the "Min Pin") is not, as many suppose, a bred-down version of the Doberman. It is a much older breed, a descendant of the German Smooth-haired Pinscher to which the Dachshund and Italian Greyhound probably contributed.

The Min Pin is a high-stepping little dog, a natural showman, and a joy to watch. It has, however, got a mind of its own and, in common with many small breeds, is likely to yap if unchecked. It is so attractive that most owners let their Min Pins get away with murder.

Standing from 10–12 in (25.5 cm) at withers, the Miniature Pinscher may be black, blue, chocolate with sharply defined tan markings, or solid red.

It did, incidentally, receive pure-bred (pedigree) status in 1895 from the German Pinscher–Schnauzer Klub.

THE COMPLETE GUIDE TO KEEPING A DOG

COURTSHIP & MATING

Once they are mature, male dogs are in a continuous state of readiness for courtship and mating. On the other hand in female dogs such readiness is cyclical, meaning that the bitch is only sexually active periodically when she is "in heat," or in scientific terms "in oestrus." On average a bitch comes in heat every six months, although the time between heats can vary from four to twelve months.

The behavior of the male is largely dictated by the sexual status and behavior of the bitch. She goes through a series of three distinct phases during her reproductive cycle. The longest phase is generally the quit period when she will not accept a mate, and a male is unlikely to make any approach to her. This lasts on average for about four months, and during this time the reproductive organs are in what can be described as a resting state. This resting phase is broken when the bitch starts to attract male dogs and, though she may show increased interest in them, she will not allow mating. Her behavior may change in other ways as well, for example she may become more excitable, lose her appetite, and urinate more frequently.

This stage of the cycle can also be detected by anatomical changes in the vulva, or external genitalia, which swells and releases a bloody discharge. The bitch also releases a chemical compound in her urine which attracts male dogs, and may cause several to congregate around her home. This may irritate her owner, but little can be done to mask the odor. While most bitches show some or all of these signs there are sometimes no indications whatever, although there can still be a successful, if unwanted, mating.

Although males are attracted to a bitch in this state, and great interest is shown by the male if he is allowed to be with her, the bitch will almost never accept a male that attempts to mount her at this stage. Generally she will either walk away, or threaten the male which normally discourages him from being too persistent. This stage of the bitch's sexual cycle can vary in length from two to fifteen days, with an average of about six days being usual.

After the resting phase when the bitch will not accept a male, she comes into heat and courting begins. The dogs meet, nose to nose.

During the courtship ritual, the dogs will sniff each other's inguinal region, as two dogs meeting do, but with much greater interest.

Generally a period of play will follow, especially in the early days of heat, and the female will display the "female standing pose."

The next stage of the cycle is the period of heat, when the bitch is sexually receptive and successful fertilization can take place. There is usually a dramatic change in the behavior of the bitch when heat begins. Whereas before she would reject the advances of males, she now does this less often and starts to display the characteristic posture known as "female standing," when she stands with her vulval region presented to the male and her tail skewed to one side.

The eggs are generally shed on about the third day of heat, but the bitch will continue to accept advances for a weeks, or more afterwards. It is quite possible for different members of a litter to be sired by two different males if more than one mating takes place.

When a male dog is allowed to meet a bitch in heat, the two of them will act out a courtship ritual, a sequence of actions which usually follows a similar pattern. First, they will greet each other by sniffing at the nose and then at the inguinal region, in much the same way as any two dogs meeting, although their interest in each other will be more intense than on a casual meeting, in particular on the part of the male. This frequently leads to a period of play, especially in the early days of heat. As a final display before mating, the male will often stand alertly alongside the bitch, facing in the same direction with his head and tail erect.

Assuming she is willing, the bitch will then stand in the presentation posture already described, and the male will mount. After mating has finished the male dismounts, but they remain joined by what is called a genital lock or tie. This can last anything from a few minutes up to an hour, and generally the dog and bitch stand quietly facing away from each other during this time. Sometimes the bitch in particular may become active, and even try to bite the male; if this happens, she should be quietened down.

Individual preference can also have an effect. While dogs do not form permanent pair bonds, studies have shown that females certainly have sexual preference, and males also, but to a lesser extent. The degree of socialization of the dogs toward other dogs and toward people also plays a part, and of course any kind of disturbance in the vicinity can upset things.

The bitch is almost always brought to the stud male, rather than vice versa. This is because, being highly territorial and needing to take a dominant role during courtship and mating, the male performs much better on his home territory than in strange surroundings. The female, as the less dominant and less active partner, is less affected by surroundings.

Once her period of heat is over, the bitch quickly ceases to be sexually attractive to the male, and at the same time

After a variable length of courting, the bitch will stand, her tail slightly to one side, to allow the male to mount.

The male mounts the bitch and mating occurs. This lasts just a few minutes, and then the male dismounts.

They then remain standing quietly facing away from each other, joined by the genital lock, which can last up to an hour.

she refuses any sexual advances he might make. This behavior change is usually rapid, but she may refuse a male one day and accept him the next. If there has been no mating or if it has not been successful, the bitch will return to a sexually inactive state for some months.

The various forms of sexual activity disappear immediately in bitches that are spayed, and rapidly, although not necessarily immediately, following castration in males. Veterinary surgeons can now give injections which will postpone, but not prevent, a bitch's coming in heat.

THE PREGNANT DOG

A bitch may act strangely during her pregnancy—perhaps carrying toys around, and even trying to curl around them as if they were puppies. The owner should be tolerant of odd behavior at this time, only worrying if it continues after the pups leave.

When a bitch has been successfully mated, the pregnancy that ensues lasts about 63 days, although there can be a variation of several days in either direction. At the start of the pregnancy, there is nothing obvious in terms of appearance or behavior to distinguish a pregnant bitch. A veterinarian may be able to detect the presence of puppies in the bitch's abdomen about three weeks after mating, but outwardly there is no change at this time.

At about five weeks the owner may be able to see that the bitch is pregnant, from a slight increase in her body weight and a distention of the abdomen. Depending on the individual, this may not be recognized until six or seven weeks. The bitch then increases in size and weight rapidly up until full term at nine weeks.

A common phenomenon in dogs is a state known as pseudo, or false pregnancy; this often occurs after a mating that has been infertile. The external characteristics of false pregnancy are extremely similar to those of a real pregnancy, but there are no pups developing in the womb. However, the bitch may show signs of abdominal swelling and also it is a characteristic of bitches during their first pregnancy, whether false or genuine, that the teats become erect and enlarge to two or three times.

A false pregnancy sometimes ends well before the full nine weeks of a normal pregnancy; the abdomen will suddenly reduce in size and the bitch no longer appears pregnant. However, in other instances, a number of behavior changes characteristic of pregnant bitches near full term may be observed.

Near to term, a bitch will generally become restless and may roam around the house as if looking for something. She may make whining or crying noises, and tear up any available material for nest building. Sometimes she may fail to respond to obedience commands.

The owner should make a few special considerations for a pregnant bitch. It is important to provide extra food from the fourth week of pregnancy working up to two or three times the normal amount by full term. An area of a suitable size for whelping should be prepared, perhaps a special box. Finally, if the bitch does behave strangely during her pregnancy, the owner should be tolerant.

Whelping Box

A whelping box should be provided for the bitch well before the puppies are due. It should be placed in a dark, quiet, and draft-free place and preferably raised slightly off the ground. Even if the bitch does not choose to use the box for whelping, after birth she and the puppies can be moved there. A playpen can be attached to the front of the box later on when the puppies start to venture out.

PUPPIES AND NEW MOTHERS

Once the pups are born, they enter a crucial period, as their adult behavior can be radically influenced by their environment and early contact with other dogs and people.

A puppy is born at a very early stage in its development, although after birth it grows and gains control of its senses extremely rapidly. At birth its eyes are closed so it is unable to see; its ears are not sufficiently developed for it to be able to hear; nor, it is thought, can it smell anything. The newborn puppy does have a primitive sense of taste, but at this early stage it relies almost entirely on its sense of touch and its sensitivity to cold.

The newborn pup's behavior is almost equally restricted, but it is highly functional. As long as the conditions are suitable, the pup spends 90 percent of its time sleeping and most of the rest feeding. The pup is able to go straight from a period of wakefulness to being asleep with no apparent signs of drowsiness in between.

During its wakeful periods, the young pup spends its time either searching for a teat to feed from, or else simply suckling. Pups normally move about by sliding along on their stomachs making swimming type movements with their front legs. At the same time, their heads swing from side to side in their search for a warm object. If a pup fails to make contact with its mother after traveling a short distance, it will set off in the same manner in a new direction. Once it touches the mother's body, the pup will move along parallel with it until it contacts a suitable area, where it will burrow in and come to rest once its head and shoulders are covered. It will behave in the same way if offered a human hand.

After a few minutes, the pup will make further exploratory movements in order to find a teat; when it finds one, it may not begin to suckle for some time, although there soon ceases to be any delay as the pup becomes practised. Unlike kittens, pups do not appear to prefer one particular nipple. Although the sense of taste is poorly developed, pups will turn away from any bitter substance, while milk, on the other hand, does seem to appeal to them.

Newborn pups have a reflex which makes them withdraw any limb which encounters something painful. If a pup finds himself away from his mother in a cold place, he becomes restless, more alert than usual and his breathing becomes more rapid; he will also make a distress call comparable to human crying, which is usually termed "mewing." Some studies have revealed the strange fact that a mother will often ignore this mewing, and may even squash a pup that is crying in distress. However, if she can see a pup moving around some distance away, she will bring it back to the nest, but not if she merely hears it. Pups also make a grunting noise, which appears to indicate pleasure when distress is relieved.

INOCULATIONS AND HEALTH CARE

INOCULATIONS AND HEALTH CARE

Within living memory, the chances of rearing a healthy pup were slim because of the scourge of distemper.

Nowadays, due to advances in veterinary science, the risks have been virtually eliminated. However, the prospect of a pup contracting Canine Distemper and several other killer diseases still exists and it would be sheer folly not to have your pup inoculated against them.The age at which your veterinarian prefers to inoculate puppies may vary slightly. Generally, a first inoculation is given at about eight weeks, with a follow-up four weeks later. On no account should the pup be taken for walks on the sidewalks, or allowed to mix with other dogs, until the second inoculation has had time to take effect.

Keeping inoculation records

It is customary, once a pup's inoculations have been carried out, for the veterinarian to provide the owner with a Record Card. Written thereon are the pup's name, breed, sex, and age; also the type, and dose of vaccine given. A reminder may be sent in 12 months' time, inviting the owner to bring the pup into the surgery for a booster. In any case, proof of up-to-date inoculation will be necessary should you have occasion to book your dog into boarding kennels.

During the first few weeks after birth, pups are protected by antibodies received from their mother's milk—this is known as "maternally derived immunity." However, the protection wears off quickly and, thereafter, the pup may fall prey to all or any of the killer diseases, which is why vaccination is so important.

The inoculations which your veterinarian administers are likely to be those which provide protection against not only Canine Distemper, but also these:

- **Canine Parvo Virus** is a comparatively new disease first recorded in 1977. By the summer of 1978 it had become widespread with large-scale outbreaks as far apart as Canada and Australia. It was first recorded in the UK in 1979.

  Parvo takes two forms—myocarditis or inflammation of the heart muscle in young pups up to eight weeks of age, and a severe gastro-enteritis or inflammation of the stomach and intestines from about five weeks through to adulthood. The death rate can be as high as 100 percent in young pups, but it reduces to around 10 percent in older pups and only about 1 percent in adult dogs.

  Pups that survive myocarditis are frequently left with impaired heart function and may die prematurely, while survivors of the gastro-enteritis may remain in poor condition for a long period of time because of damage to the gut.
- **Canine Distemper** is caused by a virus that can attack virtually all of a dog's body tissues.
- **Viral Hepatitis** can cause damage to the liver, kidneys, and eyes. It may also be responsible for respiratory infection.
- **Leptospirosis** damages the kidneys and liver.

You can see the extreme importance of not only having one's puppy inoculated but ensuring that booster inoculations are kept up-to-date.

FLEAS

In the past, fleas used to be a problem only during the warmer months of the year in temperate areas, but now the advent of central heating has enabled these parasites to plague dogs and their owners for much of the year. The presence of fleas on your dog does not indicate neglect, as the cleanest of dogs can be host to these parasites, which feed on blood. Adult fleas are equipped with sharp, piercing mouthparts to penetrate the dog's skin.

You may well notice at first that your dog scratches persistently when it is infected, in spite of being told to stop doing so. Regular grooming with a special fine flea comb should alert you to the presence of these troublesome parasites. Look for tiny specks of black dirt—these are the flea droppings.

If you are in doubt about these, sprinkle the debris from the comb on to a piece of white paper, and pour a little water over it. The dark specks will dissolve, producing a reddish-brown coloration on the paper, because of traces of undigested blood in the flea dirt. Actual fleas themselves may be harder to locate, although the base of the tail is a good point to look for them. One of the advantages of grooming your dog outside is that if any do leap off at this stage, then they are not likely to cause problems in the home.

Fleas can be treated by means of either a powder or spray, or by giving your dog a medicated bath. It is also important not to forget any cats in the household, as fleas can spread back and forth between dogs and cats, although not all canine treatments are suitable for cats. In addition, if you are treating your pets outside, avoid using a spray near a pond, as this may be toxic for fish. The same applies indoors, if you have an aquarium. Here, you must also treat the dog's bed and bedding, and possibly the carpet, because fleas breed off the dog in its environment.

On occasion, in the case of a severe explosion in the numbers of fleas, you may need to take more radical action to eliminate them. Pest control companies can undertake this task for you, with minimum disturbance.

ROUNDWORMS

One of the major concerns about dogs is the slight yet potential danger to human health which exists from the parasitic worm called "Toxacara Canis.".The risk stems from the fact that if these microscopic eggs are inadvertently swallowed by a child, then the larval stage in this parasite's life cycle can develop in the human body. Larvae can then move from the child's intestinal tract into the tissues, this phase sometimes being described as "visceral larval migrans." Should these larvae reach the eye, then they are likely to encyst and cause blindness. The number of actual cases recorded annually is, however, tiny.

Regular deworming will largely eliminate the risk of this infection, and to prevent puppies representing a danger, most veterinarians recommend that they should be treated from two weeks old onward, as well as their mothers. Apart from being spread externally, via eggs, pregnant bitches can pass the parasite directly to their puppies across the placenta before birth, and also via their milk.

Once the worms are established in the puppy's gut, they will start to produce eggs which are expelled with the faeces. These will then take several days in the environment to mature to an infective stage. After this period, however, they can remain viable for possibly years, and so heavy soil infestation is likely to build up in places where dogs congregate, such as public parks. If you have young children, therefore, you should encourage them to wash their hands thoroughly if they have touched the ground—and always before eating or drinking.

Signs of a roundworm infection in puppies are likely to be a pot-bellied appearance and poor coat condition. In older dogs, however, the symptoms are less obvious. It is often possible to identify the characteristic eggs from a faecal sample, but regular treatment against this and other similar parasites is usually deemed preferable.

CHOOSING A PUP

The choice of the right puppy for the owner's circumstances is vital, if a happy relationship between man and dog is to be created. The dog will be part of the household for many years, and the owner must take responsibility for the things which help keep a dog happy and healthy—grooming, exercise, and correct nutrition.

Choosing a pup is almost certainly the most important decision regarding his pet that an owner ever makes; the individual that is selected will be his responsibility for many years to come. A host of considerations affect this choice; the size of home and garden, the size of the dog, the facilities for exercise, personal preferences regarding breeds, the choice available, the health of the available puppies, the desire for pedigree or non-pedigree, the preferred sex, and the behavior of the puppies in the chosen litter.

Many of these decisions are matters of common sense, for example whether there is enough room for a given size of dog, although a surprising number of owners make mistakes over this; hence the need for welfare organizations to look after abandoned pets.

However, the puppy's behavior is vitally important, and here there are a number of considerations, which often pass unnoticed by even the most considerate of owners.

The temperament of a dog is crucial and depends on many factors. One of these is certainly its parentage, so at least the mother, and if possible the father, should be seen and their temperament assessed. The future behavior of the dog is strongly influenced by the age at which the puppy is purchased and brought into the owner's home. It is important for a puppy to become accustomed to socializing; generally around seven or eight weeks is the best age at which to obtain a new puppy. Certainly they must be purchased somewhere between six and 13 weeks. The

Left You should make sure that the puppy of your choice is healthy before finalizing the purchase.
1. Pick up the puppy to check that it does not object or show signs of pain; its body should be firm and relaxed.
2. Lift the ear flap and check that the ear canal is dry and clean.
3. Open the mouth gently and check that the tongue and gums are pink.
4. The eyes should be clear and bright, and there should be no signs of discharge.
5. Run your hand against the grain of the coat to check for sores and the black dust caused by fleas.
6. Check under the tail that there is no staining, which would indicate diarrhoea.

puppy will then become fully socialized toward the owner with sufficient, but not too great, socialization toward other dogs. Any puppy kept with other dogs for more than his first 13 weeks is likely to be almost untrainable as a pet.

A puppy who is purchased early is less likely to be disturbed by the sudden change of surroundings. Puppies become familiar with surroundings as they get older; a change from, say, a kennel to a house with children may be traumatic to an older puppy, while a younger one would merely explore and show interest.

Once a suitable litter of pups from which to choose has been found, the individuals must be considered, as their personalities will be different. The first choice to make is between a bitch and a dog. A dog is likely to be more assertive and need firmer handling, and there may be problems from straying or urination indoors. A bitch, on the other hand, will come into heat twice a year and so will need special attention at these times and there is still some risk of unwanted puppies.

As well as the sex differences, an examination of the litter is likely to reveal that some puppies are more pugnacious and come forward to meet a human inquirer, and perhaps start play fighting with another pup. Others may appear quiet or fearful and stay in their box away from humans.

There is unlikely to be one best dog in any litter, because differences in human personality mean that different dogs appeal to, and suit, different people. For example, a bold assertive dog would not suit a quiet, elderly person living alone; similarly a quiet bitch might not suit an outgoing person with a forceful personality.

It is best to try and judge the potential character and degree of dominance of a young puppy, and then relate this to the character of the owner. It is obviously difficult to make judgements of this kind for either party, but it is certainly worthwhile studying a group of puppies for a time and attempting to assess something of their character in terms of fearfulness, friendliness, alertness, activity, and dominance.

Do's and Don'ts

Do check that everyone in your home really wants a dog.

Do be prepared to travel some distance. It is usually only breeders of toy varieties that can be found in big cities.

Do ask to see the dam of the litter. This will give you an idea what your pup will look like when full grown.

Do make sure that the Certificate of Pedigree is in order and that this, and the Form of Transfer, have been signed by the breeder.

Don't buy a dog if you are out at work all day.

Don't choose a long-coated breed if you haven't the time to groom it.

Don't buy an Afghan Hound when you really set out to buy a Yorkshire Terrier.

Don't buy a "pet" quality dog if you plan to exhibit it in pure-bred classes.

GROOMING AND BATHING

Below After weaning, it is never too early to introduce a dog to the sensation of being groomed. The coats of many puppies may be less profuse than that of adults, and so grooming will be more straightforward.

Whether pet or show dog, your canine companion will benefit from a daily grooming. This daily beauty treatment not only makes your pet look and feel good, but gives the owner an opportunity to check for possible flea infestation or any minor injuries, or other problems.

Of course some breeds need considerably more grooming than others, so if your time is strictly limited it is advisable not to choose a breed which requires intricate preparation, especially if it is destined for a show career.

Most short-coated breeds are fairly easy to look after. All they need is grooming with a brush of short, stiff bristles, or with a hound glove. A rub-down with a velvet pad also works wonders and so does a brisk toweling. For heavy-coated breeds you need a brush with nylon bristles.

Clipping, combing, and plucking

There are some breeds, the show preparation of which is by no means easy for the novice to undertake. The Poodle, for example, needs its coat clipped about every six weeks and while the attractive lamb clip will suffice for a pet, an intricate lion cut is obligatory for show, and this can take many hours to perfect.

The glamorous Afghan Hound and popular Old English Sheepdog are but two breeds which require lengthy preparation, while terriers must be hand stripped; the Bichon Frisé is clipped and elaborately scissored and the Hungarian Puli has the thick cords of its coat separated by hand. Other breeds, such as the comical little Griffon Bruxellois, must be knowledgeably plucked.

Usually the relevant breed club can supply information and a pattern chart of what is required.

Canine beauty parlors will undertake the work for

you, but most owners take pride in personally ensuring the immaculate turnout of their breed.

There are a number of routine jobs that must be done when you groom your dog. You must, for instance, remember to clean inside its ears with cotton wool moistened with olive oil taking immense care not to probe too deeply; wipe away any stains around the eyes with cotton wool dipped in lukewarm water, or cold tea, and clean your dog's teeth with a proprietary brand of canine toothpaste.

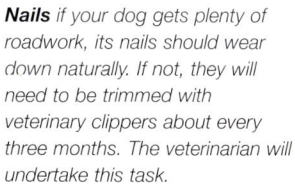

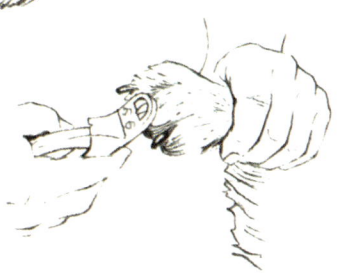

Ears *check the ears and ear flaps for any sign of wax or an unpleasant smell, which could be signs of canker. Ear wipes are available, but never probe the ear.*

Nails *if your dog gets plenty of roadwork, its nails should wear down naturally. If not, they will need to be trimmed with veterinary clippers about every three months. The veterinarian will undertake this task.*

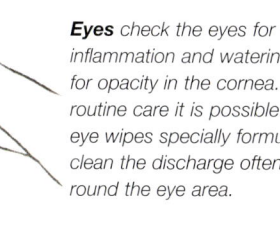

Eyes *check the eyes for any inflammation and watering, also for opacity in the cornea. For routine care it is possible to buy eye wipes specially formulated to clean the discharge often found round the eye area.*

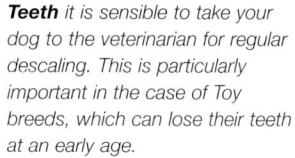

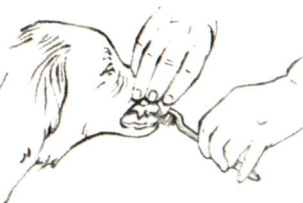

Teeth *it is sensible to take your dog to the veterinarian for regular descaling. This is particularly important in the case of Toy breeds, which can lose their teeth at an early age.*

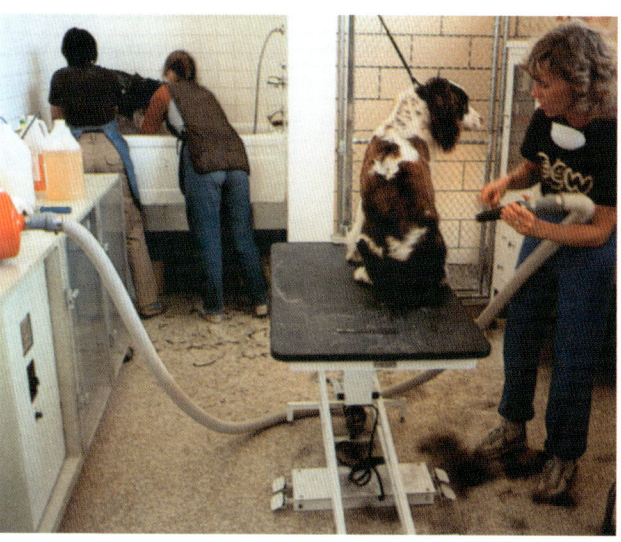

Clipping and curling

- *Some people buy a long-coated breed because they love grooming. They may sit, with their dog on their knees, all evening, meticulously working on its coat. If, unlike them, your time is limited, it is better to choose a short-coated breed.*

- *Dogs that receive regular walks on the sidewalk usually wear down their nails as a matter of course. Most breeds, however, need to have theirs clipped with veterinary clippers every few months. Take care not to clip beyond the quick (the white part of the nail) or bleeding and pain will be caused. Don't be afraid to ask the breeder, or your veterinary surgeon, to show you how to tackle this task.*

- *The perky little Yorkshire Terrier that you may see running around, covered in mud, is very different from its sedate, exhibition cousin, which spends most of its time wearing paper curlers.*

It is not usually necessary to bath pet dogs except in summer-time when, after a brisk toweling, they can run about and get dry in the garden. However, show dogs are, in the main, bathed the night before, or a few days before a show, depending on the type of coat. This is a matter on which the breeder can best advise you.

THE DOG'S SENSE OF VISION

The dog's sense of vision in daylight is thought to be inferior to that of man. A dog sees color, static shapes, and details very poorly, although it is very sensitive to moving objects and can see a waving hand up to a mile away.

Unlike his senses of hearing and smell, a dog's vision is generally inferior to that of man. In the past many people maintained that dogs were color-blind, but this is no longer thought to be true. In the eye there are two types of cells which can sense light, rods, and cones; together they form the layer at the back of the eye known as the retina. In dogs there is a much greater proportion of rods to cones than in humans. The rods are sensitive to low levels of light, but only see in black and white. The cones are responsible for color vision. Using very sensitive techniques, it has been shown that the few cones present in a dog's eye enable him to see color in a rudimentary fashion. However, it is not known if he makes much practical use of this information.

The predominance of rod receptors allows the dog to see much better than humans in poor light conditions. His ability to see at night is further enhanced by the presence of a special reflective layer, known as the tapetum, at the back of his eye. It is the reflection from this which causes a dog's eyes to shine green or yellow-green when lit by a car's headlights at night. Any light entering the dog's eye passes through the layer of rods, and is then reflected back through them again. This

increases the eye's sensitivity to light, but it also causes a loss of detail.

The dog perceives still and moving objects very differently from humans. A man can see both with ease, but a dog only seems to see objects well if they are moving, or if he himself is moving. This means that dogs see static shapes very poorly, but that they are sensitive to movement over very long distances. For example, a shepherd's hand signals can be picked up by his dog at distances of up to a mile.

Dogs are extremely sensitive to anything that makes a sudden or unusual movement, an asset made much use of by retrievers, pointers, and hunting dogs. Guide dogs for the blind use this facility all the time as they lead their owners amongst crowds and across busy streets.

Another major difference between a dog's vision and that of a human is caused by the position of the eyes on the head. A man's eyes point forward and the field of view overlaps almost completely between the two eyes, whereas a dog's eyes overlap less and point to a greater or lesser extent to the side, depending on the flatness of face of the breed in question. This means that dogs judge distance less well than humans, but can detect movement over a much wider field of vision.

The fields of vision

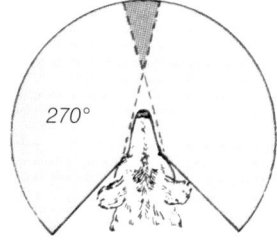

270°

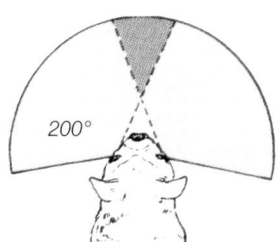

200°

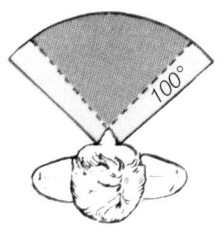

100°

The width of the field of vision is determined by the position of the eyes on the head. Dog's eyes point to the side to a varying degree, depending on head shape, giving a wide view. Human eyes point forward and are able to focus more clearly.

A DISCERNING NOSE

A dog's sense of smell is known to be at least 100 times better than a man's, and it has been rated more highly than this, up to 100 million times better.

The true difference is probably much nearer the lower figure. The variations can be accounted for by the different methods which have been used for testing, and the variety of chemicals, with widely differing types and intensities of smell, which have formed the raw material for such tests.

Undoubtedly the dog's sense of smell is more highly developed than his other senses. All dog owners know that their pets use their noses to investigate new objects, strange dogs, and unknown people, with great interest.

The areas inside a dog's nose which detect smells are about 14 times larger than a man's. Also, the part of a dog's brain which deals with smell is proportionally much larger and better developed than the equivalent part of a human brain. It has been estimated that there are about 40 times as many brain cells connected with smell detection in the dog as in the human. It is also conjectured that the cells in a dog's nose which detect smells may be more sensitive than those of a man, but this has not been proved.

All dogs rely on their sense of smell constantly, and some are used by man purely to detect odors. Dogs have been used for tracking game for thousands of years, and this continues to the present day. In France dogs have been used for centuries to snuff out underground truffles.

More recently, dogs have been used by the police and the armed forces to track people and find objects and substances. A well-trained tracking dog can follow the scent of a specific individual, even when this is crossed by the trails of many others; the very best trackers can follow a trail several days old. However, tracking dogs are not infallible; they can be put off the scent by adverse conditions, such as temperatures, humidity, rain, wind, and competing odors.

The dog's ability to follow a track after smelling an object, or piece of clothing, belonging to a person has even been used to establish that identical twins have the same odor. A dog will follow the track of either twin, after smelling an article belonging to one of them.

In the last few years, the so-called sniffer dogs have been widely used by the police and the army. These have been specially trained to smell out particular substances, especially explosives and illegal drugs, and have proved much better at finding these things than any machine.

STARTING TO GROW AND SOCIAL DEVELOPMENT

The pup's development is at its most rapid during the first four weeks of its life. By then it may weigh as much as seven times its birth weight, and its abilities to see, smell, and move around will have progressed enormously. The time spent sleeping will rapidly decrease, and the pup will begin to enjoy a range of other activities.

Vision develops extremely quickly, so that by four weeks of age the puppy's eyesight is almost as good as that of an adult dog. At birth the eyelids are closed, and the light sensitive region of the eye, the retina, is poorly developed, although the puppy will react if a bright light is shone through its retina.

When the puppy is between 10 and 15 days old, his eyelids open, but he still cannot see well, and responds inconsistently to lights or moving objects. By the time he is four weeks old, the pup will follow a moving object with his eyes in the same way as an adult dog. However, the brain is still not fully developed; for example, the pup seems unable to recognize its mother until about a week later.

The development of hearing follows a similar time pattern to that of vision. The ear canal opens when the puppy is about two weeks old, and full hearing has developed by four or five weeks. General development of the brain, such skills as co-ordination of limb and head movements, walking and responses to touch, occur at the same time, so that by the time he is five weeks old the puppy is ready to learn all the other abilities needed for adult life.

While the puppy is developing all these skills and capabilities, its range of experience remains fairly limited. Puppies continue to spend most of their time sleeping or feeding, and when sleeping they arrange themselves in a pile for warmth. When one wakes up, its movements will wake the others and all will tend to feed together.

Puppies are not able to pass waste matter or urine without being stimulated to do so. The mother generally does this by licking the pups, which causes reflex elimination. She does this for the first two to three weeks, and also ingests all the waste matter, thereby keeping the nest clean. After this time, the pups will eliminate of their own accord, and will usually leave the immediate area of the nest to do so.

Puppies will start to eat solid or semi-solid food when they are about three weeks old. They will eat anything they find in the nest box, and occasionally they may stimulate their mother to regurgitate food for them, by licking at her face and mouth. It is quite normal for wolf mothers to feed their young in this way.

At four or five weeks the puppies are ready to start playing, exploring and interacting fully with each other. It is interesting that by this time, five weeks, the facial muscles have developed fully to give the puppy its full repertoire of expressions.

Unlike cats, dogs are naturally social animals. Studies have established that there is a critical period during a puppy's development when it must have contact with both people and other dogs, if it is to develop normally into an adult pet. This period starts as early as about three and a half weeks, when puppies start to play with each other, and continues until about 12 weeks, after which the social attitude of the puppy toward its own and other species has become relatively fixed.

The importance of this socialization period in producing a good house pet has been shown in several studies. Puppies that have little or no contact with humans until they are three months old generally make poor pets. They are usually timid and afraid of people, and do not develop the dependency on the owner that most pet dogs show.

TRAINING

Experiments by the Russian scientist Pavlov led to theories of conditioning that were to form the basis of modern training methods and theories. The poorly-trained dog may exhibit a variety of behavioral problems, ranging from destructive or aggressive tendencies, to jealousy between pet dogs and attempts to dominate its owner.

Leash training

Although you will not be able to take your puppy out for a walk in public places until it has completed its course of inoculation, at about 12 weeks old, the intervening weeks up to this point will be useful in familiarizing the dog with walking on a leash. This can be carried out quite easily in the garden, especially if you have a wall or fence with an adjacent path.

Remember that puppies tire much more quickly than older dogs so do not be tempted to overdo training in these early stages since this will just be counter-productive. A brief session morning and evening is usually to be recommended, avoiding the middle of the day in hot weather. Dogs should not be exercised then, because there is a risk that they could succumb to heat stroke. The short-nosed (brachycephalic) breeds such as the bulldog are most at risk.

It is standard practice for the dog to be trained to walk on the left-hand side of its owner, so start with this in mind. Remove the collar and fit a choke chain and leash, or a head-collar. Harnesses are another popular option with owners of Dachshunds, spreading the point of control more widely over the body, rather than just the neck or head. This is to be recommended in this case because of the susceptibility of these breeds to inter-vertebral disc problems which can arise in the vicinity of the neck.

In the initial stages the puppy is likely to pull on the leash by trying to rush ahead. Continue walking at your own speed, pulling slightly on the leash in order to tighten the choke chain, accompanying this with the command "heel." This should then encourage the puppy to slow down, as the sensation of the chain tightening will be unpleasant. Similarly, pulling on the head-collar will also tend to slow the dog down.

Left *The steps in training your dog to walk correctly on the leash are shown here. At first, it can be helpful to speak quietly to your pet as you walk along, by way of encouragement. Again, consistency in approach is important. While the leash may be held in the right hand, the dog is invariably positioned on the left.*

By this stage, you may already have booked into a dog training class. These are held in many towns, but as more people appreciate the need to train their dogs properly, so courses usually fill up quickly. It is advisable to make enquiries early on to be certain of obtaining a place. Once you have started the course, you may well be given specific routines to accomplish with your pet between these lessons. This can be particularly useful, because although your dog may well master these quite readily in the privacy of your garden, it will also need to perform them with your encouragement in the totally different environment of the training hall, in the company of other dogs.

Never assume because your dog does respond properly in its own environment that it will continue to do so elsewhere; this can be a dangerous fallacy. Your pet may be distracted by a scent, for example, and run off regardless of your instructions to sit; this type of reaction is inevitable at some point. To minimize the risk of any accident, you should take your dog to a quiet spot, as far away from roads as possible, when you first extend the training process beyond the immediate confines of your garden.

The command "sit"

Leash training should also be linked with other basic commands which will be essential when the dog is walking along the sidewalks. For example, it must learn to sit, rather than straining to rush across a road. You can begin this aspect of training right from the outset, encouraging the puppy to sit in advance of every meal.

Apply gentle pressure to the dog's hindquarters to encourage it to sit. This can be repeated at the start of every session of leash training: hold the leash in your

Left With the dog standing still, give the command "sit." Gentle pressure over the hindquarters as shown may first be necessary to evoke the required response.

Left Sitting is a natural posture for dogs, and they should feel quite happy in this position.

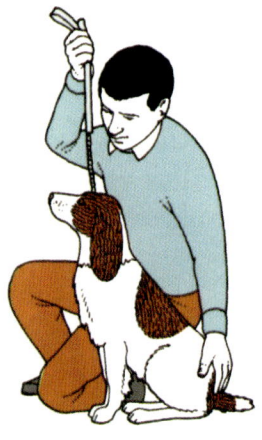

Left You should be able to kneel down, keeping the leash held high without upsetting your dog.

right hand and then apply a light touch with your left hand. Do not allow the leash to slacken at this point, but try to keep it taut as this will help to ensure the puppy adopts the required position rather than jumping up.

If you encounter problems, you may want to kneel down alongside the dog, keeping your hand in place over the hindquarters and the leash in an upright position. Do not be too keen to give praise in this instance, but allow the dog to settle down first for a few moments. You will soon find that the dog will sit of its own accord, before you place the food bowl in front of it, as this is a natural posture for dogs to adopt.

Having started on the leash from the sitting position, you should also break the walk with the command "sit," as will be necessary when you are opening the car door, for example, or when you come to a road. You can also encourage your dog to sit when it is playing in the garden. Such behavior is essential when you are training your dog to run free outside as you will want to put it back on the leash at the end of the period of exercise. Sitting is a relatively straightforward command to teach, and because it is such an important part of many other routines you should concentrate on this command during the early stages of training.

By the time your young dog is about six months old you should be developing other commands which will form part of its outdoor training requirements, in preparation for allowing the dog off its leash. These sessions should not be too long, just five minutes or so, two or three times every day. Continuity is important, and the dog is likely to respond best to one person, especially when learning new routines.

Once these routines have been mastered, then other members of the family can encourage the dog to behave in the required fashion. As an example, whoever feeds the dog should always insist that it sits before placing the bowl down on the ground. Make sure that the same commands are given, however, to prevent confusion and a likely lack of response on the dog's part. The word "sit," for example, should be used at all times rather than simply saying "food" in this instance, and hoping that the dog will respond accordingly.

Lying down

The sit and stay routine is to encourage your dog to lie down and remain in this position until called. It is usually learnt quite quickly once the initial response has been mastered. At first though you may well have to encourage your dog to alter its posture from a sitting to a lying position. You can do this quite simply by lifting the forelimbs together and gently pressing down on the top of the shoulders.

When the dog is lying down stay nearby and give the command "down." If this is carried out after a period of exercise your dog may readily remain in this position since it may be relatively tired. Alternatively it may simply attempt to stand up or sit. If it does, simply repeat the procedure until it is lying down. Obviously, do not expect your pet to settle down readily on a wet or uncomfortable surface. You can reinforce the message by holding the leash close to the ground which will make it harder for the dog to stand up if it persistently tries to do so. This is possibly more effective than having to reposition the dog repeatedly in the "down" position.

Again, as with the sit and stay command, you can gradually back away, leaving the dog lying on the ground. Having learnt this routine previously, then dogs soon adapt to the new version. It is important for a dog to sit and stay when instructed, once you allow it to run free off a leash; while it must also be prepared to lie down, both in the home and when waiting with you out of doors. In an emergency this may prevent a dog from straying into a potentially dangerous situation, for example if you should suddenly encounter riders on horseback when you are out for a walk along a narrow path. If the dog drops down as commanded then it will be unlikely to disturb the horses, which may otherwise be unnerved and could even attempt to bolt off.

Another situation where the command "down" is essential is within the home itself. While it may be pleasant to have a young exuberant puppy bounding out to greet you with great enthusiasm, you do not want a large adult dog behaving in a similar fashion, leaping up and bowling people onto the floor.

This again requires consistency in training from the outset. It is unfair to expect an adult dog to appreciate that such actions are no longer welcomed if you have allowed them since it was a puppy. Try to provide just a welcome pat when you return home or first thing in the morning, rather than a more exuberant greeting. If your dog does try to jump up, simply encourage it to lie down by using the technique described previously. Be calm and firm throughout so that there is no question of the dog interpreting your anger as excitement, and striving to obtain more attention by this means.

Left The command "down" is especially important for larger dogs, so that they do not cause problems in the home. From a sitting position, the dog's front legs will need to be lowered as shown here.

Left The dog should then be reasonably comfortable. It is best to carry out this exercise in the home, or on a dry patch of grass, so that the dog can rest happily.

Left Using a hand signal to show that you want the dog to stay in position, you can give further encouragement by holding on to the leash in the early stages of teaching this command.

REWARD AND PUNISHMENT

The second type of conditioning is easier to understand because it is based on rewarding the dog when he has done something that pleases the owner. The principle of this type of conditioning is simply that when a dog is rewarded for behaving well, this increases the likelihood that he will behave in the same way again. As a corollary, if a dog is scolded or punished for doing something, this ought to make it less likely that he will do it on future occasions.

Most dog owners will be able to think of several occasions when these techniques have apparently been unsuccessful. A common reason for this is that a dog can get confused by what appears as a lack of consistency in the owner's behavior. A dog can only relate a reward or reprimand to its most recent behavior. Although a human sees that a puppy is scolded because it wet the carpet while the owner was out, it is quite unreasonable to expect the puppy to associate the two actions unless one follows immediately after the other. A delayed scolding only causes confusion in the dog's mind, because it will be behaving in a quite unrelated manner when the owner discovers the misdeed.

Although there is a place for both reward and punishment in the upbringing of a dog, as a general rule reward is always the best policy. Punishment is normally used to stop a dog doing something, or as a reprimand for a misdemeanor, but it only works if the dog is caught in the act. For example, if a dog has chewed up a pair of shoes while his owner is away and on his return the owner punishes the dog as they enter the room where the shoes are, the dog will see this as a reprimand for going into that room. The dog may then be afraid of going into the room, but he will continue to chew up shoes.

When a dog is actually caught in the act, some consideration should be given as to just how the punishment should be administered. Physical reprimand should never be too severe, and a slap on the rump or a shaking by the scruff of the neck is quite sufficient. As with reward training, it is useful to associate punishment with a verbal command such as "bad dog," so that later on the command alone will stop the dog from behaving badly.

Punishment can have both beneficial and detrimental effects on the general behavior of a dog. A certain amount of punishment reminds the dog that the owner is the boss, and thereby reduces the likelihood of the dog asserting himself too strongly. On the other hand, the use of too much punishment can detract from the ideal dog-to-owner relationship of loving obedience. A dog that is frequently punished can become very confused by the unpleasant treatment given him by his owner, who is also the source of what care and love he gets.

It must also be remembered that punishment may not always be received by the dog in the way it is given by the owner. To some dogs, the physical contact involved in most forms of punishment also acts as a positive stimulus. While a slap may hurt momentarily, the fact that the owner is interacting with him physically may be seen by the dog as part of a game. If a dog sees punishment as partly rewarding, its effectiveness is obviously greatly reduced.

That there are these problems associated with punishment has led some people to advocate and make electric shock collars, which administer a very small but punishing shock by remote control. While these remove the problem of the owner being directly associated with the punishment and make it easier to catch the dog in the act, they have caused a number of problems in practice. For example, if a dog is given a shock during a fight with another dog in the hope of stopping it from fighting, the dog is likely to fight more furiously than ever because of the pain it has received. Since conventional training methods are perfectly satisfactory and electric shocks are as unpleasant to dogs as they are to humans, there seem no grounds whatever for the use of these shock punishments.

HOUSE-TRAINING

It is unlikely that a pup will come to you ready house-trained, if for no other reason than that breeders, perhaps with several litters to look after, simply do not have the time.

Some pups are house-trained within a matter of weeks. Others take considerably longer. It is something that is achieved by diligence and patience, not by bullying or adopting the unpleasant habit of rubbing the pet's nose in the offending spot.

Most likely the pup has been conditioned to answering the call of nature on newspaper, and further paper training is recommended.

Once your pup has grown up it will be able to control its bladder for a matter of hours. In puppyhood it cannot do so, and you must be prepared for mistakes.

Do's and don'ts

Spread newspaper fairly liberally on the kitchen floor and, whenever you see the pup about to squat, lift it up firmly but kindly, point to the paper and place it on it. Do this even if it has erred, but NEVER hit it if it has not used the newspaper.

Once the pup shows signs of understanding what is required, continue the practice, but substitute the generously spread paper with just a sheet or two at the back door. Once pup knows to toddle to the door when it wants to relieve itself you can start opening it and let it out into the garden, praising it lavishly when it does what is required. But don't leave it out in the cold for an inordinate length of time. Some dogs, like people, take a little longer to understand what is required of them than others.

Obviously one does not want an adult dog to relieve itself in the house as a matter of course. However, the mere fact of having been paper trained in puppyhood

When your pup relieves itself, place it promptly on the sheets of newspaper that you will have placed on the kitchen floor.

Soon the puppy will look for the newspaper when it needs to answer the call of nature and toddle onto it, but be prepared for the odd mistake.

can be enormously beneficial in the case of tiny breeds, if, for example, you are going out and know that your return may be delayed. In such a case, simply leave a sheet of newspaper by the door. The dog will know what it is there for.

How long to leave your dog

New owners often ask how long they may leave their pet before returning to let it out into the garden. Bearing in mind that it is always best to leave a young dog only for short periods until it has had time to build up confidence in your return, it should, in adult life, be capable of being left for about five hours. There are, in most people's lives, the odd occasions which compel them to extend this period. However, the truth of the matter is that the person whose job demands their being out of the house from nine to five should not consider dog ownership. The dirty, noisy, and destructive dog is usually also a lonely one.

Some basic rules

- *If you are out at work all day, it is unfair to keep a dog no matter how much you may love them, unless, of course, you have a friend or helper who could be relied upon to call at your home every mid-day to exercise the pet in your absence.*

- *Never, ever hit a dog. Your tone of voice should be sufficient to express displeasure and a dog wants only to please. Be generous with praise whenever a dog does well, patting it, and saying "Good boy" or "Good girl" as the case may be.*

Gradually decrease the amount of newspaper and leave a sheet or two by the back door.

Soon, if the weather is warm, you can open the back door when the pup heads toward it, and encourage it to go outside.

LEARNING OBEDIENCE

Puppies vary considerably in the rate at which they mature, but informal training, especially house training, should start as soon as they are moving around independently. This is the time to teach a puppy its name and then a few basic commands. It is best to choose a short name that can be spoken clearly, will be quickly learned by the puppy, and will not be embarrassing to shout out in public.

Formal training at registered training clubs does not start until puppies are six months old, and it can be completed in about three months. However, informal training should certainly begin much earlier than this, otherwise bad habits will develop. Some of these may not become apparent until later in life, and a particularly common example is the dog that jumps up. In a small puppy this presents no problems, and indeed many owners may enjoy their puppy playing in this way. However, when dogs grow larger, it can become undesirable, irritating, or even dangerous in extreme cases, such as a Saint Bernard jumping up to place its paws on a small child.

It is useful to consider why a dog starts to jump up in the first place. If jumping gains the attention of the owner and results in play or affection, this is taken by the dog as a reward for the act of jumping.

A reward for a dog can take many forms. A tit-bit of food is one of the most common rewards used to encourage a good dog, or one that has just done what the owner wanted.

If food was the only possible reward, a dog would very likely overeat excessively during a formal training session. An alternative is to associate in the dog's mind a phrase such as "good boy" by saying it each time a reward is given. "Good boy" will then come to be considered as a reward in itself, just as the bell caused Pavlov's dogs to salivate. The other great alternative to food is affection; dogs are particularly easy to reward in this way, and this is the underlying cause of most instances of jumping up.

One of the simplest ways to eradicate an undesirable habit, such as jumping up, is simply to stop rewarding it. For example, each time a dog jumps up, the owner should walk away and ignore him. The dog should get the message fairly quickly unless the habit is too well engrained. It is also a good idea to reward the dog with affection when it behaves in the desired manner, such as standing quietly.

An alternative to ignoring the dog and hoping that undesirable or awkward behavior will stop, is to use punishment, say a slap on the rump (not on the nose because this is very delicate). As has been seen, punishment can be useful in some circumstances, but with a jumping dog, it is unlikely to help. This is because the dog may well be totally confused by a change from the previous reward for this behavior to sudden punishment for doing what to the dog is the same thing. Looked at from the dog's point of view this is illogical and disturbing and may therefore lead to other behavior problems.

CARS & KENNELS

Most dogs are likely to travel fairly frequently in cars. The vaccinations already mentioned will necessitate a visit to the veterinarian, and in many cases this will be by car. Unfortunately treatment at the veterinarians will almost always give some discomfort to the dog, and this can make any visit after the first one a fairly traumatic event, once the dog senses where it is going. If the dog's first car journey is to the vet, this may make him frightened of all car travel by a process of association. It is therefore worth thinking ahead, and perhaps giving the puppy a brief ride to a place he will like, such as a park, before the first visit to the vet.

Some dogs dislike car journeys for other reasons. Travel sickness affects some dogs, as it does some people, and the reason is the same, the influence of the car's movements on the balance organs. On the other hand, many dogs enjoy car rides immensely. Most of them regard the car as an extension of their own home territory and may bark at any strange person that approaches when they are left alone in the car.

It is not good for the dog to stick its head out of the window while the car is moving. Not only is there a danger of it hitting something, but also the fast flow of air can dry out the eyes, causing irritation. When the car is parked and the dog is left inside, it should be in the shade and a window should be left open a few inches to provide air.

Dogs are very dependent animals, and are unhappy even when their owners are absent for short periods. Any potential owner who is at work daily with no one else in the house should think carefully before buying a dog. When left alone, dogs become bored and sometimes destructive.

If the owner is to be away from home for a period of days or weeks, the dog may need to be boarded in a kennel. Here he will not suffer from loneliness in one sense, because he will at least be in the company of other dogs. Nevertheless, the change in surroundings, the low level of human contact, and the absence of the owner can have a psychological effect on the dog. Most dogs cope with a kennel for two or three weeks very well, but it is probably a good idea to leave a familiar toy at the kennels and if possible the dog's normal food, although it may eat less than usual.

Some kennels are not just for boarding, but act as sanctuaries for stray and unwanted dogs. Many people prefer to acquire one of these instead of buying a young puppy, because these unfortunate dogs are in great need of a home. Dogs of this kind are likely to present more problems than a puppy because their characters are already formed. Also they may have been mistreated, and being older are less adaptable and less easy to train. However, with love and patience, many such dogs can become excellent house pets—no different from those reared in one home since they were puppies. The quiet, planned introduction into the new home, and the necessary basic training should be just the same as for any younger dog. However, it may well take longer for the dog to become a fully socialized member of the family.

A PROPER DIET

Basically, dogs have the same nutritional requirements as ourselves. They need a balanced diet containing protein (meat), carbohydrate (cereals), and fat with minerals and vitamins added. Almost all types of meat are suitable excepting liver, which is a laxative and should be fed only in strict moderation.

Water is essential and must be supplied either (almost always) as drinking water, or in the food itself. Minced meat contains about 70 percent water.

Fresh meat versus branded pet food

It does not seem so long ago that conscientious dog owners insisted on feeding pets fresh meat, using prepared dog foods only as a standby. And indeed a diet of water, and suitable meat and biscuits do meet the basic food requirements of the dog in full.

Nowadays, however, branded pet foods have been

scientifically prepared to meet the nutritional requirements of the dog and are fed by most kennels and individual owners, as much for the benefit of the dog as for convenience.

These prepared foods come in the form of meaty canned products, to which dog biscuits should be added, cans of complete or soft, moist foods which do not require the addition of biscuits, or a complete dry dog food to which only water is added. The dry foods do increase a dog's thirst, so if they are used, it is necessary to ensure that the drinking water supply is well topped up.

And while many dog owners still insist on feeding pups on lightly cooked, lean minced beef for the first few weeks from weaning, canned puppy food is now available, which has been specially formulated to give pups a good start in life.

Puppy feeding schedule

Age	Feeds per day	Approx time of feeds
From weaning to 3 months	4	Breakfast, Lunch, Tea, Supper (optional bedtime drink, perhaps an egg swirled in milk for large breeds)
3-6 months	3	Breakfast, Tea, Supper
6-12 months	2	Breakfast, Tea (or early supper)
One year and over (the dog is an adult at one year)	1 or 2	Mid-day and/or early evening (if mid-day meal only is decided upon a few biscuits should be given at bedtime.)

Note: The exact time of feeds is flexible, but once chosen must be strictly adhered to.

Initially the pup should receive two milky meals (a prepared baby food such as Farex is ideal) and two meals of lightly cooked, lean, minced beef or canned puppy food, with puppy biscuits.

Feeding the adult dog

Quantities based on average 14½oz (400g) can

Toy sized dog	e.g. Yorkshire Terrier	¼–½ can
Small sized dog	e.g. West Highland White Terrier	½ can
Medium sized dog	e.g. Cocker Spaniel	1 can
Large sized dog	e.g. Labrador Retriever	1½–2 cans
Very large sized dog	e.g. Great Dane	4 cans

It will be appreciated that some dogs burn up more energy, and have a greater need for food, than others, so once you have ascertained the correct weight for your dog you can adjust its rations accordingly. Consult your veterinarian if in doubt.

Dog food comes in a variety of forms. In the beginning you will need to try out different types of food to see which suits your dog best.

Mealtime tips

- *If you feed a dog late at night you only have yourself to blame if it is not clean until morning.*
- *It does not matter whether you feed your adult dog once a day, or twice, dividing the food ration into two portions. However, toy breeds with small stomachs often fare better on two or three little meals a day.*
- *Never give your dog poultry bones. They could be swallowed whole and splinter inside its stomach.*

complete
dried food

fresh meat

tinned
meat

semi-moist
meat

dog biscuits

puppy
mixer meal

raw-hide chew

chew sticks

vitamin treats

217

THE THINKING DOG

Whether dogs and other animals think, or in other words use reason when making a decision, is a question which has bothered philosophers and scientists for centuries. After a lot of thought, the Greek philosopher Aristotle decided that although animals could learn and remember things, only humans were capable of reason.

Humans can also talk to one another using language. All animals communicate with one another in some way—vocally, visually, or by some other method—but the level of communication possible with the human languages is thought by many experts to be in a class of its own. Sentence structure, vocabulary, and subtle intonation can be used to communicate original thoughts which have never been expressed before.

A dog can understand a number of commands, such as sit, come, wait, and heel, but it cannot understand sentences. The way dogs communicate, although there is still much to be learnt about it, seems to take the form of fairly simple signals. Only man's nearest relatives, the apes, provoke any serious argument as to whether animals possess language.

The ability to think and reason is partly related to brain size, so it is hardly surprising that the dog's mental capacity is much smaller than that of a human. For example with a dog of comparable weight, such as a Saint Bernard, the brain weighs 15 percent of that of a man.

If the dog has no command of language and a much more limited mental capacity than man, does it think at all and, if so, how? It is impossible to go inside a dog's mind to see how it works, but relevant observations can be made.

It is certain that dogs dream. When they sleep, they sometimes twitch and move their eyes rapidly under closed eyelids. These are both indications of dreaming in humans, but what a dog dreams of no one knows.

There are other parallels between human and canine mental processes. There are many recorded instances of dogs showing grief at the death of their owners. Probably the most famous case was a dog called Bobby, to whom a monument has been erected in Edinburgh. Bobby followed his master's coffin to the graveyard and stayed near the tomb for the rest of his life; he survived his owner by 14 years. Was he displaying grief, or did he simply establish a new territory, feeling that this was where he belonged?

Another important question is whether dogs have special abilities which humans do not possess, a sixth sense or any kind of extra-sensory perception. There are many stories of dogs, left behind when their owners move house, finding their way to the new home several hundred miles away.

Animals may well have better powers of navigation than humans—birds certainly do—but it is a mystery how a dog knows which way to go in such instances.

Other evidence of an apparent sixth sense can be explained more easily. Some of their five known senses are attuned differently from those of humans. For example, they can detect more highly pitched notes; their sense of smell is superior; and it is possible that they can detect warmth through special receptors in their noses. This may explain some of their more unusual feats, such as detecting a bugging device from its high pitched emissions and giving early warning of a fire using their sense of smell. It may even explain how dogs have apparently predicted earthquakes by suddenly behaving in an odd way some time before the event; one theory is that dogs can smell gas seeping from the ground. Another is that they detect low frequency warning vibrations.

It is still unclear whether any of a dog's behavior is motivated by thought. As more research is done, it may be possible to explain some of the oddities of dog behavior, where it appears they may be thinking. Trying to make a dog understand human language does not reveal much about the dog's mind. A better approach is to discover more about how dogs communicate with each other, and even how they try to communicate with us.

Unfortunately, if it is difficult to determine whether dogs think, it is even harder to measure their intelligence. First of all, intelligence is difficult to define, even in human terms. Most people think of it as something similar to being smart, clever, brilliant, or some other word which broadly describes academic, or problem-solving prowess. However, the following definition may help up to a point: "the mental pattern or framework which a person or animal uses to tackle a problem, based on its physical abilities and upbringing."

Even if a broad definition of this kind can be agreed upon, reasonable tests have to be devised. This is difficult enough for humans, and almost impossible for dogs and other animals.

Clearly, any test of intelligence must be tailored to suit a particular species; it is impossible to make more than the broadest of comparisons between species. However, even within the dog species problems arise because there are so many different breeds. To take an extreme example, a Pekingese and a Great Dane can hardly be given a test which involves jumping up to retrieve an object. Most of the breeds have special aptitudes, and this makes it almost impossible to devise a general test of dog intelligence.

This leaves the possibility of assessing intelligence merely by observing a particular dog's behavior. Some dogs certainly perform extraordinary feats, which apparently require great intelligence. There are dogs that collect the morning newspaper from the newsagent; others can get out of a room by undoing the latch; many dogs learn strange tricks such as riding along with two or three legs on a skateboard.

Acts of this kind appear to reflect intelligence, but they must be looked at against the inbred qualities of the dogs in question, and also the behavior of dogs in general. Some breeds of dog have been trained to retrieve objects for generations; to them the collection of a newspaper is an admittedly more complex form of a process which comes to them very easily.

A dog that opens a door with the latch is likely to have found the solution by chance, perhaps by nuzzling the latch in an attempt to push the door open, rather than by thinking the problem through.

Growing old together

- *Should an elderly person keep a dog? What if they should predecease their pet? This is a question that often crops up, particularly in the case of lonely old people who live alone, and would love to have a canine companion.*
- *Obviously it is ill advised for a frail, elderly person to keep a large, powerful dog. But there is no reason why they should not keep a pet as long as arrangements are made in advance for the animal's welfare in the event of its owner's death.*

GLOSSARY

Achondroplasia Improper development of cartilage at the ends of the long bones, resulting in a form of congenital dwarfism. A defect in most breeds and a requisite in others like Dachshunds and Basset Hounds.

Afterbirth The placenta and foetal membranes expelled from the uterus following the birth of each newborn puppy.

Back The area of a dog's body extending from the withers to the croup.

Back crossing A form of inbreeding in which a dog is mated to its parent.

Badger A grayish-brown color that may be mixed with a few dark hairs (Great Pyrenees, Sealyham Terriers).

Bad Mouth Crooked teeth; when the mouth is closed, upper and lower teeth do not line up according to the standard of the breed.

Bandy Legs Legs that bend outward.

Barrel A rib region that is round in cross section.

Barrel Hocks Hocks that turn out, causing the feet to toe in. Also called spread hocks.

Barring Striped markings.

Base coat The primary color of the coat.

Bat Ear An ear that stands up, with a broad base, rounded at the top, with opening facing forward. An erect ear that is broad at the base and rounded on the top.

Bay The prolonged bark or voice of a hunting hound.

Cafe Au Lait Usually used to describe Poodles, this color is the typical color of the French coffee of the same name.

Camel Back An arched back.

Candle Flame Ears A type of dog-ear that is large and erect with uneven edges.

Canid A family (Canidae) of carnivorous animals including dogs, wolves, coyotes, foxes, and jackals.

Canine An animal of the family *Canidae*, especially a dog.

Canine Distemper A viral infectious disease in dogs.

Canine Teeth The large, sharp, curved teeth that are located on each side of the mouth. Also referred to as eye teeth.

Cap Darkly shaded color pattern on the skull of some breeds.

Cape Long, thick hair covering the shoulders.

Dam The female parent.

Dapple A mottled or variegated coat color pattern.

Deadgrass Tan or dull straw color.

Deep-Chested Term describing the rib cage structure of dogs like German Shepherds, Great Danes, and Irish Setters.

Dehydration Excessive loss of water from the body or from an organ or body part, as from illness or fluid deprivation.

Demodex A mite that causes mange.

Dentition Forty-two adult teeth, including incisors, canines, premolars, and molars.

Depth of Chest An indication of the volume of space for heart and lungs, and commonly referenced to the elbow (i.e., above, at the level of, or below).

Dermatitis Inflammation of the skin.

Dewclaw An extra claw on the inside of the leg; a rudimentary fifth toe, removed on most breeds.

Dewlap Loose, pendulous skin under the throat and neck.

Ears The auditory organ, consisting of three regions: inner ear, middle ear, and the most important pinna (or leather), which is supported by cartilage and which affects the expression of all breeds.

Ear Mites Microscopic insects that survive by feeding on the lining of the ear canal.

East-West Front Incorrect positioning that causes the feet to turn outward.

Eclampsia Coma and convulsions during or immediately after pregnancy, characterized by edema, hypertension, and proteinuria.

Elbow The posterior region of the articulation between the arm and forearm.

Elbows Out Turning out or off from the body; not held close.

Embryo An undeveloped foetus.

Fall Hair overhanging the face.

Fallow Pale cream to light fawn color; pale yellow; yellow-red.

Fawn A brown, red-yellow with hue of medium brilliance.

Feathering Longer fringe of hair on ears, legs, tail, or body.

Femur Thigh bone. Extends from hip to stifle.

Fever In dogs, a body temperature reading over 103°F.

Foetus The unborn young of a viviparous vertebrate having a basic structural resemblance to the adult animal.

Gaskin The lower or second thigh.

Gastric Of, relating to, or associated with the stomach.

Gay Tail A tail carried above the horizontal level of the back.

Genealogy Recorded family descent. Pedigree.

Genetically Linked Defects Problems with health or temperament that are passed to offspring by their ancestors.

Genetics The science of heredity.

Genotype The genetic makeup, as distinguished from the physical appearance, of an organism or a group of organisms.

Hackles Hairs on neck and back raised involuntarily in fright or anger.

Hackney Action A high lifting of the front feet accompanied by flexing of the wrist like that of a Hackney horse.

Half-Prick Ear Also known as the semi-prick ear, ears carried erect with just the tips leaning forward.

Hallmark A distinguishing characteristic.

Handler One who trains or exhibits an animal, such as a dog.

Hare Foot Foot on which the two center digits are appreciably longer than the outside and inside toes of the foot, and the arching of the toes is less marked, making the foot appear longer overall.

Harlequin Patched or pied coloration, usually black or gray on white.

Harness A leather, nylon, or cloth strap shaped around the shoulders and chest, with a ring at its top for the lead.

Haunch Bones The hip bones.

Haw A third eyelid or membrane on the inside corner of the eye.

Immunization To produce immunity in, as by inoculation.

In Whelp Pregnant.

Inbreeding The mating of two closely related dogs of the same breed.

Incisors The six upper and six lower front teeth between the canines. The point of contact forms the bite.

Inflammation A localized protective reaction of tissue to irritation, injury, or infection, characterized by pain, redness, swelling, and sometimes loss of function.

Interbreeding The breeding of dogs of different breeds.

Internal Parasites One celled protozoan, larvae, and worms that survive by living off the host animal's meals or blood.

Iris The colored membrane surrounding the pupil of the eye.

Jacobsens Organ A sense organ located in the roof of the dog's mouth that functions somewhere between smell and taste.

Jowls Flesh of the lips and jaws.

Keel The rounded outline of the lower chest.

Kennel Building or enclosure where dogs are kept.

Kennel Cough Tracheobronchitis of dogs or cats.

Kink Tail A deformity of the caudal vertebrae producing a bent tail.

Kiss Marks Tan spots on the cheeks and over the eyes.

Knee See Stifle.

Knee Joint See Stifle.

Kneecap The stifle, with the bone known as the patella.

Knuckling Over Faulty structure of wrist joint allowing it to flex forward under the weight of the standing dog.

Lactation Secretion or formation of milk by the mammary glands.

Lame Irregularity or impairment of locomotion.

Landseer Newfoundlands that are white dogs with black markings, named in honor of Sir Edward Landseer, the 19th century artist who used these dogs as models

Layback The angle of the shoulder blade as compared with the vertical plane viewed from the side.

Layon The angle of the shoulder blade as compared with the vertical plane viewed from the front.

Lead A strap, cord, or chain attached to the collar or harness, or sometimes simply around the neck, for the purpose of restraining or leading the dog. Also called leash.

Leather The flap of the ear; the outer ear supported by cartilage and surrounding tissue.

Lemon Used to describe pointers, this color is a brilliant, medium-saturated yellow.

Leptospirosis An infectious disease of domestic animals, especially cattle, swine, and dogs, caused by spirochetes of the genus Leptospira and characterized by jaundice and fever.

Level Bite When the front teeth (incisors) of the upper and lower jaws meet exactly edge to edge.

Level Gait Dog moves without rise or fall of withers.

Mahogany Used to describe several breeds, this color is a medium-saturated, dull, reddish brown.

Marking An instinctual behavior in which male dogs urinate in certain locations to establish their territory.

Making a Wheel Term given to the circling of the tail over the back.

Mandible The bone of the lower jaw.

Mane Long, thick hair on top and sides of neck.

Mantle Dark-shaded portion of the coat on shoulders, back, and sides.

Manubrium The first sternabra of the chest.

Markings Contrasting color or pattern in a dog's coat.

Mask Dark shading on the foreface.

Mastitis Inflammation of the breast or udder.

Mate To breed a dog and bitch.

Natural Breed A breed of dog which occurred naturally without the interference of much selective breeding.

Neck Well Set-On Good neckline, merging gradually with withers, forming a pleasing transition into topline.

Nesting Behavior Behavior of a pregnant female who prepares a place to give birth and nurture young.

Neuter To castrate or spay.

Oblique Shoulders Shoulders well laid back.

Obliquely Placed Eyes Eyes with outer corners higher than their inner ones.

Occipital Protuberance A prominently raised occiput characteristic of some sporting and hound breeds.

Occiput Dorsal, posterior point of the skull.

Odd-Eyed Eyes of different color, such as one brown eye and one blue eye.

Omnivore A person or animal that feeds on both animal and vegetable substances.

On-Dog Identification A system of tagging, tattooing, or microchipping used to uniquely identify a dog.

Pack Multiple hounds cast at one time.

Pads Tough, shock-absorbing projections on the underside of the feet. Soles.

Paper Foot A flat foot devoid of arch to the toes.

Parainfluenza In canines, a disease characterized by fever, vomiting, and diarrhea.

Parasite An organism that grows, feeds, and is sheltered on or in a different organism while contributing nothing to the survival of its host.

Parti-Color Two or more definite, well-broken colors, one of which must be white.

Parvovirus A highly contagious febrile disease of canines and especially dogs that is caused by a parvovirus (genus Parvovirus), is spread especially by contact with infected faeces.

Quarantine Enforced isolation or restriction of free movement imposed to prevent the spread of contagious disease.

Quick The vein running through a dog's claw.

Rabies An acute, infectious, often fatal viral disease of most warm-blooded animals, especially wolves, cats, and dogs.

Rat Tail The root thick and covered with soft curls; at the tip devoid of hair, or having the appearance of being clipped.

Red A reddish orange color of dog.

Red Sesame Red with a sparse black overlay (Shiba Inu).

Registration Papers Documents showing proof of registration, date of birth, parents, breeder, and owner issued by a dog association for a particular dog.

Renal Of, relating to, or in the region of the kidneys.

SabreTail Carried in a semicircle.

Sable Coat color produced by black-tipped hairs on a background of silver, gold, gray, fawn, or brown.

Sacrum The region of the vertebral column that consists of three fused vertebrae that articulate the pelvic girdle.

Saddle Markings in the shape of a saddle over the back.

Saddle Back Overlong back, with a dip behind the withers.

Sandy Used to describe several breeds, this color is a dull, yellowish gray of medium saturation.

Tail-Set How the base of the tail is set on the rump.

Tapetum Lucidum The highly reflective portion of the interior of the canine eyeball that aids in night vision.

Terrier Front Straight front as found on fox terriers.

Testicles The male gonads, which produce spermatoza.

Testosterone A potent androgenic hormone produced chiefly by the testes; responsible for the development of male secondary sex characteristics.

Thoracic Vertebrae The thirteen vertebrae of the chest with which thirteen pairs of ribs articulate.

Throatiness An excess of loose skin under the throat.

Thumb Marks Black spots on the region of the pastern.

Umbilical Hernia A usually self-correcting hernia of the intestines in which protrusion occurs through the abdominal wall in the region of the navel.

Underage Dam Dam under eight months of age at the time of mating.

Underage Sire Sire under seven months of age at the time of mating.

Undercoat Dense, soft, short coat concealed by a longer top coat.

Unsound A dog incapable of performing the functions for which it was bred.

Urethroliths A general term referring to mineral deposits that form an obstruction in the urethra of male dogs.

Uterus A hollow muscular organ located in the pelvic cavity of female mammals in which the fertilized egg implants and develops. Also called womb.

Varminty A keen, very bright, or piercing expression.

Veil The portion of the dog's forelock hanging straight down over the eyes or partially covering them.

Vent The anal opening.

Vertebral Column The bones of the central axis of the dog posterior to the skull, including cervical, thoracic, lumbar, sacral, and caudal vertebrae.

Walleye An eye with a whitish iris; a blue eye, fisheye, pearl eye.

Wean The process of making a pup eat solid food instead of its mother's milk.

Webbed Toes Toes connected by a skin membrane; important for water-retrieving dogs, providing help in swimming.

Weedy An insufficient amount of bone; light boned.

Well Let Down Having short hocks; refers to short metatarsals.

Wet Neck Loose or superfluous skin; with dewlap.

Wheaten Pale yellow or fawn color.

Wheel Back A marked arch of the thoracic and lumbar vertebrae.

Whelp Date The date of birth of a litter.

Whelping The act of birthing puppies.

Xiphoid Process Cartilage process of the sternum.

Zoonosis A disease of animals, such as rabies or psittacosis, that can be transmitted to humans.

Zygomatic Arch A bony ridge extending posteriorly (and laterally) from beneath the eye orbit.

INDEX